Love at the Border

An Adoption Memoir from Mexico

Anna Maria DiDio

LOVE AT THE BORDER. An Adoption Memoir from Mexico.

Copyright :copyright: 2019 Anna Maria DiDio

ISBN-13: 978-0-9997356-8-8

Chasing Kites Publishing House
Book design: Matías Baldanza

Dedication

For Richard, Isabella,
and Priscilla with all my love.

This book is an honest account of an international adoption and how important it is for the parents to try to understand the experience from the baby/child's point of view. Not only is the child not with the mother who gave birth to her or her first caregivers, but she is not experiencing anything familiar to her. The baby or child doesn't experience it as a rescue or a happy event, but rather as a terrifying, confusing, and disorienting disruption of anything familiar to her.

Anna Maria DiDio's experience can help all adoptive parents to be patient, go slowly, take their cues from their children and "tune in" to their experience. These children, whether from a different country or not, are apt to be very different from their parents and it is important for the parents to notice, make room, and celebrate those differences.

—Nancy Verrier, LMFT,
adoptive mother and author of
The Primal Wound and *Coming Home to Self*

Contents

Prologue

S he bit me!" howled Isabella. I dropped what I was doing and ran into the family room. Isabella held out her arm for me to inspect. My fingers tenderly touched the red welt outlined by teeth marks on her forearm as Isabella stood stunned, her brown eyes wide, shifting from her arm to my face. I snapped my head around and stared incredulously at Priscilla. "Did you really bite her?" I asked. It was one of those mother-states-the-obvious-questions and, when I affirmed the fact, Isabella wailed again. "She bit me."

Priscilla backed away from the sofa clutching a needlepoint pillow to her chest. Her black eyes welling up, she covered her face with the pillow.

My husband's footsteps echoed down the stairs in hurried thumps. Richard's office was on the third floor. When he heard Isabella's cries of pain he rushed into the room, Spanish dictionary in one hand, glasses in the other, and started to say something. He then realized he needed to check the dictionary, so he put his glasses on.

After a two-year journey, we had adopted seven-year-old Priscilla from a Mexican orphanage only weeks earlier, thrilled to finally have a sibling for eight-year-old Isabella. But when Priscilla realized her home was now in suburban Philadelphia, she cried and pleaded in Spanish, begging to return to Mexico.

Squeezed in behind the sofa, Priscilla was now crying along with her big sister and plopped down in a defeated heap on the

1

floor. With both girls sobbing in stereo at full volume, Richard broke into the mix with an authoritative, *"Nos disgustan con tu comportamiento."* Grammar errors aside, we thought we communicated, "We are disgusted by your behavior." I gave us an "A" for effort because it was close enough.

The Spanish words hung in the air a moment. I think we were all surprised. Richard and I had tried to learn some Spanish in order to communicate with Priscilla. My night-owl husband had done his homework, poring over a dictionary and his high school Spanish textbook. Up to this point, we communicated like cavemen—pointing, gesturing, and saying words like: *la cuchara* (spoon); *comida* (food); *basura* (trash).

After hearing her native tongue in a fully formed sentence that was a strongly worded admonishment, Priscilla blinked, took a deep breath and let out another mighty sob. She stood up, tears streaming down her cheeks, then ran for her room and slammed the door. I walked Isabella to the bathroom, my arms around her shoulders. "Why don't you get ready for bed?" I said softly.

She nodded, still sputtering and hiccupping, her lower lip protruding in an exaggerated pout. As I closed the bathroom door, she turned to look at me with eyes that were angry and sad. I nodded my head and tried to give an encouraging half smile. Who was I kidding?

After both girls had fallen asleep, I retreated to my bedroom and closed the door. I sat down on the green-flowered coverlet at the edge of the bed, crossed my arms tightly across my chest and began rocking back and forth. Our creaky old house had no air conditioning and it was a hot July night, yet my insides were shaking as if I were chilled, and my stomach churned with a regret and dread that I had never before experienced. It was too late to begin crying. If I made a sound, it might be screaming, so

Prologue

I sat there thinking about the only question that turned over and over in my mind. What had I done to my family?

The knob turned with a squeak, and Richard came in. He closed the heavy wooden door with a thud. Wordlessly, he sat down on the bed and put his arms around me. I looked up to see his brown eyes rimmed in dark shadow. Priscilla hated me, and our family was changed forever.

CHAPTER 1

The Beginning

B y the time we slipped into our narrow seats aboard US Air
Flight 421 to Mexico City on that steamy August morning
back in 2002, I had a sharp, pulsing pain over my left eye—a sure
sign of the headache to come. My husband Richard, eight-year-
old daughter Isabella, and I were traveling to meet a six-year-
old girl selected for us by our adoption agency. The agency had
promised to send a picture, but by the time I left work on Friday,
it had not arrived. We knew almost nothing about this child we
hoped to adopt, but we smiled at Isabella anyway, having told
her a few weeks earlier of the upcoming adventure.

What we did know was that this would be the first international adoption for *Ministerios de Amor* (Love Ministries), which
are shelters dedicated to the rescue and transformation of home-
less children "through love and comprehensive care." I did not
understand at the time what a major leap of faith it had been for
Ministerios to agree to this arrangement.

The plane tilted upward, and I leaned my head against a pillow and closed my eyes. My friends who had adopted seemed
to have accomplished it rather effortlessly. Other couples with
biological children, I was betting, had never given a thought to
"having" a family. Now at forty-six, I had spent the last fifteen
years trying to get my family life together. Was I crazy, stubborn, or both? Calculating the ages of the mothers in attendance
at parties, barbecues, and church events was my social tic. "I

must be the oldest mother on earth," I pouted to Richard at a neighborhood dinner.

Shifting in my seat, I tried to stretch my too-long legs in the uncomfortably tight space, made smaller when the passenger in front of me reclined his seat,. I concentrated on our mission: to get to know a six-year-old Mexican girl who had lived in an orphanage her whole life. We had so many questions. It had been just the three of us for so long. We started this journey wanting a sibling for Isabella. Sisters are so much more than family. I treasured my relationship with my sister, Kathy, who is my confidant, sounding board, and friend. I wanted the same for my daughter. The "sisters" would come face-to-face tomorrow. Was this how our family was supposed to turn out?

Looking down, I realized I had just about twisted my wedding ring off my finger. I had stored my diamond band at home so as not to have precious jewelry on the trip and this stand-in felt odd on my finger. I folded my arms tightly around me and concentrated on breathing.

We had been up early and I was tired, but my eyes were open for good now, so I grabbed my book. The paper bookmark, with Isabella's childish scribble of "MOM" encircled by hot pink and purple flowers, made me smile. I thought back to the hot July day one month before when the phone rang. The agency we had worked with for almost a year had some questions for me. Would we want to meet a little girl?

The information about her was sparse, and later we discovered that most of it was incorrect. Initially, we were told that the child's name was Pamela and she was five years old. The agency called back two days later to say Pamela was not part of a sibling group, was actually six years old and liked to be called Priscilla.

As the plane floated skyward, Isabella dug out her playing cards for a game of Crazy Eights with Richard. Her sandals were on the floor, bare legs tucked underneath, ash-brown hair caught up in a ponytail which fell back over her shoulder. While pondering her card choices, she twirled her purple hair-tie ribbons. "Spades," she cried out, her brown eyes twinkling. I could see that she had only one card left. Father and daughter loved to play games—Monopoly, Checkers, Yahtzee, Parcheesi. Games were not my thing. They made me impatient and fidgety and I couldn't wait for them to end. Richard and Isabella delighted in any card game, and also mental gymnastics like "20 Questions" and "Sit on Your Hands Math." Richard, after all, was a math professor and loved that kind of thing. My handsome, dark-haired husband had a quiet intensity, even at cards, his bushy scientist eyebrows furrowed in thought.

As I watched father and daughter interact, I thought about our own unique family chemistry. My inevitable strategy was to worry about things as much as possible, starting way in advance—the logic being that by the time the event takes place I would be all worried out. The trouble with this approach was that this was our third attempt at adopting a child, and as much as I wanted to believe in "third time's the charm," I was coming close to the end of my emotional rope.

When we married eleven years earlier, we both knew that I had a history of fertility problems. In a previous marriage, I had become pregnant after almost two years of trying, only to lose the child after approximately eleven weeks. At the time, an ultrasound revealed an abnormality of my uterus. I didn't know what to make of it or how to fix it. That marriage had started to crumble years before. When we divorced, my yearning for motherhood was stronger than ever.

When Richard and I married, the anxiety came back in a big way, flooding over me just as I was starting a new phase of my life. A new marriage is stressful for any couple. Add one partner recovering from a bad relationship AND infertility issues, and that marriage is bound to have its difficult moments.

As newlyweds, Richard and I settled in southern New Jersey, both of us eager to have children. I immediately scheduled an appointment with an infertility specialist. It just drove me crazy whenever someone said, "I got pregnant...just by accident!" or "We weren't even trying!" Why was it so effortless for some people to have children while I had to work so hard?

"Trying to have a baby" — a phrase that sickened me — actually seemed to give us so much power and purpose as a couple. Shortly after Richard and I married, a so-called friend boldly asked me, "Are you one of those career women who put off having a child and now that you want one, you can't?" I felt like screaming back at her — It's not that simple! I did not choose this sequence of events. Richard and I both wanted a family and when one of us was defeated, the other swooped in with a life-saving technique like chocolate chip ice cream. Any doubts I had about getting married for the second time dissolved as we leaned on each other.

Type A. Driven. Bossy-pants. Call me what you will, but I knew what I wanted. As this was pre-internet, I dove into piles of books and magazine articles. I quizzed all the doctors, nurses, therapists, and other health professionals with whom I came in contact about the reproductive cycle, treatment options, and holistic medicine alternatives. After choosing a doctor, who coincidentally was a college friend of Richard, I came back from my first appointment reporting what a great guy he was — totally dedicated to our cause. What I didn't tell Richard was that I had cross-examined the good doctor about his background, training, standard treatment plan, and a hundred other things — the normal questions any intensely crazy infertile woman would want to have the answers to at her first appointment with yet another reproductive endocrinologist. The guy probably thought that Richard married a nut job, but I didn't care.

They say a little knowledge is a dangerous thing, but my information quest definitely increased my appreciation for the delicate miracle of birth. It's a wonder everything goes right as frequently as it does. But the cynical side of me kept noting that every time I turned around someone else I knew was pregnant. Why couldn't it happen to me? Couldn't God see that I would be a terrific mother? I was meant to have my own child. Richard and I would make such a beautiful child together. Lord, hurry up and make it happen!

As my infertility problem became clearer, we mapped out a plan for surgery, recovery, waiting, waiting some more, possible fertility drugs, bigger doses of fertility drugs, and the seemingly inevitable in vitro fertilization. It was all too much to comprehend, and I focused on one month at a time. Surgery would come first. It turned out that my uterus had a septum through it, sort of like a wall dividing the uterus. That "divide" did not have blood cells, making it impossible for an egg to adhere and grow. This was the most likely reason for what was now two pregnancies that resulted in miscarriage, the second one occurring shortly before Richard and I married. Surgery was the only recommended course of action.

My doctor assured me that the surgery would be "pretty routine" and could be performed on an outpatient basis at a local surgical center. There would be no scar because the surgery would be done laparoscopically, which is pretty common now, but at the time made me even more nervous.

The day of the surgery, I worked in the morning and had a friend drop me at the surgery center at lunch. Richard was due to pick me up after his classes were over. Five hours later, the center was closing and we had to leave. Richard arrived to find me nauseous, crying, and not able to walk. He practically had to carry me to the car. I was sore for days afterward, taking small baby steps while holding my tummy.

We then started the regimen of standard fertility drugs, which quickly progressed to stronger drugs. Once the shots started, I went to the doctor's office at seven o'clock every morning for an ultrasound. The nurse expertly read the images in order to determine the size and number of eggs that had been produced. At various points in the cycle, hormone levels were evaluated for the readiness of egg development. When the time was right, another shot was needed to release the eggs. I could administer this one myself, then schedule the evening's activity. It was then that those hopeful feelings would begin to grab hold of me, and I would start to think... maybe this time.

Some months I would have eight to eighteen eggs ready to be released and hopefully fertilized. "You're tall," my doctor would say, his head bobbing in a little laugh, his light brown hair combed back perfectly, not moving at all. "There's plenty of room in there for a few." He always encouraged me, taking the time to carefully explain and present my options when I cried in his office after yet another unsuccessful cycle—another month with my life on hold, waiting for motherhood.

These treatments can easily lead to four, five, and six or more children—the feel-good events that show up in the news occasionally. I marveled at how easily it could happen. Month after month of disappointment would cause any woman to lose perspective, increasing the dosage—loading the dice with more follicles and more eggs in the hopes of a baby payoff. Imagine all the doctors out there, trying to help women who have become slightly unhinged in the process as they sacrificed everything to reach their goal. I guess that included me.

Despite our support for one another during this time, Richard and I did our best not to get on each other's nerves. The truth is that we tried to make it fun, but it was stressful and just generally depressing to me that we had to work so hard at conceiving. Richard attempted to set a romantic mood—music, wine, a roaring fire. As time went on, we decided to leave less to chance. Richard's sperm was treated to enhance swimming ability. With super-charged sperm, I was sure one would find its way. *God, we only need one!*

At the start of each monthly cycle, I felt that conceiving could almost happen. Of course, I was afraid to even think this, but I couldn't help feeling that success was just within our reach. But then, at the end of the month when my period arrived, I would be crushed, feeling as if I had let both of us down. The realization of yet another failure usually reduced me to a tearful puddle.

I had been trying to have a baby for ten years. I could not even verbalize it without feeling sick and stupid. Was this normal? Who volunteers to be poked, prodded, criticized, second-guessed, and written off as a bit looney? I was hell-bent on being a mother and no one was going to get in my way.

But during that time, not only did I hate myself, I hated anyone who was pregnant.

One weekend while at the beach, Richard and I were relaxing, digging our toes into the sand and listening to the surf. As had become typical, I was so preoccupied with my "situation" that I sat in my own world. Richard spotted Sue, the wife of his boyhood friend, John. Married just a month before us, John and Sue were both about our age; it was the second marriage for both. Sue did not have children from her previous marriage and had mentioned at the wedding that they wanted to start a family right away. *Good luck,* I thought to myself. I had wanted the same family for years and was nowhere close. Well, of course, Sue got pregnant about two months after the wedding and delivered a healthy baby boy right on schedule. When Richard told me about their news, he avoided my eyes and quickly changed the subject. I experienced a wave of anger that was impossible to communicate. How could I not be happy for them?

Until now, my rage had been an internal simmering, but suddenly Sue was coming toward me and that anger spilled over to truly horrible behavior. She was making her way across the hot sand lugging the baby, diaper bag, beach chair, and God-knows-what-else. Richard ran to help her, and I started to have an anxiety attack. I could not face this woman and her baby. As if in a trance, my body got up and simply floated away. I walked on the beach for what seemed like hours, circling back to the house later that afternoon. My actions had no logic, but Richard understood. He nodded as I babbled, and I think he even said that Sue had said hello and was rooting for us. We hugged, and I squeezed hard, grateful that Richard picked up the mental slack. He was always so positive and hopeful—a perfect balance to my pathetic and needy state.

I had to wonder; where did my determination come from? My mother and I were not particularly close. She loved us but did not seem to enjoy motherhood even a little bit. Four children in six years was too much for her. We always seemed to make her angry, her temper flashing at a moment's notice. Things improved as she got older, but whenever my sisters and I would get together, we would recall the screaming and histrionics of our youth. She was not really a bad mother, just simply not interested in us at all. Our after-school activities were often done in a whisper because we did not want to wake her from her nap.

When I was growing up, babysitting was the only reliable way to make any money, but I had no interest in expending any energy on the children. My goal was to put the kids to bed as early as possible in order to eat anything chocolate and read "literature" that could not be found in my ultra-Catholic home. Years of being unnoticed as a middle child must have motivated me to mother my own child. I can't really explain it. I loved Richard and wanted a child to love together.

The Beginning

~

My memories of how we got to the point of sitting on a flight to Mexico were interrupted when the pilot announced upcoming turbulence, and instinctively, I looked at Isabella bouncing up and down in her seat. I watched Richard rummage around in his black carry-on bag for another game. He pulled out a pencil and paper. What were they up to? Isabella looked at me and asked, "Mommy, do you have any candy?"

"How about a Jolly Rancher?" I asked, waving her favorite green apple flavor that she immediately grabbed out of my hand. She put her head close to Richard as he made a list of numbers and then drew a few blank lines. Isabella took the paper and then chewed on the tip of the pencil in concentration as she thought of the next few numbers in the pattern Richard had written. Father and daughter were "two brains in a pod," or whatever that saying is.

I couldn't help but think about what would happen when another little girl was added to the mix. What kind of games would she want to play? I began reflecting not only on our unknown future, but on just how our story began.

CHAPTER 2

Union

R ichard and I met in 1988 at *Carolina's*, a bar and restaurant just off Rittenhouse Square in Center City, Philadelphia. I was newly single after almost ten years of marriage and worked in the Human Resources department for a local brokerage firm. My sister, Kathy, worked nearby and at the end of the day, we planned to meet up with a few of my co-workers. My office mates and I were also coping with the fact that our company was closing, gobbled up by a larger financial firm; ultimately, we would all lose our jobs.

Kathy was four years younger, and as my *singlés* mentor, was helping me through this new independent phase of my life. She delighted in showing me around town and we loved hanging out together. She explained that *Carolina's* had a setup particularly well-suited to mingling, including a long, narrow bar area that patrons had to squeeze through to get to a larger open room in the back. We had been there a few times and enjoyed the mix of regulars and corporate types. Kathy was neither. My sweet artsy sister, a graphic designer, was the perfect complement to my snarky and cynical personality. She laughed at my jokes, re-worked my wardrobe, and provided encouragement every step of the way. What more could you ask of a sibling?

When I declared that I was ready to socialize, she told me, "You will have to get some clothes other than your boring corporate suits." She added, "Oh, and while we are on the subject, why is all of your underwear white?"

"Because it's practical and does not show through my suit blouses." I then added, "We can't all dress like Madonna." It was the eighties, after all. But she was right. That was me in a nutshell—boring, corporate, and even underneath, conservative and no frills.

It was a beautiful end of summer day and we walked to the bar, cutting through the Square. We had a drink or two and then I headed to the restroom, which was at the back of the bar.

"How's it going?" were the first words Richard said to me as he slid behind me into the unisex bathroom line.

"OK," was my brilliant reply. I took in his dark hair and eyes and noticed that I could look directly in them. Was I taller than he was? He wore a red, yellow, and black checked shirt, khaki pants. *Cute but nerdy*, I thought.

I suddenly felt the gawky teenager in me reemerge. How do I make small talk? Did I look OK? Was I doing this right? "We're a coupled world," a friend told me over coffee one day as I told her my observations of being single again.

As I closed the bathroom door to join Kathy and my friends, Richard almost jumped in front of me with an earnest, "When can I see you again?"

Honestly, I got a kick out of that... a man in pursuit but with a sense of humor. I told him that I was with a group celebrating eventual unemployment and then blathered on and on that I planned to travel, perhaps to Europe, Italy maybe. Even as I was sharing the details of my life, I noticed that he listened intently, taking in my every word. For some reason, I couldn't stop talking.

"That's just great," he said, then repeated, "when can I see you again?"

"We are joining a big party at the Bourse Building," I offered happily, the next location planned for our office countdown celebration on the following Friday.

"What's your name?" he asked as I turned away.

"Anna Maria," I replied without thinking. Why had I said that? Usually, only my family called me that.

"That's a beautiful name," he said. "I'm Richard." We shook hands and our eyes met again. I turned to rejoin my sister and thought, *Nice, but definitely not my type.*

The next Friday, Kathy and I made our way to the Bourse Building in the Old City part of town. The bar had a reputation for a lively happy hour, attracting the after-work crowd. We arrived to find a rowdy scene with most of my office co-workers out on the dance floor already, singing "Don't Worry, Be Happy," which had become our office theme song. Out of the corner of my eye, I saw Richard approaching our group. He stood there looking at me, holding a large brown paper bag.

"Hello Anna Maria," he said with a little wave.

"Look who it is," I said, nudging Kathy.

Until that moment, I had completely forgotten that I had told Richard about the gathering. He looked like a lost puppy standing there. I elbowed Kathy and said, "Remember, it's the guy that I met last week at *Carolina's* bathroom. Go talk to him." My instinctive reaction was to avoid any conversation that would ask something of me. I was there to play and did not want any expectations.

Still shaking my head, I ordered another drink. Kathy made her way over to talk to Richard and I could see them chatting and laughing. After an hour or so, preparing to leave for happy hour number two, Kathy leaned in to yell in my ear over the music, "Where should we go?" I could see Richard lingering in the background still holding that paper bag. "What are you doing?" I hissed loudly at her.

"Anna, he's really nice and he just wants to talk to you. He drove here to meet you, why don't you just say hello?"

"He drove here?" I asked. "Well, that's great. Will he drive us to the Irish Pub?"

Kathy looked at me and said, "Be nice," then shrugged her shoulders and headed toward the door. My guard was up. I had avoided him the entire happy hour. While I drank and talked with my friends, I could see him at the edge of the bar. He had no trouble mingling and chatting, all the while also keeping an eye on me. Something in my head said it was too soon for anyone to be checking me out.

We piled into his beat-up red Toyota and headed toward West Philadelphia. *I was right*, I thought, eying the worn gray interior and grimy dashboard, *definitely not my type*. Pulling up to the bar, Kathy and my two co-workers got out.

Richard and I lingered on the sidewalk. "When can I see you again?" he asked. I felt bad that I had not really talked to him up to that point. After all, he was nice enough to drive all of us to the pub, and I felt guilty that I had basically ignored him.

"Gee, you are persistent. I don't know," I began to babble. "I just recently separated from my husband; I have a lot going on. My company is closing, and I am losing my job. What's in that bag you have been carrying around all night anyway?"

"It's a present for you. I just heard this music and thought you might like it."

"A present for me?" I am not surprised easily and now I stood on the sidewalk not knowing what to say. The traffic on Market Street whizzed noisily by. We looked at each other. Feelings of stupidity and regret—not a great combination—stopped my chatter. Why had I been so rude?

I reached out for the brown paper bag, which was clearly an album and looked inside to read the cover.

"*Union*, by Toni Childs. I've never heard of her," I said. "Plus, I just moved out of my house and don't have a stereo." I started to babble again, not knowing where this was going.

"I'll make a tape for you and give it to you the next time I see you. It's wild music; you haven't heard anything like it."

I folded the bag over the album and tucked it under my arm. "Thank you," I managed to stammer. He smiled, and a sweet look of relief and happiness crossed his face as we talked. He had tried to find me during the week, searching the phone directory for my number, but had no luck. Check one for persistence. We made a date for the next weekend, which turned out to be a disaster. At a Thai restaurant, I ordered soft-shell crabs and became deathly ill. He felt terrible a week or so later when he called. He promised to make me a germ-free dinner at his apartment.

That night, before my stomach issues, we really had fun. Richard made me laugh, and we never ran out of things to talk about. He was interesting, smart, and not so nerdy after all. His home-cooked meal was delicious and special, complete with pink cloth napkins and a yummy dessert.

Gradually, we spent more and more time together. He got the "single life" theme of my divorced existence immediately and deferred to doing whatever I wanted. The list included: late night clubbing, movie marathons, New York, Jersey shore, Indian food, parties, neighborhood bars— everything I had never had a chance to do because I married so young. By the end of the year, I had landed a new job and we talked about taking a vacation in Europe when his semester was over in the spring. As a university professor, his summers were free, and so we began to plan the itinerary together.

It was not all smooth sailing, however, and I started to ask myself if this was meant to be. During the time that we had become a regular paired item, my family had been wondering what I was up to. Richard and I kept to our separate family routines around the holidays. Then around April, my mother called and asked if I would introduce him at a get-together planned for Mother's Day. I agreed.

Richard planned to take his own mother out that Sunday, so we arranged to meet first at my parents' house for drinks. We arrived at the same time, pulling up in the driveway of my childhood home. He opened my car door and said, "I love your dress," gave me a quick kiss, and we went to meet the family. Because it was warm outside, my mother had set up the cheese and crackers on the deck, so we walked around to the back of the house and I made the introductions. Kathy was also there and everyone greeted Richard warmly.

When we went inside to make our drinks, I had a déjà vu moment unlike anything I had ever experienced. Suddenly, I was seeing Dave, my ex-husband, everywhere in the house. All the memories of family dinners, holidays, and parties flooded my head. We had been together since I was seventeen. The feeling was disorienting, and it stopped me cold. The last time I brought a guy home to meet my parents, I married him. It was sixteen years later and now I was already too serious with the very next guy. Was this a mistake? Were we moving too fast?

I made Richard a drink and then excused myself to the bathroom. I closed the door, looked up into the mirror and did a double take. The dress that Richard said he liked was something from the back of my closet with a high neck, long sleeves and a full gathered skirt that stopped below my knees. The fabric was a soft jersey material of bright red and pink roses on green vines. It looked like a garish square dance outfit, and I could not even recall when I had worn it last. Richard and I had an easy relationship and I thought that bringing him to meet the family would be no big deal, but my headache and now sweaty flower dress said otherwise. Cold water felt good on my face, and I held onto the sink for support.

I looked into the mirror again at my smudged mascara when suddenly, a flashback of applying makeup to a black eye appeared in front of me. How could I have been so wrong about my choice for a husband all those years ago? On the edge of making another decision, my hand was shaking as I grabbed a tissue.

Kathy knocked and opened the door without waiting for a response. "What are you doing in here? Everyone is on the deck, and you should be out there with Richard." She paused and grabbed the edge of my skirt, pulling it out. "Whuuuuuuut are you wearing? Where did you even buy that?"

"Stop," I said defensively, smoothing down the fabric. "Spring. Flowers. It seemed like a good idea when I pulled it out of the closet this morning." Now I felt ridiculous.

I turned to Kathy. "I am seeing Dave everywhere in this house. It feels like a mistake to be here with Richard. I was married forever. How am I ever going to move on?"

"Stop thinking about it too much. You are having fun with Richard, aren't you?"

"Yes, but why did I agree to do this today? It feels awkward and weird."

Kathy had no sympathy for me. "It's okay to feel like you are out of practice with the dating thing. But you've jumped back in. C'mon, we are all waiting outside."

I went back up to the kitchen. Determined to disappear, my parents' alcohol offerings were just the ticket. Grabbing some ice, I filled a tumbler and poured vodka to the top of the glass, added a splash of 7Up for something sweet and drank it down. I made another and pushed the screen door open.

"Hey, what is there to eat?" It had been many hours since breakfast, and with no lunch, I started to jam all the cheese and crackers in my mouth, intent on soaking up the vodka. Then I noticed my glass was empty, so I returned to the kitchen to make another drink.

I am a happy drinker, and after two huge cocktails, I was already laughing and singing to myself in the kitchen as I cracked more ice. Richard came in with a concerned look. "Everything ok?"

"Yes. It. Is." I sing-songed, and gave him a huge vodka kiss. After making myself another tall one, I went back outside and devoured the entire roll of pepperoni. Everyone and everything was suddenly hilarious.

Soon it was time to leave for the country club. Kathy and I were in the back seat with my dad at the wheel. Richard was driving behind us, on the way to see his mother. I turned around and waved crazily at him until he turned off down another road. My parents had a worried whisper-talk all the way to Doylestown. Kathy laughed and rolled her eyes. I put my head down on the seat.

My goal of dodging the chit-chat had been achieved. With enough alcohol, no one would expect me to contribute to the conversation, a state I hoped would last all through dinner. Turns out I didn't have to worry about that. I found my way to the ladies' golf locker room and promptly threw up. Luckily, I made it to one of the stalls. The locker room was lovely, decorated in a pink and green theme with white wicker furniture and some sort of trellis thing that separated the sitting area, lockers, and bathroom. A foursome was lingering there chatting casually, but all conversation stopped once I started puking. The ladies were gone when I came out to wash my face for the second time that day. I plopped my flowered dress onto a similarly flowered couch and fell asleep.

The next thing I knew, Kathy was tapping me on the arm. "It's two hours later and time to go," she said, laughing and shaking her head. "You missed dinner, and honestly, you have got to get it together. What is wrong with you? Richard is nice, and you need to relax."

But the feeling lingered all summer. We would be having a good time, then suddenly a memory or mistakenly calling Richard "Dave" would produce waves of doubt and uncertainty that I could not shake. It was the same story when we traveled to Europe. I wanted so much to do something else, see something else, and couldn't wait to go. But when we got there, it felt like three steps forward and two steps back. We would be walking hand in hand along some of the most romantic streets in Venice or Florence and I would get in a mood or want to go back to the room and read my book. I had to give the guy credit though. Whatever I threw at him, he took it all in stride.

Because Richard had several weeks of vacation remaining, he decided to stay in Europe and visit other friends. I left to return to my new job as time off was in short supply for me. When I resumed my routine, I discovered something significantly important: I missed him. It was really noticeable in the evenings. Richard lived in Philadelphia and I lived in New Jersey, but we talked for hours on end some nights. Whatever my head case issue was, Richard would listen and work it through with me.

Yet it was during this time that the feeling of us being a mismatched couple persisted. We were so different. He was a professor of physics, math, and computer science—his apartment was wall-to-wall books. However, he was not your standard introverted geek. He had lots of friends and could talk about an infinite number of subjects. When he wasn't teaching, he performed in a comedy theatre group, played in a band, and finished the New York Times crossword puzzle in no time. I, on the other hand, was firmly immersed in the corporate world. I had many colleagues, but few close friends. In my spare time, I had mastered a diverse array of handicrafts, but they were all solo efforts. In college, I dropped my Intro to Theatre class when we had to roll around on the floor pretending to be an animal in search of food.

Richard did not let me get away with that for too long. He had a comeback for every one of my objections. We were having fun. In fact, it was always important to Richard that I do what I wanted. When I had my heart set on attending a black-tie fundraiser, he was less than thrilled about renting a tuxedo. But he did it for me.

It felt like I had been married forever, and now that I was single, I was still finding out who I was. When it came to marriage the second time, my decision boiled down to two words: tick tock. The life I wanted included children and my biological clock was not going to wait for me to figure out all the mysteries of life. I paid attention to how I felt when we were together, and I liked it. He loved being with me and told me over and over in so many ways. Honestly, when a guy is that into you, it's hard to argue. After one year of dating, my arguments were wearing thin, and we began to talk about a life together.

It all came down to this: I gave myself permission to fail. We had developed a sense of trust, and yes, I loved him and told him so. My hesitancy reflected my lack of confidence in the ability to choose a mate. Was I sure that this marriage was going to last? Since I just was not there yet, I came up with my five-year plan. If we did not have a child and were not happy in five years, I would move on. It sounds a bit cold and calculating now, but it was a way for me to say "yes" and walk down the aisle a second time.

Now, several years later, here we were flying to Mexico to complete our family. Without a doubt, he was exactly the type of guy for me.

CHAPTER 3

Good and Bad Videos

A s our plane passed out of the invisible turbulence, I squinted to see the glare of the sun blazing through the window. I reached across the seat, wordlessly asking Richard for his hand, and squeezed. The beverage cart moved ahead of us as we began sipping our coffee. Isabella gave me the thumbs up, drinking her orange juice. Looking for something to absorb another Advil, I opened our airline "snack"—an ice-cold bagel, cream cheese, granola bar, and apple. Isabella was impressed and tore into the box. On our way to Mexico to perhaps meet her new sister, I couldn't help but wonder at how far we had come since the dark times of fertility drugs and injections, ultrasounds, and dejection.

I thought back to the years when each month's end arrived with no good news, I would try to get physically and mentally ready for the next cycle. About a year later, when the verdict came that my diagnosis was "unknown," I cut my doctor off in mid-sentence.

"What do you mean, unknown? Do you think it is all in my head now? My equipment has been fixed; why doesn't it work?" I had a similar angry conversation with God, demanding His co-operation. It was in this fantastically positive frame of mind that we entered the world of adoption for the first time. Actually, I don't remember it being that big of a decision. The drugs made me crazy and set the stage each month for failure, which seemed to go on forever. We easily came to the decision to adopt, thinking that in vitro treatment or a surrogate parent was not for us. It came down to: Did we want a baby? The answer was "yes," so we got in line.

On the advice of an adoption "expert," we began to share our plans in the hope that someone would know someone who was having a baby, thus supporting my fundamental philosophy of life—everything is about networking. I answered a few crazy personal ads and gave my name and number to just about anyone who might come in contact with a pregnant teenager. It was through one of those calls that I met up with Betty who was taking care of the pregnant daughter of a local pastor whose family had thrown her out of the house. As Betty told us the story of this girl's childhood and now her second pregnancy, it was clear that this situation was not for us. The fact that we were meeting with this woman at all spoke to our desperation on so many levels. At the end of the dinner at our local mall, she offered no hope and no encouragement, telling us in all likelihood that the daughter would probably keep her baby and try to work things out with her family. Her first child had been adopted and now there was regret. OK, thanks for nothing.

But that was the way things were if you were hoping to adopt a child. We went out of our way to cross paths with anyone who would be able to help. Of course, we could not rely on our friends and family to be successful. It was obvious that some of them were not thrilled with our news and felt compelled to share their minimally informed opinions with us.

"Adoption is not right for us," a girlfriend told me. She and her husband were a bit older. They had no children, and I knew they had been to see a fertility specialist. She summed up her feelings by explaining, "We don't want to raise someone else's child," as if she were going to catch some deadly disease.

Well, good for you, I thought. I hope someone else's son or daughter is willing to take care of you in the nursing home.

It was critical that we find an adoption agency we could trust. Searching for the one that would connect us to a baby who was right for us was intense work. My methodology was pretty simple in the pre-computer era. I began to call every listing in the Philadelphia phone book under the word "adoption." The results were a truly bizarre mix of hope, help, and hell. One Christian agency had a Preliminary Application, an Initial Statement of Faith Application, and a Statement of Faith Part II Application. The third questionnaire — sent to us before we had spoken to a single person in the agency face-to-face — asked: "If you were to die tonight, do you know beyond a shadow of a doubt that you would live forever with God?" Give me a break… all I wanted was a baby, just like every other couple out there. Did I have to carry the cross, too?

We settled on Choices, an open adoption agency in a suburban location near our home. We had already learned a great deal about open adoptions from the various information sessions we had attended. In an open adoption, the birth mother chooses the parents for her child and contact is negotiated then maintained after the child is born. We were told that these were the conditions, so we agreed.

After completing the required paperwork for Choices, we began attending their training classes and preparing for the home study visit. We wanted to impress them and do all of the right things, but honestly, my eyes were rolling out of my head most days. Why did I need lessons on how to be a mother? When the social worker assigned to complete our home visit showed up, I was a bit surprised that she had just graduated from college the year before. The house had been cleaned top to bottom, which

27

she efficiently noted on her clipboard. However, the most important answer that could not be checked on any list was: when would this happen for us?

But wait—there was more stuff to do. We endured a thorough psychological evaluation including multiple choice questions, essays, and an interview. Once we had the green light on the mental front, the agency needed a way to promote us as potential parents and we received instruction to create our oddly unique infomercial. We watched the agency's version of "good" and "bad" videos, both of which felt cheesy and insincere. Thinking about it now, all these years later, I wonder if I sounded as exasperated and frustrated as I recall feeling. I have always been bad at hiding my feelings and I cringe now thinking of that video. Talking to the camera in my "alone" segment, I spoke of our efforts and desire for a family, all the while thinking, *Please like me enough to give me your child. I'm a good person. See how nice I am?*

Maybe that's why no one called us. Months went by with no word from Choices. To me, our prospects for a family seemed close to zero. Of course, I then proceeded to rant at the only person who was in my corner: Richard.

Coming home from shopping, we happened to run into another couple that we did not know well, but who had adopted two children several years before. They were shouting to us across the street when they saw us get out of our car.

"We heard you are going to adopt. That's terrific and good luck." They were smiling and waving, and I waved back and then went into the house.

It was a nice and thoughtful thing to say, but I was hell-bent on feeling crappy about the whole situation, which seemed to be dragging on forever. Once Richard and I were inside, I asked him, "How can anyone say that they are happy for us? This whole process is horrible. They should have said, 'Hey—we feel sorry for you! You could be waiting til hell freezes over!'"

I know Richard felt terrible that I was so sad. It must have felt like I was determined to drag him down with me. He never had any answers for my rants, but always hugged me and said encouraging and positive words that I needed to hear. I persisted in my role of high-maintenance wife even when we had other things to celebrate. On the evening after Richard was promoted to Associate Professor, we went out to dinner to celebrate with a few other faculty members. I knew that I looked miserable and just wanted to wallow in it. Richard was upset that I could not put it aside for a night. It was one of our few fights, and I felt terrible for days afterward.

Not long after finishing our paperwork, I called the doctor's office asking, "What's wrong with me?" I felt so bloated. I had cramps. The nurse was used to these types of calls and advised me to buy an over-the-counter pregnancy test and then call the next day with the results.

"I'm not pregnant," I snapped at her.

"Well," she said, "Let's just try this and see. It will be one thing to rule out."

Of course, being the know-it-all that I was, I was as wrong as could be. Later, the doctor said that it was common to have residual "rebound" cycles after several courses of fertility drugs. Richard came home a little late that night. Jumping up from the couch as soon as the door opened, I ran toward him, sliding on the hardwood floor in my socks and waving the blue stick in the air.

"We're pregnant!" I yelled, wrapping myself around him. Richard inspected the positively bright-blue colored end of the white plastic stick. We were wildly happy, yes, but deep, deep down, I was desperately trying to prepare myself for the ultimate letdown.

The first ultrasound showed our little baby's heart beating away. I cried with relief. Because I was thirty-seven, we were advised to take advantage of genetic testing. We held our collective breath until the results were final. I was having a healthy baby girl! Once again, the tears just poured out. It was a few days before Christmas and I was the happiest I had been in a long time. I waited until the beginning of the second trimester to call Choices and tell them the good news: take us off the list!

Isabella was born healthy after an uneventful pregnancy. I caught a miserable cold on a business trip to Davenport, Iowa. That was about as dramatic as it got for nine months. The fun thing about a late-in-life pregnancy was that I had so many showers plus hand-me-down gifts. Everyone was so happy for us—they all wanted to share the moment. My family, church, neighbors, and work all hosted wonderful celebrations. Richard and I had to buy absolutely nothing. However, not one of those shower gifts was put away or opened to the point of removing the plastic wrap. All the tags were still attached and the boxes stacked in the closet. It was another one of my management techniques. If I did not have the baby, the presents could all be returned much more efficiently in their original boxes and wrapping.

A few days before my due date (that I revealed to absolutely no one), I was up to go to the bathroom at 1:00 a.m. when I had the feeling of a huge rubber band snapping inside me. My water broke in a flood and I sent Richard to the phone to call the doctor. Even as the labor pains were pressing down on me in the car, I was paralyzed with fear that I would be disappointed again. It was painful to visualize myself with a child in my arms, and I deliberately pushed those thoughts away for months. Richard and I never discussed a name for our new baby girl. To do so would have been a display of confidence that I thought was over the top. How could we be so brazen as to name our child? I am not superstitious, but that struck me as clearly crossing the line.

Even after the pain-killing medication was given, I told the nurse that I wasn't going to be able to do it. She didn't listen, and Isabella arrived at 3:11 p.m. that afternoon. I looked down at her and immediately began to cry. My salty tears hit her face, causing her to scrunch up her nose and eyes. Richard and I both laughed and took turns cuddling her and smiling in awe.

Motherhood filled me with a happiness that I had never experienced. Watching our baby grow day by day was our entertainment. Richard and I were totally content.

In the years leading up to becoming a threesome, we were active socially and kept up with the latest TV, music, movies, and cool things to do around town. Suddenly, those things were all so unimportant. We had no interest in the happenings that used to occupy all our free time. It felt so natural to stay at home and play with blocks and read stories. I didn't see it as giving up anything. We had this little girl who now adored us. After years of watching everyone else's sweet baby at the grocery store, mall, or walking around town—now I felt like yelling, "Look at me! I have a baby and isn't she cute?"

Thankfully, Isabella was such an easy baby. At nap time, she dove into her crib. At first, we chose a daycare close to my office where I would go over during my lunch hour and feed her a bottle. Eventually, in an effort to have more time and control over our schedule, we hired a nanny who came to our house during the day, managed a consistent feeding schedule, and took Isabella on walks to the playground.

As much as this was my dream come true, I never considered staying home full time. Maybe if the sequence of events had been different I would have made another choice. But at thirty-eight years old, my career was firmly established and I had worked hard at that, too. I had to feel good about my choices and I think that made me a better mother. When we were with her, Richard and I hugged and kissed our baby constantly. Richard used to say, "There is not a more loved child in this world."

As Isabella grew, the thoughts of infertility and adoption faded quickly. Her early childhood in New Jersey seemed to go by in a blink. As we watched her grow, we eventually arrived at the thought... if we were over the moon happy with one girl, wouldn't it be great to have two? We decided we wanted a sibling for Isabella. I thought it would be ideal for her to have a sister to share in the experience of growing up. Now, sitting next to me on the plane after changing seats with Richard, she stared intently at me with the deck of cards in her little hands and begged me, "One quick game, Mommy, please! I'll deal."

She fanned her cards and hid behind them, then clutched them to her chest so Richard would not peek. Who could resist? She was so worth it all.

CHAPTER 4

From New Mexico to Old Mexico

W hen Isabella was four years old, we moved to Pennsylvania, settling into a one-hundred-year-old stone colonial home. It was my dream house which turned out to be a bit of a money pit as old homes often do. At least we got the location right, landing on a street with an unusually high number of parents about our age with a child Isabella's age to match. Maybe it was nesting instincts taking over my psyche, but it made me want another child even more.

Isabella fulfilled our parenting dreams in a big way, but for me, our family felt unfinished. My sisters were an important part of my life, particularly my younger sister, Kathy. Our shared experience resulted in a closeness that I could never have with a friend. As the years passed, Kathy and I managed many a family crisis together. The plight of an only child seemed lonely to me.

After a year of assorted drug treatments with a new and not-so-friendly infertility specialist, I found out I was pregnant. During my first two routine check-up appointments, the exam and bloodwork were all progressing well, according to my doctor. We were thrilled at the timing and were cautiously optimistic. During my third appointment at about ten weeks pregnant, the nurse performing the ultrasound could not find a heartbeat. I remember lying there not even able to comprehend what was being said. I left the office in tears and called Richard, choking out the news, "We lost our baby again." This miscarriage (my third) was the most devastating, but helped us to conclude that whatever magical or miraculous event that brought Isabella into our lives, it was not going to happen again. Facing this finality was incredibly difficult because we knew the adoption journey would be a tough mountain to climb.

Because we had been absent from the world of adoption for several years, we wondered if and how it may have changed. We began the search again for an agency we could work with. A friend who worked as a family attorney in New Mexico recommended an agency in Albuquerque. He assured us that it was an active agency because New Mexico laws were quite favorable for adoptive couples.

Similar to Choices, the Albuquerque agency specialized in open adoptions. Richard and I were determined to make it work, and once again agreed to an open adoption. I can't say that I welcomed the prospect of the birth mother in our lives. Although I would have agreed to almost anything to have another child, an open adoption scared me. Again, we were asked to sign a contract agreeing to scheduled visits with the birth mother, photos at six months until age three, and then once a year after that. We signed the agreement, but I secretly prayed that this birth mother would just leave us alone. How was I going to compete with this other woman? How would our child see this relationship as the years progressed? What if the birth mother wanted more?

At the time, I viewed an open adoption as a road to continued heartache. My logic went something like this: Wouldn't it just be better for everyone to move on with me starring in the mommy role? Let's rip the Band-Aid off. I would be her mother in every sense of the word while the birth mother would somehow realize that this was all for the best and allow me to take over all parenting decisions. Then, I would acknowledge what a horrible person I was for thinking these thoughts. Who would deprive a woman of seeing her child?

I knew deep down that secrets were not the formula to a healthy family. Of course the birth mother must be involved. That did not change the fact that the whole thing terrified me. Finally, I would sum it all up in my head with something like, *God damn it! Why can't I have a uterus that works? This sucks.* I would then repeat these ponderings each day for what seemed, at the time, for the rest of my life. The only person who I felt comfortable enough to share these feelings with was Richard.

We signed up for the mandatory orientation held at the agency's main office in Albuquerque, which included developing a scrapbook that would tell our family story. We were advertising ourselves again to potential birth mothers—just like the video we had produced for Choices Agency five years earlier. Another project, I thought miserably. I just wanted to take a baby home with me and shut the door.

Toward the end of the day, Richard and I sat through a tense interview. Linda, a tall social worker with a long skirt and flowing ponytail, asked tough questions, trying to narrow in on our preparedness for adoption. I almost gulped when Linda asked, "Would you adopt a child that is the result of rape or incest?" Richard and I both answered a scratchy "yes" to this final inquiry. At this stage in our lives, you would think we would know how we felt about these issues, but now, coming face-to-face with making the commitment to raise another child, I wasn't so sure. Our home was a happy place, and my husband and daughter were a dream. Now the prospect of child number two had the possibility of a dark cloud.

I didn't know what to do with that thought and pushed it away. For years in the corporate world, I prided myself on facing the tough issues head-on. I scoffed at those who ducked out of meetings where there was conflict. Yet now, facing the issue of adding to our family, I didn't take the time to think through what that disruption could mean. We were so confident that this child would be integrated seamlessly into our family. I dismissed the thought that our new daughter could have possibly been exposed to trauma. Since these scenarios had little chance of happening, theoretically at least, I didn't waste time or thought on them.

Now who was dodging the issues? I was beginning to understand that every adoption has its own bit of trauma, and these are coping skills worth learning. I would not learn until years later that the adoption itself is a disruptive event. Because the world was clapping so loudly at our efforts, I was not able to hear anything else. There is no question that I viewed adoption as a good thing. From the perspective of the child, however, it's a loss, and I had no clue about what would be necessary for Priscilla to ultimately succeed when faced with the biggest challenge of her young life.

Richard and I were both guilty of being ill-prepared for the tough questions. We both wanted another child, but our definition of child-rearing was the sum of our experiences with Isabella. There was no way for me to comprehend what a more difficult child would be like. This focus allowed us to move forward with naive confidence. We were able to communicate to anyone and everyone that we would be adding to our family— no matter what.

That day in Albuquerque, however, the end of the interview couldn't come soon enough. I had answered all the questions with a smile frozen on my face, but inside I was seething. At a coffee and doughnut break, I whispered to Richard, "Do you believe that we have to go through this all again?"

"We'll get through it," he promised with his usual optimism.

As we anxiously waited for "the call" that we were sure would come at any moment from New Mexico, we checked in with Linda, our caseworker. She kept us filled in on the latest developments at the agency and adoptions across New Mexico. While we waited, we also busied ourselves with the remaining agency orientation requirements, which included reading several adoption books and writing a short summary. The titles represented a comprehensive overview of the adoption process and stages of family adjustment. Some books were negative and somewhat depressing, but there were also uplifting stories about families with biological and adopted children. The joy and love they experienced gave me hope.

Richard and I spent time talking about the view of adoption presented by these books. We found the material simultaneously fascinating and distressing. So many adopted children displayed attachment issues no matter when they were adopted. Even with all of this information, we were still thoroughly positive that this was the path for us, determined that we would manage whatever happened. We never took this decision lightly and honestly thought that we were abundantly well-suited for this undertaking.

After a few months, it was painfully obvious that there were only non-developments and rationalizations about why we weren't being picked by a birth mother. Linda did not mince words, telling us that one of the most frustrating aspects of adoption is predicting when it would happen. She said that many adoptive parents are forever attempting to get staff to commit to waiting times, and that was something she could not do, reiterating the unpredictable availability of children. We clung to every word on the phone as she spoke in reassuring tones, emphasizing that our timetable had nothing to do with our parenting abilities.

When more than a year had passed and our picture book had not even been chosen for review, we were exceedingly worried. Still, we waited—for another year. In addition to the despair, we now faced a bureaucratic hurdle. It was time to renew all of our paperwork, which would be a massive undertaking. Before we went looking for our old files, we received even worse news: the agency was closing because the number of adoptions in New Mexico had dropped dramatically. This was a terrible shock, and we couldn't help feeling that two years had been absolutely wasted. As we reflected on our predicament, we concluded that the time for an infant was passing us by.

It wasn't that we were unhappy—far from it. There are not enough adjectives for me to list how crazy I was about Isabella. She was as eager for life experiences then as she is now as a beautifully grown woman. As a baby, she quickly transitioned out of the "nanny" phase. At almost two years, she had a spirit that needed some external stimulation. We decided that Richard would take her to *Building Blocks*, a community and faculty day-care facility. It was her first exposure to a playgroup type situation. On her first day, a boy bit her arm while they both waited for the swings. As I looked at the round bruise surrounded by teeth marks, I wondered if we had made a mistake. Isabella was not used to standing her ground. She was a quick learner and spoke up when she needed to. Delicious food, songs, music, and artwork filled her day. At dinner, she shared tales of buttermilk pancakes and performed all of the "choreography" while singing *Itsy Bitsy Spider*.

There was not a day that I didn't think about another child so I could do this all over again. It was like I was chasing another high. But after giving up on having another baby, I was in a funk. Isabella had graduated from daycare and would soon start kindergarten. So much precious family time had already slipped away.

What now? My prayers started to have a distinctly familiar theme: help me, help me. No matter how many times I acknowledged that we were already a happy family, I still came back to the thoughts of another sibling for Isabella who had just started first grade.

One day, while riding the train into town, I saw an article in our local newspaper about a program run by a small adoption agency in the suburbs. The agency specialized in bringing children from Mexico to the Philadelphia area for a summer camp. The couples who hosted children were encouraged to consider adoption. In many cases, they did go on to adopt the child who stayed with them — even when they hadn't been considering adoption before.

I looked at the picture of about a dozen cute Mexican faces smiling for the camera. I called the agency as soon as I got to work that day and discovered that it was a Catholic agency, but one that encouraged all Christian couples to apply. Richard and I had been raised Catholic, but we now belonged to the Presbyterian church. I set up a meeting with Juan, the Director of Adoption Services.

A few days later, I left work early and hopped on the train to Bryn Mawr where Richard was waiting. The office was right around the corner, in a cozy house on a small side street. Built-in shelves overflowed with piles of documents, books, and religious pictures. Inspirational messages adorned the walls of the first-floor office. Juan came over and introduced himself and led us to a table directly under an enormous picture of Our Lady of Guadalupe.

The image was vaguely familiar, but I did not immediately know the story behind it or understand the significance of Mexico's most popular religious and cultural symbol. The Blessed Virgin is pictured serene and prayerful, surrounded by what I would describe as a gold cloud. The poster was the focal point of the room and had a calming effect on me immediately as I recalled the hundreds and hundreds of times I recited the *Memorare* in the hopes of getting pregnant. The *Memorare* is a special kind of prayer asking for Mary's assistance at times of dire need. The text of the prayer is concise and implores Mary's help in a specific and urgent way. Catholics are immensely fond of memorized prayers of all varieties, and I relentlessly used this intercession to Mary to quiet my nervous mind and battered spirit. Maybe it was the incessant reciting in my head, but during all of those doctor visits, treatments, and waiting, it was the only thing I could physically do that was comforting and gave me courage. As I sat down at the small table next to Juan's desk, I knew we were in good company.

Juan had brown, wavy hair and an easy smile, his dark eyes intense and focused as he greeted us. He wore his spirituality happily, starting off our meeting with a prayer, communicating with God in a kind and gentle tone—like he was talking to his best friend. His voice was soft as he asked for faith and guidance and gave thanks for bringing us together. I remember liking and trusting Juan immediately. After what we had been through, I wasn't quite ready for my own personal chat with the Lord. I wanted answers and was perhaps a tad direct when I asked Juan almost immediately about what our chances would be to adopt a girl who was between five and seven years old.

"Would you say that we are guaranteed to find a little girl?" I pressed. I didn't plan on leaving until I knew the task at hand start to finish and likelihood of success. My steno pad question list was lengthy and I jotted down Juan's every word. Sometimes, I just can't turn it off and I was feeling like we had lost so much time already.

"Yes. From what I know of the children, you should have no problem."

Juan talked us through the Mexican adoption regulations. It was extremely reassuring to learn that he had guided many couples through to a successful child placement. He had so many stories of happy endings, I wasn't really focused at all on the challenges. Probably one of the most obvious hurdles was that the children did not speak English and we did not speak Spanish. Juan did not see that as a drawback for us, saying that the children learned English incredibly quickly once they were in the United States.

I began to sketch out a timetable as Juan reviewed the international adoption requirements. All I could focus on was how fast I could possibly finish the paperwork. He was patient and walked us through each handout page by page while I scribbled. I had already started to plan my calls for the next day. Once our paperwork was finalized, the information would be sent to a dozen orphanages. After waiting *years* for an open adoption to work for us, I could not even picture the possibility of so many children eligible for adoption *now*. We were doing something perceived as good for both sides of the border, and I became more determined than ever to make it happen.

In the car on the ride home, I marveled at Juan's spiritual confidence. He had a total "give it up" kind of faith that floored me. Exhibiting a peace and serenity that I longed for, he was happy and confident that the Lord would be there for him.

"How does that happen?" I asked Richard as we stopped for a pizza. "How is it possible to believe that *strongly*?" I wondered as I chomped on a veggie slice. Once again, Richard shrugged. Over the years with all of my questions, ramblings, musings, and marvelings, Richard had perfected his answers. But this time instead of answering, he simply said, "I don't know," and picked up his soda and car keys as we stood up to leave.

We began the paperwork checklist in earnest. As a way to keep myself occupied on the home front, I threw myself into a kind of domestic whirlwind. Motherhood the second time around was delayed and this was my hurry-up strategy. To pass the time, I took a quilting class. Then, after not owning one since the '70s, I bought a crockpot and began preparing large quantities of food. My *Mrs. Fields Cookie Book* got a workout: drop cookies, fancy cookies, filled cookies—you name it—I baked and we ate them all. During one frenzied cooking craziness, I smashed two fingers in the mixer the day before our fingerprints were to be processed and was beside myself that I had possibly delayed our paperwork.

Seven months later, soon after finishing our dossier, Juan told us he would be taking a job in Florida. I had a panic attack. How could he leave us? Juan had been married a year earlier and just had a baby girl. Now, another child was on the way. This was a wonderful career opportunity for him, and he assured us that we would be in good hands. I vowed to keep the faith as we bid Juan farewell. Thankfully, the paperwork had been completed.

Time passed in fits and starts. It was hard to shake the self-absorbed stupor reminiscent of our infertility days. No news was just no news with a dose of anxiety. To make matters a bit worse, I had not told anyone at the office of our plans, and the secret weighed on me.

Summer came early in its full humid vengeance to Philadelphia that year. It had been almost a year since our first meeting with the agency. Then, suddenly in July, the phone rang and the agency director had a question for me. Would we want to meet a five-year-old girl named Pamela? Did we need time to pray about it?

Heck, who needed to pray any MORE at that point? God was sick of hearing from me. I called the agency back the next day, saying that we would be overjoyed to meet Pamela. Before we hung up, I asked, "May we see a picture? What do you know about her?" We never did see a picture, and later found out that Pamela was actually six years old and had been brought to the orphanage as a baby. Not only that, but nobody called her Pamela. Everyone used her middle name: Priscilla.

It didn't matter — we were headed to Mexico City to meet her!

It was already about eighty degrees at 5:00 a.m. on our August departure day, the air humid and still. We were sweating as we dragged the suitcases to the train platform. Would Philly transit be on time?

"Round trip for three to the airport," I said as the conductor stopped at our seats.

"I hope you're headed for someplace a little cooler," the conductor offered as he punched our tickets and stuck the receipt in the plastic tab all in one quick motion.

"Unfortunately, no," I responded. Our dream was turning into reality. I didn't care if it was monsoon season. It was a thrill to be on our way! The familiar rocking of the airport train soothed me a bit as we headed for the complete unknown. As I looked at Isabella, I thought back to her excitement when we told her about the trip. She came home from school a few days later and announced, "I told everyone at school that I was getting a sister!"

"Really," I said, "What did you say?"

"I said that we would be best friends and that we would play together and that I would help her with her homework."

It made me so happy to hear that Isabella was as excited as we were. We knew so little, but I could cope, as nothing was going to be *final* because of this trip. Representatives from Mexico made it clear that this was a "meet and greet" trip. We tried to explain that to Isabella, but in her mind, this could be her sister. Yes, that was true, but the bottom line was that we were not committing to anything. Right now, we all had a dose of magical thinking. It all felt so new. The anxious and unsettled feelings lingered around the edges and I didn't know what to do with them. At some point, we would be forced to reckon with them, but not now. At this moment, we were preparing for a hugely important family adventure. It was all falling into place.

Years later, some of our friends opened up to us about how frightened they were for us, wondering why we would take on such an obligation. We were already a family. Perhaps they knew we would likely have to confront the complications that often accompanied international adoptions like timing delays, unforeseen expenses or cultural issues. Even at the time, I recognized this too. I'd read the exact same news stories and was hyper-alert to these possibilities as we prepared for the trip, but I'd pushed those concerns to the side. In agreeing to go to Mexico, we were taking the next step. This was the child that had been chosen for us and nothing would keep me from her.

I did not know much about Pamela Priscilla, but I knew myself and my capacity for love. I felt like I had so much more to give. After all of the fertility heartache to become a mother, it turned out to be something I was good at and loved. In hindsight, the agencies could have done more to prepare us on both sides. We would come back to that thought time and time again.

I sat on that plane with my arms around Isabella, worried and excited all at once, but feeling overwhelmingly that the odds were in our favor. My dream of a larger family would be realized. As the plane began its descent, Isabella leaned against me, closed her eyes, and I kissed the top of her head.

CHAPTER 5

Adoption
American Style

He's adopted, you know," my mother said in a hushed voice, even though just she, I, and my sister, Mary, were in the room. She had been talking to us about Joey's upcoming birthday celebration scheduled at our grandmother's northeast Philadelphia basement.

No, we didn't know. My sister and I looked at each other, mouths open.

"What about Linda?" we almost said together, asking about Joey's sister.

"She's adopted, too," my mother said.

It was the mid-sixties and my older sister, Mary, and I were about twelve and ten years old. Joey and Linda were our first cousins, and we had spent many a birthday, First Communion, and holiday together.

We were following our mother around as she cleaned the house, and the news that our first cousins were adopted hit us like a thunderclap. Wanting to know all of the details, we started asking questions.

"Why didn't you tell us before? How were they adopted?" we asked.

"I don't know a thing about it," mother said, fluffing pillows and dusting off the coffee table with her cloth diaper rag.

45

"Why couldn't Aunt Delores have children?" we persisted.

"I never asked her."

My sister and I looked at one another again, aghast, then laughed, falling back on the sofa. The thought that sisters would not know this crucial piece of information struck us first and foremost as funny. "Well, why didn't you just ask her when she was adopting Joey and Linda?" we chimed in again.

"It was none of my business."

"Yes, it was. You're her sister."

All of these years later, this conversation has come back to me as I struggled with my own issues and questions. In my mother's generation, adoption was not discussed and celebrated like it is today. Once the children were part of the family, there was no need to mention it again. What was the point? No one discussed fertility or inquired as to any of the reasons for adoption.

From the initial days of our adoption journey, my family members who were adopted were never far from my mind.

Now in our global existence, families can be created from many corners of the globe. The international adoption route is understandably attractive, in part due to stories of domestic adoptions where biological mothers appear months later with a change of heart.

With international adoptions, once a child is approved, there is little to no concern about birth mother interference, however there are other hurdles. The process is not for the faint of heart as it's longer, costlier, and much more complex than a domestic adoption. It's also almost impossible to prepare emotionally and culturally. The child is clearly different and there is the occasional rude stare or comment, but the challenges go above and beyond that. Parent motivation must be all about family and not political crisis or natural disasters. Americans tend to have the view that they are giving children opportunities that would not be possible in their native country. In nations where the reality is unrelenting poverty, separating children from the culture of their birth is viewed as a favorable solution. Still, many nations have struggled with the balance of what is in the best interest of the child.

The Catholic agency we were working with had deep ties to Mexico. In addition to Juan, representatives from the agency had a significant presence in the Philadelphia Catholic community and had been operating a summer camp for Mexican children for years. The agency's literature emphasized adoption as a positive and desired outcome. We were thrilled to take part in this international adventure but later came to realize that the country of Mexico was not as delighted.

At the time, adopting had been part of our neighborhood trend. Within a mile of our house, we knew of three babies from China, two from Africa, two from Guatemala, and at least five from Mexico, all embraced by loving families. The Child Citizenship Act of 2000, which automatically confers U.S. citizenship on foreign adoptees at the time of adoption, significantly increased foreign adoptions, making them front-page news with stories of celebrities traveling to distant countries to adopt. As we waited for Priscilla to join our family, I wondered what the family reaction and reception would be. Would they love this cute Hispanic girl?

Soon after we first started working with Mexico, I volunteered at the largest Human Resources conference in the world, which, as luck would have it, was held in Philadelphia. As a volunteer, I was admitted to the conference free of charge. Before ten thousand HR professionals descended upon the city, I attended a pre-conference meeting where volunteers received assignments for the next three days. It was a hot June day and the convention center was cool after a warm walk down Market Street. In a room on the second level, hundreds of volunteers chatted excitedly. At the check-in table, a former colleague recognized me and handed me my badge. We were then separated into groups of about a hundred each. Some of us were assisting speakers, vendors, and special guests. Others were helping with the large numbers expected in the exhibit hall, while another group was to provide directions to all of the attendees looking for room locations or a good cup of coffee. I was assigned to the last group. After partnering, we were given our assignments for the next few days.

My partner, Helen, and I introduced ourselves to each other and coincidentally found out that we worked in the same building at 20th and Market Street. A petite, perky brunette, she was the manager of a temporary employment agency, and had in fact called on my company. We had hired several people from her firm, and we had many colleagues in common. On the first day of the convention, Helen and I were scheduled to work a few hours near the connecting hallway of the convention center to the Marriott hotel, directing the conference attendees to their breakout sessions. When no one was around, we chatted about our work and our chosen profession. In an effort to create small talk, I inquired about her vacation plans, as it was late June and time to head "down the shore," as we Philadelphians like to say.

"Going anywhere interesting?" I prompted.

"No," Helen replied, "I am just about to take maternity leave."

Glancing quickly at her belly, it was obvious that she was not pregnant. There was an awkward pause.

"Really," I said, nodding my head hoping to encourage her to continue with an explanation. We suddenly entered a danger zone even for innocent girl talk.

"Yes, my husband and I will be leaving for Mexico next week to adopt a little girl. We have named her Michele."

"Get out," I squeaked. "Are you by any chance working with the agency in Bryn Mawr?" Helen nodded as I gushed, "Would you believe that we are also waiting to hear about adopting a girl from Mexico?"

Helen and I plunged into an in-depth conversation about infertility, adoption, and our Mexican connection. At that point in our timeline, Richard and I had finished our paperwork and were waiting to be called. We had hit the wall, just waiting and wondering what would happen next. The uncertainty of it all had depressed us no end. Helen and her husband had the finish line in sight and were acquainted with all of the players. She happily filled in the blanks for me, telling me about their trips to Mexico (three!) and how they came to adopt a girl with special needs (it shortened the time frame by months). In addition to maternity leave, Helen was also going to take family leave because baby Michele had a hole in her heart and was scheduled for surgery about a month after their return. Michele was not from the same orphanage as Priscilla and, because she needed immediate medical attention, the timetables and Mexican connections were a bit different.

During my train ride home that evening, I sat dazed, but smiling and looking out the window. Any doubts I had about Mexico just faded away as I saw the encounter with Helen as the ultimate sign that we were going to be successful. Suddenly the world felt supportive, loving, and, best of all, the adoption process, once so secret, now seemed downright commonplace. I couldn't wait to tell Richard. We had made hundreds of family decisions to get to that point, yet I had never felt more confident about our choices than I did at that moment. With one sentence, Helen and I discovered our bond and talked for hours. We kept in touch for years after that.

Meeting Helen was more than just a fun coincidence though. As strangers, we discovered a uniquely personal bond totally by chance, sharing every detail. My own sisters ultimately decided not to have children, and I don't really know any more than my mother did about her sister's circumstances. Why were we so hesitant to discuss it? I was particularly close to Kathy, but when it came to this topic, we didn't venture far from the boundaries set all those years ago. It was a fact that my sisters' plans for childbearing were not my business, but I wanted to have the same conversation with my sister that I had with Helen and that was not in the cards.

When I told my sisters about our plans to visit a child in Mexico, we had already submitted all of the paperwork. I don't recall their reaction, but I know we didn't share much on either side. The ups and downs of our journey seemed like too much information. When it came to adoption and my family, I instinctively time-traveled back to the sixties. I thought it would be so different. Perhaps we have not come that far after all.

CHAPTER 6

Mexican Treasure

Our Delta flight landed in Mexico City right on time. After immigration questions, we walked through the doors into the throng of relatives and friends waiting for arriving passengers. Lugging our bags toward the international terminal exit, we spotted Sari right away. At about 5'7" she was quite tall by Mexican standards. She waved to us from the edge of the crowd. I could see her black overstuffed purse slung over her shoulder, one hand clutching papers and a cell phone, the other enthusiastically signaling us to follow her.

Sari was the main contact in Mexico for our agency in Pennsylvania. She was a volunteer who made sure that adoptive couples arrived at the various official destinations in and around Mexico City. In a huge, sprawling city of over twenty million, this was no small feat and not a job for one woman alone—Hector, her faithful driver, handyman, and all around personal assistant did most of the ferrying.

In a bob-style cut to her chin, Sari's auburn brown hair had a slight wave. She always wore colorful pantsuits set off with a dramatic flair, usually a contrasting scarf or trademark silver jewelry. Bright red lipstick, meticulously re-applied during the day, topped off her sophisticated look. Now in her sixties, Sari had an energy and enthusiasm for her work that was truly remarkable.

We had met Sari the previous fall as we were preparing our paperwork. Sari was in Philadelphia for the agency's *Family Fun Day,* sponsored by a local Catholic church. The day was a celebration and reunion for all of the adoptive couples and children who had been placed by the agency over the years. Sari had no children of her own but worked tirelessly to create families. "Oh, that will be another one out of jail," she would chirp happily as she recounted her success stories to us. From what we knew, the shelters did not even remotely resemble jail, but a family for a child represented success and that made Sari happy.

Sari spoke with authority, but always with a smile. Although not professionally trained, she knew all of the rules and regulations of international adoption laws that pertained to Mexico. Her interest in and commitment to adoptive families had grown over the years, largely because of her faith and love of children.

At the airport now, Sari watched us drag our suitcases through the throng of animated family members waiting outside of the customs area.

"Helloooo," she trilled, almost screaming. "How are you doing... you must be tired... no?" Hugs and two-cheeked kisses were traded all around as we began to weave our way to the parking garage. As she was helping us with our bags, she told us that her driver Hector was not able to meet us today. I admired Sari's nerve, pulling out of the airport garage into the chaos of Mexico City congestion as she chattered and gestured, turning around to look at us a bit too often for the traffic. No sooner had that thought passed through my mind when WHAM! we were sideswiped by a car with four young men who barely flinched and kept on driving. Within a second, their car disappeared into another lane and the endless honking traffic. No one was hurt, and Sari was able to keep driving. There were so many cars whizzing by that we were afraid to stick our head out of the window to look at the damage. Sari wailed loudly (and I think cursed in Spanish) and immediately grabbed her cell phone, frantically calling Hector. Richard and I exchanged nervous glances when we realized that no one was going to pull over to trade insurance information. Ten minutes of Spanish later, she declared, "It is no problem. Hector will fix it and call my insurance company." Thankfully, her two hands now clutched the wheel. It was our first lesson on Mexico road rules.

The streets of Mexico City stretched endlessly before us. The sheer size of the city left me weary. The neighborhoods soon became indistinguishable as we rode from one section of the city to another. We passed low, flat-topped buildings, stores, road-side stands, and small strip mall-type shopping area where we picked up provisions for our stay. We marveled at the prices, especially for the baked goods. Huge pastries of all shapes, with cinnamon, glazed sugar, or chocolate were stacked on large, wide metal trays. Most of the goodies were thirteen cents or less!

For our three-day visit, we would live in an apartment owned by Sari's family located in what you would not exactly call a tourist area of Mexico City. Loaded with our mixture of junk food and essentials, we climbed two stories and stopped on a small landing with two cream-colored doors. Sari proceeded to unlock the apartment deadbolt with seven complete turns. At each click of the lock, the U.S. State Department warning about the safety of Mexico City came back to me: *Sporadic bursts of politically motivated violence occur from time to time in certain areas ... click.*

Crime in Mexico continues at high levels and is often violent... click, click.

The kidnapping of non-Mexicans continues at an alarming rate and in some instances... click.

Americans have become victims of harassment, mistreatment, and extortion by Mexican law enforcement... click Click CLICK!

I pushed the thought away, refusing to believe that anything bad would happen to us. We were here on a mission and the angel of adoption would surely watch over us.

The door opened into a spacious, two-bedroom dwelling with a large room for eating and living. The décor was 1970s green and blue, with a large, overstuffed sofa facing a TV just inside the door. A maple hutch and matching table with four chairs sat at the other end of the room. Through a set of swinging doors, we could enter the kitchen, which was just large enough to turn around. The second bedroom was small and, once Isabella saw the large, king-size bed in the master, she announced that she would not be sleeping in the second bedroom by herself.

Sari breezed through the apartment announcing mat-ter-of-factly, "Remember, do not throw the toilet paper in the toilet. The plumbing… it cannot handle."

We put our bottled water in the bathroom and the kitchen and made sure the bathroom trash can had a plastic bag. Richard turned the bolt all seven times after Sari kissed us goodbye.

"Can I go out onto the balcony?" Isabella asked as we re-laxed and then readied for dinner. "No," we responded together. Remote control in hand, she plopped onto the sofa and channel flipped through English and Spanish entertainment.

~

Meet-Pamela-Priscilla-day dawned with butterflies all around. The itinerary included a short visit to the *Ministerios de Amor* office, where we would meet Luisa, the social worker assigned to us, and then travel to the orphanage. *Ministerios* was the Mexican agency that partnered with our Pennsylvania agency.

Sari and Hector were already outside at 7:30 a.m., tooting the car horn. We ran down the stairs and when we opened the apartment building door, a beautiful breeze hit our faces. What a glorious surprise! The sweltering heat of home was just a memory as the forecast for sunny Mexico was a pleasant eighty-five degrees, no humidity, and an evening cool enough for a jacket. It was easy to be optimistic as we piled into the car that morning.

We pulled away from the curb and entered the roaring morning traffic. I lost all sense of direction after only a few blocks and many turns but in Hector's capable hands we made it to the *Ministerios* office in only twenty minutes. On a quiet side street not far from the heart of the city, it looked more like a house nestled in a cozy neighborhood than an office building. From the street, only the surrounding concrete walls and part of the sloping, red tile roof were visible. The gate opened up to reveal the most treasured commodity in Mexico City—parking. Cars were parked two-wide and four-deep on a long pathway up to the door. Green vines with fuchsia flowers clung to the walls. Pots of green, pink, and yellow were everywhere.

As I stepped into the lobby, the low ceiling, dark walls, and blue pillow décor put me in a tranquil mood. Sari walked down the hall, telling us she would be back in a moment. In the conference room where we waited for our caseworker, Luisa, I noticed a guitar leaning against the wall near the corner. We waited about thirty minutes; the office was still totally silent. At 9:00, an administrative assistant delivered water. Still, no one else was around. Another half-hour passed until the office started to come to life. My mind wandered. In the background, I heard Sari's rapid Spanish in a room down the hall. Isabella circled the large oval conference table again and again, first walking, then skipping. Eventually, Luisa walked in dressed in a simple tan suit, her dark hair pulled back in a sleek chignon.

After inquiring about our trip, Luisa gave us the details we had been waiting for. She explained, "Pamela is a happy child, full of personality with many friends. She was brought to the orphanage as a baby, yet no one has visited her in seven years. Her name is Pamela Priscilla, but everyone calls her Priscilla."

Luisa began to sift through a file while she talked about the various activities scheduled for us that day. Continuing to sort the thick pile of papers in the folder, she shared a few more tidbits. We were hungry for information, and I watched her carefully measure every phrase. She seemed almost guarded as to what she shared.

Setting down the folder, Luisa explained, "Priscilla began her life at another *Ministerios* location, but has been at Cuernavaca for the last five years. She has been well cared for. The staff at the shelter is highly experienced."

Priscilla's home was not called an orphanage because many of the children living there had parents. Luisa deliberately used the word *shelter* and went on to explain, "It's just that some of the parents cannot afford to raise their children." Parents were required to visit their children only once a year in order to retain parental rights.

"The women at the shelter are referred to as '*Tías*' (Aunts) and they have been preparing Priscilla for today's visit," she added. "One *Tía* in particular has been very close to Priscilla. Her name is *Tía* Vero and I know they are fond of each other."

My mind was a jumble of images as I tried to imagine what we would discover over the next few hours. Snapping back to reality, I extended my hand to take the photo Luisa was holding out to me. Other than an impossibly grainy fax we had received just a few days prior to our trip, this was the first time I would actually see the girl who could potentially be my new daughter. My heart beating loudly, I looked down at the picture to see Priscilla, her black hair flying straight back behind her. A group of children were on a Moon Bounce. Priscilla seemed intent on capturing the attention of another child and was obviously saying something mid-bounce. She wore a simple white T-shirt, dark shorts, and white ankle socks. Her skinny legs were tan, with the taut little muscles of a kid at play. I could not stop looking at her face. Focusing intently on the photo, I saw a little girl with big brown eyes, small button nose, and sweet, perfect, bow-shaped lips. Isabella and Richard strained across the table for a look.

"She's so cute," I said, and heard myself exhale a little too loudly. Chiding myself to have a little faith, I shot a quick thank you prayer to God. Priscilla looked happy and content with the world, eager to play and engage with others. All of this captured in a picture. Yes, I wanted this to work.

I didn't hear what was said next because I couldn't stop staring at her. My mind and body felt numb as I tried to sort out what I was feeling. We had worked tirelessly to get to this point and anxiety began to overwhelm me. Could the day possibly live up to my sky-high expectations?

Our meeting ended, and as I got into the back seat of the car and fumbled with my seat belt, I was lost in thought. Sari was pointing out the highlights along the route to Cuernavaca, explaining that it was a popular tourist destination and a favorite vacation spot for families. All of the talk faded into the background for me as I tried to picture myself meeting Priscilla. The thought was mind-blowing, and, for as much as we had prepared, I had my arms wrapped around myself like a pretzel and could feel my throat tightening. When I am overly nervous, I try to use a visualization technique for each successive step. I could see the car stopping and me getting out and walking toward a child, bending down for a hug, maybe stroking her hair. It was the first instant where I would lay eyes on Priscilla that had me in a knot. Even though we were driving into the complete unknown, I knew deep down that this was exactly where we were supposed to be.

The scenery was green and tranquil, and, after spending so much time stuck in Mexico City traffic, it was a relief to be almost speeding up through the mountains. We were headed about fifty miles south of Mexico City. I had been holding Isabella's hand for a while, but it was all clammy, so I let go and gave her a hug. She was quiet, and as always, happy and excited to be with us. Richard and I had agreed immediately that she should accompany us on this trip; she needed to get to know Priscilla and be a part of the adventure of meeting her for the first time. I took her ponytail and gave it a twirl. She smiled and squeezed my hand.

I tapped Isabella's shoulder, trying to get her to look out the window at the changing scenery. As we approached the outskirts of Mexico City, the buildings gave way to neighborhoods and roadside stands filled with colorful pottery, jewelry, sombreros, blankets, and trinkets. The highway to Cuernavaca was a toll road, and, as we slowed down to approach the toll booth, I could see men with machine guns patrolling the area. Suddenly, as we stopped, a girl no more than five years old and about two inches higher than the hood of the car darted in front of us. She held up three small, red balls and began to juggle them furiously. I gasped and began to fumble for change and roll down my window. No, no, no, Sari and Hector were saying, shaking their heads and impatiently waving her away. When the bumper inched closer, she ran into another lane. Isabella and I exchanged silent glances as our car passed her by.

We were getting close. By now we had all fallen into a noticeable silence. Mexico is our neighbor, but life there could not be more different. As our car climbed the hills to our destination, I looked out at the makeshift structures that passed for houses. In this beautiful country of sun and flowers, the windows of these one-story dwellings were small and dark. Some had clotheslines stretched across the front porches, with toys and occasional appliance in the yard. The natural beauty of the mountains was in stark contrast to the poor living conditions. For the native Mexican, this is a fact of life.

We turned down a small narrow road, and there it was. The orphanage/shelter turned out to be a converted hotel. We stepped out of the car and approached a tall, white, corrugated-metal fence and pressed the doorbell. A high, shrill sound brought one of the *Tías* running to the door. A young woman who looked to be in her twenties with shoulder-length shiny black hair unlocked the gate.

Sari introduced us and explained the reason for our visit as other staff members came out to the patio to meet us. The *Tías* were dressed in skirts with tailored white blouses, black stockings, and black dress pumps, hair pulled back in elaborate ponytails and curled updos. They wore their makeup perfectly applied, including colorful eyeshadow and glossy lips. The one male in the group had on long black pants (men NEVER wear shorts in Mexico) and an open-neck, long-sleeve, white shirt. I was distracted for a moment by their ultra-dressy appearance, only later realizing that the staff had dressed up so beautifully for us.

We shook hands with everyone and stood awkwardly for a moment, feeling all eyes on us. Isabella was clinging to me, not sure what to do. Sari graciously intervened and asked to see the shelter.

We walked across a gravel path to the lobby area. A few feet in front of the doorway, four steps led down to a living room, which had been the hotel lobby. Two tweedy, dingy, gray-brown patterned sofas and a small TV were the only items in the room. Stairs at the opposite end of the lobby led to an eating area with six long tables and chairs. A small group of boys sat at two of the tables, paper and pencils in hand, apparently completing a lesson.

Although we did not know it at the time, Priscilla was upstairs hiding. She knew enough to understand that her life was about to change, and it frightened her.

Sari asked one of the *Tías* about the living arrangements and then dutifully translated for us. The boys' and girls' rooms were on different floors, with boys on the second and girls on the third. Each room contained at least two sets of twin-sized bunk beds, with two children assigned to each bed, which meant eight girls to a room.

Meanwhile, we were all growing restless still waiting for Priscilla to come downstairs. To the left of the living room was a large sliding glass door through which we could see a brick patio and an oval-shaped swimming pool. We stepped outside to have a look. The pool was large enough to have both a shallow and deep end as well as a Jacuzzi. I hoped that there would be no swimming any time soon though, as white scum floated on top of green water. The sides of the pool were dark with a feathery moss covering that moved as the water rippled.

The stairway leading to the bedrooms to the right off of the pool area had assorted buckets and mops piled on the landing. The stone around the edge of the building was crumbling and the gray stucco was dirty and cracked. Flowers, though breathtakingly beautiful, were everywhere, contributing to a look of overgrown neglect. There was laughter coming from the kitchen area. About a dozen boys were working at the table looked happy, well fed, and cared for. Resources may have been stretched, but I sensed that the *Tías* loved the children.

That's when I saw them both out of the corner of my eye. A precious girl, her eyes cast down, descended the stairs, her hand firmly clasped to *Tía* Vero. Those big brown saucers looked a bit sad as she met my gaze. Her jet-black, shoulder-length hair was perfectly combed, parted in the middle with two little ponytails on either side of the part. The hair was tucked through and pulled back, holding the thick, black mane off of her face. Short, straight hairs escaped across her forehead and those wisps moved in the blowing breeze as she walked toward us. Tan and glowing, Priscilla was one week shy of her seventh birthday, yet I remember thinking how tiny she was! I smiled. Priscilla smiled back to reveal a mouth full of perfect baby teeth.

After Sari and *Tía* Vero helped with the introductions, Priscilla dutifully gave each of us two-cheek kisses, then stepped back, her big brown eyes focused intently on us. The girls eyed each other. Isabella brought a doll to give to Priscilla, which was dressed in American-flag-type clothes. Isabella held up her own similar doll. Priscilla reached for the doll and hugged it to her chest. We had both girls sit on the sofa to pose for a picture. It's my favorite shot of our entire Mexican experience. Isabella and Priscilla are sitting side by side, neither sure of the future. Both were probably wondering what the adults were talking about.

There was a quick *Tía* huddle and Priscilla once again disappeared up the curved staircase. Sari quipped, "They are taking her to change her clothes." Priscilla had been wearing a simple white t-shirt and baggy blue shorts. We were all dressed to impress, ready for our lunch date. Soon Priscilla reappeared in an orange smocked dress that tied in the back, white lace-trimmed socks, and black shiny shoes.

Strolling around Cuernavaca holding hands with two little girls was wonderful. At lunch, Priscilla sat up straight in her chair and was extremely positive that she wanted a chicken taco. After dessert, she joked with Hector, "Why did you order that big piece of chocolate cake for dessert and not give me any?" Of course, she said this in Spanish. We had to wait for Sari and Hector to stop laughing before they could tell us what she said.

After lunch, we walked through the lovely town center. We stopped to browse through an open-air market of crafts, jewelry, and other handmade items where Sari purchased matching necklaces and bracelets for the girls. I had my eye on pottery and found a vase with a hand-painted sunflower. Isabella was thrilled to buy souvenirs for her friends at home. Priscilla, however, was not to be denied. Grabbing my hand firmly, she pulled me to a shoe store and pointed to a lovely pair of black patent dress shoes, then pointed to herself. Sari had told us earlier that the children do not own any clothes at the shelter. All clothing is shared.

"She knows what she wants," I said to Richard.

When we stopped for ice cream, Priscilla ordered a scoop of vanilla with a hard chocolate shell. I watched in amazement as she made a small hole at the base of the mound, eating all of the ice cream from inside the shell, leaving the chocolate covering perfectly intact until the end. She then proceeded to crunch the chocolate shell, announcing that chocolate was her favorite. (*"Me gusta!"*)

When we dropped Priscilla off at the shelter, we stood together at the front gate as Sari took our picture. Our first family portrait produces an amazing rush of memories when I look at it now. It was such a happy day. Our idea of a family was finally happening. We had no idea of the struggles ahead.

After more goodbyes and quick kisses on the cheeks, the *Tías* took Priscilla back inside. We were left with thoughts of our child, now separated from us, wondering what she was thinking about.

The next day we picked up Priscilla and traveled to a nearby park. The girls played on the swings and monkey bars, laughing and running, looking for all the world like two kids just being kids. After a while, we went to eat at a nearby restaurant where Pris was the center of attention and loving every minute of it. The girls colored and drew with the crayons and paper that Isabella had in her backpack. Priscilla drew the exact same tree that Isabella did, matching each color and pen stroke. Priscilla then wrote her name perfectly at the bottom of the paper, much to the delight of all the adults. She was clearly at ease with grown-ups, able to behave during a lengthy meal, unbelievably cute.

When it was time to say goodbye after day two, I squeezed her hard not knowing when I would see her again. We gave her gifts of candy, more coloring books, and coloring supplies. She was happiest about the candy, telling us, "I will have to hide it so the other children will not eat it."

As we drove away we turned for one last look at our daughter—a word that no one dared say aloud. One hand was clasped to *Tía* Vero, one was waving. I imagine that Priscilla felt nothing but relief at this point. We had no idea what it was like to live with fifty other children. At the time, we understood that Priscilla was told about the upcoming adoption. Priscilla later said that nothing was really explained to her. She was so young and, in all likelihood, did not comprehend the purpose of our visit. I am sure she was anxious to return to her friends and not think of us again. She was probably happy for the treats and the lunch—but did she understand what it meant to be adopted? Did she imagine a life with us, leaving behind all that she knew and loved? Definitely not.

CHAPTER 7

Hanging by a Thread

I n the back seat of the car, weaving our way back toward Mexico City, I began to turn green. Ever alert to intestinal distress, I mentally took inventory of the meals during the last two days, deciding which food was the culprit of my queasiness. It had to be the taco—no, maybe the fruit. Then I noticed that Hector's technique of descending the mountains was gas, brake, gas, brake. My stomach was churning, and my eyes throbbed with all of the tension that a life-changing experience can bring.

We were headed back to the *Ministerios de Amor* office to meet up with Ceci Blanchet Pezet, Director of *Ministerios*, lovingly referred to as "Mommy Ceci" to the hundreds of children whom she has helped over the years. Sari reminded us that Ceci would be anxious to hear all about our visit with Priscilla, as this was *Ministerios'* first venture into adoption. Luisa, also eager to hear our impressions, would be there as well. Ceci was legendary in Mexico for her work with children, and we wanted to make a good impression. Meanwhile, I was trying not to throw up.

We walked into the office to meet a tall, broad-shouldered woman with short sandy blond hair that framed a round full-cheeked face. Dressed almost totally in white, she was a towering presence and gave us the customary greeting with a kiss on each cheek. Her light brown eyes had bright yellow flecks that gave her a lively, engaging, warm expression. Still, I could tell that she was all business as we followed into her office. It was clear she wanted to talk, and my stomach was just not ready.

"You are not feeling well?" Ceci gave a concerned frown and then signaled for water from an assistant hovering in the hall. The sunny corner office was inviting, with plain, light wooden furniture, blue and yellow cushions and pillows, plants, and lots of books. I settled on a bench seat and Isabella plopped down next to me.

My insides were reacting to my outside, and I fought an impulse to flee. At any moment, I thought the whole business could unravel and we would be leaving Mexico with broken hearts. My dad used to have an expression that he would say when he was exasperated or annoyed or wanted to joke around with us. "Bean," he would say, using his nickname for me. "You are hanging by a thread!" The comment always made me laugh. A serious proclamation for just about any mostly minor annoying thing I was doing. It seemed to sum up the story so far today.

I pulled Isabella a little closer to me on the bench, wanting to grab onto something. It really did feel as if I was hanging by that thread. What if Ceci did not like us? What if we were not approved as adoptive parents? I was forever telling Richard about people that I would see on the news or TV that should have been hanging by a thread. People and families who had endured unspeakable tragedies and dire circumstances were always climbing back into the ring. I needed to find the secret to keep me going.

Luisa and Sari chatted in Spanish for a few moments and Richard gave me a tense look. Luisa realized we were waiting for them to stop and then asked us, "How do you like working with your agency? They are wonderful people, no?"

I related the details of Juan's departure to Florida and how the agency was still there for us, praying for us, and helping us through all of the details. I could tell that Ceci wanted to speak and she jumped in, her hands outstretched to us, "Tell me about your visit with Priscilla."

Richard took the lead describing our experience as I nursed my water and headache. By this time, Ceci had convinced Isabella to sit on her lap and then we all began to chime into the discussion. Priscilla had many charms and it was easy to see her as a part of our family. We laughed as we recounted her sense of humor and playfulness with Isabella. But Ceci wanted to be sure about us, so the conversation then turned to focus on our family. Ceci was sitting back in her chair and her tone was lightly prodding. Did we think Priscilla would fit into our family? Did we go to church and how were we involved? Where did we grow up? What were our families like and did they support us in this process?

Richard and I laughed as we recounted Priscilla's spunkiness and sense of fun.

"She has her own mind, that's obvious," I said. "But also so polite and she had beautiful manners at our lunch."

I explained how well she played with Isabella. But as far as our involvement in church, I hesitated a bit.

"We were brought up in the Catholic church, but are now active in the Presbyterian church. Isabella goes to Sunday school there."

Ceci smiled and nodded. I talked about our tiny community, the small school district where we lived, and how our extended family was cautious but supportive. Richard and I shared details about our families, both from the Philadelphia area.

I could tell Isabella was starting to squirm. Ceci saw it too and asked, "What flavor ice cream did you have?" to which Isabella immediately responded, "Strawberry with sprinkles!"

I sat there looking at Ceci, Luisa, and Sari. These are the kind of people who have dedicated their lives to children. The afternoon sun warmed the room and Luisa drew back her dark hair into a ponytail to cool off. At the time Richard and I became involved with *Ministerios de Amor*, Luisa and Ceci had forged a close friendship and partnership, united in their work for children.

Now, here in Mexico City several months later, we wanted to convey that we were serious about this process. For a second, it looked as if I had given my headache to Richard. He sat with a stunned look on his face as we began to ask Ceci and Luisa questions about the paperwork for Priscilla to be declared legally free. Luisa started to list the requirements, the first of which would be to advertise for Priscilla's "parents."

"What?" I asked, confused. "I thought you said that no one had been to visit her in seven years. Why is it necessary to go through with this when she has lived at the shelter all of that time?" I think I was whining, although I didn't mean to.

Luisa explained that this was the only way to satisfy the law. After the three-month notification period, Priscilla's case would then be assigned to Mexican Family Court for their approval—a task that could take many more months. On our next Mexico trip, when all the paperwork was in order, we would attend an adoption hearing in family court. The third trip would be approximately two-weeks long, including a side trip to Juarez where Priscilla's entry visa would be acquired. All told, we could be looking at another one or more years of waiting and paperwork!

We had been told many times by our agency that we would be required to visit Mexico twice to finalize the adoption. But Ceci had asked for this initial introductory trip to introduce us to Priscilla. Three trips to Mexico City was an overwhelming thing to comprehend in that moment.

If you have ever been on vacation in a foreign country, you know the drill. You play by their rules. Sometimes, there are no rules, or the rules change. You hope and pray it works out.

"Do not worry," was the response from Ceci when I questioned the advertisement requirement. "No one will come forward." Ceci did her best to look reassuring but, at that moment, I had a definite sense of defeat. Luisa added, "Remember, we are over ninety-million Mexicans, so this process will take time."

My nausea started to come back. Ceci stroked Isabella's hair, hugged her, and said, "It's only time. I have also adopted two boys and, when you finally have Priscilla, you will know all of the obstacles are worthwhile." But my mind was nowhere near "having" Priscilla. I could no more picture that than I could picture driving my own car around Mexico City. It all felt so strange and oddly sudden in a way.

"What are your boys' names?" Isabella asked shyly.

"Pablo and Santiago," Ceci said, pointing to a black frame, the two of them smiling, their heads tilted in toward one another.

'"Are they twins?" asked Isabella.

"Yes, Santiago is older by two minutes. They are the love of my life."

The room grew quiet and Ceci said, "I was not sure if I would ever have children. But when the call came about Pablo and Santiago, I knew they were meant to be mine and I decided to adopt them immediately after meeting them."

"Ceci," I ventured. "We really don't know that much about you or *Ministerios*. How did you get started?"

Ceci looked down at her hands and closed her eyes briefly for a moment. When she started to talk, her voice was soft. "I had a wonderful family who gave me everything in the world, but I wanted more." She paused to adjust Isabella on her lap, pulling her in a bit closer and continued.

Ceci was raised with parental expectations to have a career in business. Conquering many industries and roles, she was an accomplished, professional woman. After describing her successes in many ventures including banking and wine sales, Ceci told us of her longing for something that mattered. Her eyes focused on some faraway place as she spoke.

"The Lord was calling me to do something else with my life," she said looking right at Isabella.

Ceci said she felt called to minister to youth, but she didn't quite know how. One night on the way home from work, she took a wrong turn and found herself at a large garbage dump in the heart of Mexico City. As she pondered her predicament, rifling through the car for a map, she became aware of her surroundings. Re-tracing her errant steps on the map, she saw something moving on the mountains of refuse. It was not "something" but instead many "someones." Children were digging in the pile for something to eat. Dirty and disoriented, they didn't pay any mind to Ceci, who by this time had gotten out of the car for a closer look.

As she began to speak to the children and hear their stories, she felt that familiar stirring again. Ceci knew she had found her life's work and described the happiness she felt in sharing her faith with the children. She came to understand that providing a place where children would have a chance to find their faith and not worry about how to live was her dream. Her ministry grew as she created one of Mexico's first outreach programs just for children. Her shelters were a place where children of all ages could go to hear more about the Lord, be safe, and eat balanced meals.

Ceci explained further that our agency in Pennsylvania was always looking for new adoption partners in Mexico. After working with a variety of Mexican government agencies, they were trying to connect with people like Ceci in the private sector. Private agencies presented less red tape and were more agreeable to assisting U.S. couples. Ceci was known to our agency, but so far had not agreed to participate in the program. The agency appealed to Ceci during a personal visit to Mexico just a few short months prior to our involvement.

How did I get to be with all of these religious do-gooders? They were so giving and caring. As I thought about the sequence of events that led us to this place, I knew that this was how our family was meant to be. There is a saying about the company you keep that I was trying to remember as I was sitting there with these passionate women. I knew that I could learn a lot about patience and divine intervention from them.

"Feeling better?" Ceci asked.

"Yes," I smiled. I was weary and thought it was time to focus on getting home, yet desperately wanted to live up to Ceci's expectations. As we talked through the last of the details of our future trips to Mexico, it started to make sense in my still-foggy head.

Ceci turned to Isabella. "Are you ready to share your family?"

"I don't know," Isabella delivered her sing-song response as she squirmed in Ceci's lap. She looked down at the floor and then at me.

Ceci thought for a moment and said, "You have time to get ready. It will be a big change, but I want you to be sure that this is what you want to do."

"We fell in love the instant we saw her," I testified for the whole family.

Isabella looked as if she wanted to be saved from the conversation. She walked over to where I was sitting and put her arms around my neck. We all stood up to go. Hugs and kisses traded, Hector drove us back to the apartment and Sari gave us specific instructions for the cab ride to the airport the next morning.

On our flight back to Philadelphia, my mind was restless and uneasy. We began with the objective of finding a sibling for my daughter. Now, having put the process in motion, it was bigger than I had anticipated. Richard and I talked about seeing

Priscilla in her natural habitat. She was so at home there—happy and content. We kept coming back to Ceci and Luisa choosing her as the first child to be placed as part of an international adoption. I believed she was chosen because of her resilience and grit. They had seen the signs that Priscilla was ready for this change and we believed that to be true. Still, there were so many unknowns.

Richard and I were encouraged with what we had seen—a small girl who could focus on a lunch, a playdate, and interact with another child and the adults. Developmentally, we thought she was right on track and had a fun and interesting presence. We were thoroughly excited yet cautiously optimistic; however, questions lingered about what she had been told and what her reactions to leaving Mexico would be. Ultimately though, my mind returned to the power of the love of family and what we could all achieve together. The shelter was a distinctly special place, but there was no substitute for a mother's love and caring.

One obstacle that I did not fully understand at the time was that everything I knew about adoption was from a book, workshop, or observations from family and friends. It's one thing to know something at arm's length, but without the emotional experience behind it, that knowledge sometimes doesn't amount to much. I look back here and marvel at my determination, my positive outlook. I knew what difficulties could lay ahead but didn't really think they would be part of our story. After all, I had a social work background and then years of experience in dealing with people at all levels within an organization. I had become quite familiar with adoption issues through our first two attempts and, even though Priscilla was a bit older, I was confident that our love would win her over. Still, how much did I really know about Mexico and her experience? I would not see her again for months, maybe a year. Those were enough unknowns to give anyone pause.

Despite my aisle seat, I couldn't get comfortable with all of these thoughts whirring about, and I just stared out into space. Isabella was excited to give her classmates the gifts she had purchased in Cuernavaca and she wanted to know if I thought Priscilla would play on our swing set. When I asked her how she liked Priscilla, she responded enthusiastically that Priscilla was "so cute" and couldn't wait for them to be sisters.

The next day at home, Richard and I experienced some serious stomach distress. We realized that we both cheated a bit with the water when brushing our teeth. At least we were home, and we had scheduled Sunday as a recovery day. Thankfully, the stomach cramps and other intestinal problems were short-lived.

The rest of the summer was an uneventful exhale. I looked at the calendar and tried to picture Priscilla far away. What was she doing? Was she thinking about the family who did not speak a word of her language, who came to visit her bearing gifts, hugs, and kisses? I began to plan out my key to survival for the next few months. There would always be elements out of our control, but after hearing the legal and logistical hurdles explained, I was anxious to map them out on a spreadsheet and color code each task. In my driven, project-management-focused way, I knew it was the only way I would be able to manage it. There wasn't a to-do list that I couldn't execute. Rules? Workaround solutions? Deliverables? Timetables? Mexican bureaucracy was not going to defeat me. I had met my daughter and she *would* be a part of our family. I knew now that I was no longer hanging by that thread. My grip was firm, and I was determined not to let go.

Love at the Border

CHAPTER 8

June 30

B y April, our Pennsylvania agency and Mexico City's *Ministerios de Amor* adoption agencies decided to take matters into their own hands and arranged for Priscilla to live with us until the adoption could be finalized by Mexican Family Court. We were told that this sequence of events did not exactly comply with U.S. adoption law. Priscilla had not been officially approved by Mexico as our child. Because we were bending the rules a bit, I worried about being found out. Richard waved away my concern, yet I couldn't shake the visual image of the Department of Homeland Security at our door and headlines splashed across the nation: "U.S. Couple Defy International Adoption Laws."

Priscilla's arrival date was scheduled for June 30. Because she was declared legally free in March, we were given the go-ahead to have contact with her. From that date forward, every Sunday at 6:00 p.m. we called the shelter. We were not quite sure what she was being told but thought it important that she hear our voices and get to know us before coming to live with us. In the beginning, we scripted a few things to say in Spanish:

¿Qué usted hizo esta semana? (What did you do this week?)

¿Quiénes son sus amigos? (Who are your friends?)

Le llevaremos a la playa este verano. (We will take you to the beach this summer.)

We wanted to converse with Priscilla in her native tongue, but it turned out to be a pretty futile exercise. Our agency had experience with many other children adopted from Mexico and assured us that within a few months of Priscilla living with us, she would be able to speak English. Those first few calls, however, were an English and Spanish jumble. Karen, our neighbor and friend, came to our rescue to translate for us as we spoke to each other. Karen had many years of foreign language translation experience, and with her soft voice and contagious laugh, our conversations with Priscilla became more natural and flowed much easier.

Still, they were not easy phone calls. We were trying to communicate to a child a world away about what awaited her. Priscilla participated in the calls because *Tía* Vero found her and brought her to us. She waited for us to ask questions. We had many so that it was not a problem, but the conversations left me wondering what she knew about her situation. Did she know the reason we were asking her about riding a bike was that we were looking forward to her riding together with Isabella?

Her consistent level of spunk impressed me. We attempted to ask her questions about her daily routine and she tried to answer those questions telling us about how she would fit into ours. Priscilla was not shy about turning the phone calls into opportunities to receive chocolate, clothes, or toys for herself and her friends. We sent small gifts occasionally which probably spurred her on even more.

Isabella was especially eager for the calls and always participated in our most fun and important Sunday event. She was decidedly into being in charge as a big sister, offering opinions about how they would share and do things together. During the calls, I was ever alert to Priscilla's interest in us as a family. The glimmers were few and far between, but one Sunday gave me hope.

A few days before one of our Sunday calls, I had a terrible fall and broke my ankle. When it came time to contact the shelter on Sunday, I was still a bit out of it and not sleeping well due to the pain, the hard cast on my leg, and a massive headache. Richard, Isabella, and Karen went ahead with the call as usual. When the conversation was over, I heard from Richard that Priscilla asked why I was not there, and when she heard about my accident asked if I would be all right. At the end of the call, she said that she hoped I would feel better. It was a departure from her usual somewhat-detached demeanor, and I took it as a sign that just maybe this was the beginning of her feelings for us.

June 30 dawned hot and sunny. I awoke with the thought: *Our lives will never be the same.* It was a refrain repeated over and over to me when I was pregnant with Isabella. Funny thing though, as parents of an only child, all of our love energy was focused on that baby. How could we possibly love another? As our desire for another child became clear in our minds, what also became clear in our hearts was that there was still plenty of room.

It's the families with more than one who are still "funny" about an only child. At parent-teacher meetings or playdates, I was often asked "Why did you have only one? Did you want another one?" At my high school reunion, a mother of three said to me, "Having an only child is like having a cat." She went on to explain that when she had her first child, the care and feeding times were pretty minimal. Giving me a smug look, she cocked her head to one side and gasped, "I don't know what I did with all of my free time back then."

Why do people feel the need to be so judgmental or insert their thoughts about private family matters? In my quest for child number one, then two, some mothers were always eager to add their two cents. Frequently, I took these comments with a "consider the source" mentality. I suppose we all want to feel that we have made the right decisions about significant others, children, our profession, and everything else. Sometimes the discussions were helpful, and I appreciated an attempt to connect. At other times, the comments clearly overstepped and showed a lack of compassion or even simple manners.

Pursuing this adoption was right for me, right for us. I wanted a sibling for Isabella. We wanted to parent another little girl. I now laugh at my pre-child existence with zero tolerance for children on planes, trains, and in movie theatres. After all of the difficulties in becoming pregnant, almost adopting twice, and now managing an adoption for the third time, I was as sure as I had ever been of anything in my life that this would be our family story.

These experiences have also made me hyper-aware of the multitude of ways to become a family—or not. To this day, I still hear the "judgy" comments. It happens when the waitress takes our order and says to me while pointing to Priscilla, "She doesn't look like you." Or when Isabella is standing outside of the dressing room where Priscilla is trying on jeans and the saleswoman comments, "Is she really your sister? She looks Hispanic." In this age where we are super aware of everyone's business on social media, the boundaries are fuzzy, and people think they have a right to share whatever comes into their heads.

***

"Luisa said that Priscilla would want to speak English," Richard reminded me as we readied for our trip to the airport. It was true. Luisa encouraged us during her visit months ago. Her suggestion for establishing communication was simple. Priscilla could learn English words for familiar objects if we created our own living, tangible dictionary. We wrote the English word on one side of a Post-it Note and the Spanish word on the other side: CHAIR/SILLA, TABLE/MESA, DOOR/PUERTA. Those multi-colored papers were affixed to as many surfaces as we could name.

Suddenly, looking around the house full of yellow, orange, and pink papers, a wave of hopeless desperation passed over me. Was this going to work? "Everything will be fine," Luisa wrote to me. I know that she was trying to reassure me, but as Priscilla's arrival crept closer, I was extra anxious about the initial Spanish to English transition. I wanted to get off on the right foot.

Luisa had spent time with us, had been to our home, and had given her overwhelming approval that we were a good match for Priscilla. Eventually, Priscilla would speak English, and maybe that is what Luisa was focused on. Truthfully, I think she probably downplayed the whole language issue. That, or we were just not focused on it as an initial hurdle. My Spanish accent was terrible and, if Priscilla laughed at me, then maybe it would break the ice!

Priscilla would be traveling to the United States with about a dozen children who would go to a church-sponsored day camp and stay with local families. The visiting children would return to Mexico in thirty days. This was the summer program I had read about well over a year ago in the article that set us on our Mexican adventure. But there was a big difference—Priscilla would have a six-month tourist visa, staying with us as we prepared for the family court hearing.

I went into Priscilla's room one more time to straighten and pat down the blue and white bedspread. This bedroom had been filled with miscellaneous furniture and functioned as my ironing and sewing room for the last five years. Now with a new white metal bed and matching dresser, we were ready for the arrival of our little girl. I loved the cheerful wallpaper of pastel flowers and butterflies. Three large windows with lace panels allowed a summer cross breeze. The curtains fluttered over deep blue painted window sills where assorted toys, dolls, and beanie babies sat waiting for her.

During the sewing, cooking, and decorating whirlwind of the last year, I went to a local craft show and saw a handmade Raggedy Ann doll. My neighbor, who had also taught my quilting class, gave me the pattern. I made these dolls for the adopted children in the neighborhood with dresses and hair to match their heritage. It was the perfect strategy to take my mind off visas and court papers. I also made one for Isabella in her favorite colors and with brown hair.

"It's better than sitting around," my friend said as she showed me how to cut the pattern and piece it together. Priscilla's Raggedy Ann doll was about twenty-eight inches high with a blue and white dress, covered muslin pantaloons, with a white eyelet apron on top. Her hair was black fabric tied in knots and frayed in crazy directions. Best of all, the hand-embroidered heart on her chest said: "I love Priscilla."

Satisfied that our home was ready, I went to the kitchen to eat potato chips and drink water. Isabella came skipping down the stairs and we headed out into the steamy afternoon, on our way at last to the airport.

Terminal D baggage claim had the air conditioning blasting at subzero level, but I was still sweating. Isabella and Richard were eating soft pretzels slathered in mustard. We had all stopped talking. The airport buzzed around us with flight announcements and excited conversation. The flight carrying fifteen children and Luisa was due to land at 4:00 p.m. How did Luisa manage to supervise all of those children by herself in Mexico City?

Families who were part of the summer camp joined us at the bottom of the escalator, anxiously awaiting the arrival of the children. Passengers were now coming off the plane, but we were told that the children would be the last to exit. One well-dressed, middle-aged woman remarked with a chuckle that Luisa had her hands full. Fifteen to one—I would say that those are pretty tough odds. Just at that moment, the children, all dark-haired and wide-eyed, came tumbling down the escalator like puppies out of their cages. Chattering excitedly in Spanish, the children caused the decibel level to switch into high gear.

After a few seconds, I spotted Priscilla. It had been almost a year since I had seen her, but those eyes were unmistakable. Two dark beads fixed on me. I knelt down as she ran toward me. When she wrapped her arms around my neck and squeezed hard, a few tears slid out as an instant reflex. I reached for a tissue but found only a Dunkin' Donuts napkin. Wiping my eyes and nose, I watched her catch up with the other children. Luisa was at my side in a flash and gave me a hug.

Priscilla's black hair was parted in the middle and on each side of the part were three neat, tiny, inverted ponytails—hair pulled under and through so that it was kept out of her face. I marveled at how tight and smooth her hair was combed. Straight and thick, the rest of her hair fell to her shoulders and moved side to side as she darted about. Her face glowed with a summer, bronze color. Even though it was over ninety degrees, she wore a long-sleeve, orange turtleneck, light tan corduroy pants, and a matching corduroy vest adorned by two dancing teddy bears. Blue suede Mary Janes covered her tiny feet. The shoes had a small red heart Velcro strap over light blue Winnie-the-Pooh socks.

I was taking it all in somewhat in a daze when I realized bedlam was breaking out around me. The children were running in all directions and the adults were doing their best to keep up with them. Three laughing boys jumped on the moving baggage carousel. Two more boys darted into a waiting elevator and began pushing all of the buttons. More children ran in and out of the automatic doorway, while still others pounded on vending machines. The din seemed louder because I did not understand a word that was being said. After a few minutes of chaos, the families and helpers herded the children into a corner. As the luggage showed up on the carousel, we couldn't hold them back as they ran to look for their bags.

All of the adoption agencies involved in this effort hosted a reception at a nearby office building. Priscilla and another child named David climbed into the back seat of our car with Isabella. Priscilla and David were having a loud and overly animated conversation, none of which I could understand. We tried to speak to Priscilla using some of the Spanish phrases we had practiced, but she ignored us completely.

At the party, all of the children quietly ate pizza together. A huge sheet cake with white icing that said *"Welcome Niños"* in royal blue was cut and distributed. Isabella would not leave my side through the adult talk even though we encouraged her to try and play with the other children. It was an inkling of how tough this was for her, but I was too distracted to notice.

Parents mingled, attempting to get any last minute advice. Most of the families were already quite large with many biological children. The visiting Mexican children would just be added to their routine. After almost nine years of truly knowing every aspect of Isabella's presence, I found myself now staring at Priscilla, my new daughter-to-be. It felt funny calling her that even silently in my mind. As I watched her observing the whole party scene, it was slowly sinking in that another child would be coming home with us. After so many months and years, there would be two girls. Mostly, I was just as happy and relieved as could be, but with the festivities swirling around, it all felt so strange. To come face-to-face with this little girl who did not understand a word we said was frightening and exhilarating at the same time.

When it was time for the families to depart, Priscilla and David would not let go of Luisa. David was crying hysterically and had Luisa in a choke hold. Luisa knelt to put him down, attempting still to comfort him, then coaxed him to walk on his own. Priscilla had come around behind Luisa and tried to climb on top of her, piggyback style. David's summer family went to bring the car right to the door to avoid a further scene. We stood in the lobby of the building waiting for Priscilla to disentangle herself from Luisa. Not quite sure what to do, we shifted uncomfortably on the polished floor.

Isabella looked up at me and asked, "Doesn't she want to come home with us?" I answered with a silent hug.

I looked at Luisa and Priscilla, my smile frozen. As Priscilla clung stubbornly to Luisa and turned her face away from us, I agonized again about what we were in for as a family. Isabella held tightly to three colorful "Welcome!" balloons, which drifted in the breeze of the open doorway. We stood there, all eyes on Pris, waiting for her to decide. David, still crying, was being carried out by his family to the waiting car. Priscilla was now standing next to Luisa and watching wide-eyed.

I knelt down at eye level and put my hands on her shoulders. She was hot and her shirt damp from all of the running around, but that could have also been because of the corduroy. I turned Priscilla gently toward me and looked into her eyes. Our faces were just a few inches apart. Squeezing her shoulders, I asked, "Are you ready?"

Priscilla met my gaze, her dark eyes settling on me, sad and tired. Then she started to look over each one of us, as if she were checking us out for the first time. She did not answer me, but, after taking in the whole scene, she loosened her grip on Luisa and stood on her own. She put her hand in mine as if to say, "Let's go, Momma!"

Isabella hurriedly made a move to grab my other hand. Giving Luisa a quick kiss goodbye, Richard and I hurried the girls out to the car. *Check one for motherly instincts*, I thought, as I admired her brave heart and strong will, so apparent at even the young age of seven.

In the car heading home, Priscilla's reward was a purple Ring Pop, which Isabella dispensed as only an older sister can. I can still see the both of them sucking on those sticky candies, with colorful, wet rings around their mouths. The sun was setting and the air a bit cooler as Priscilla gazed out onto the glowing Philadelphia skyline, looking particularly small and alone.

With the lollipops almost finished, Isabella was anxious to try out her Spanish, *"Te gusta?"* she said, holding the stick aloft. Priscilla would have none of it, looking over at Isabella as if to say, "What do you want from me? I am not going to entertain you." Her expression was sour and maybe even a little mad.

Priscilla squirmed in her seat and repeatedly moved the lap belt behind her. Richard's admonishments of *"peligroso"* eventually had an impact and she eventually sat still. I turned around every few seconds to check out the scene. Priscilla, sitting behind Richard, had wiggled almost sideways in the car seat, turning her back to me as she looked out the passenger window.

Our Spanish had improved since our first trip, but it was still not that good. We arranged for Karen to meet us at the house so that we could orient Priscilla and answer any questions.

Karen was coming up the walkway as we pulled the car in the driveway. *"Buenas noches,"* she called out to Priscilla as soon as the car stopped. In the months before Priscilla's arrival, it was Karen's voice that she heard on those phone calls, and I was so grateful for her help. Priscilla pretended not to remember Karen's voice and just stood shaking her head back and forth. Priscilla's whole demeanor had become extra subdued. She didn't say a word as we gave her a tour of her room, the house, and backyard.

As we circled back to the house, the fireflies were still blinking. Priscilla pointed to them, wordlessly dragging herself up the stairs. When she reached for the front door, a train whistle sounded in the distance. Priscilla stopped and turned her head. Her eyes were wide, but still no questions and no reactions. Karen provided all of the explanations and when she finished, Priscilla heaved a weary sigh.

Inside the living room, Priscilla opened half a dozen welcome gifts with a ho-hum silence. She examined a music box, hair accessories, and clothes without any comment. My coworkers had given me an adoption shower and I had been so excited to watch her open those gifts. I chalked it up to complete overstimulation and fatigue as she neatly stacked the gifts, still in their boxes.

Upstairs in her bedroom, I picked up Raggedy Ann and asked Karen to tell Priscilla that I made this doll for her. It was another piece of information to process and at that late hour we had reached our limit. Priscilla turned the doll over in her hands, first expressionless, then frowning. Karen and I nodded that it was time to call it a night.

As we said our goodbyes, Priscilla clung to Karen. Her communication link to the world was heading out the door. For a child who loved to talk, I could only imagine her thoughts. I tried to reach out to pull her a little closer as we headed upstairs, but she shrunk back from me so that we would not touch.

I opened her flowered duffel bag, reflecting on a life contained in this tiny blue and pink carry-on. When we were bringing the bags into the house, Priscilla told Karen that the bag had been a gift from *Tía* Vero. I sorted through well-worn slacks, shorts, faded tops, underwear, towels, and bath products.

By pointing, and with various hand gestures, Priscilla asked to sleep with Isabella. We thought this might happen and prepared Isabella who said that it was OK. Priscilla's body language told us to stay away. Meanwhile my heart was breaking. All I wanted to do was hug her. Instead, I kissed my index finger and planted it on her cheek. She recoiled away from me, curled up in a fetal position, moving as far away from Isabella as she could get without falling off the mattress and almost immediately fell asleep—or pretended to anyway.

Turning out the light I looked at them both side by side. At that moment, I was exhausted but proud of all that we had endured to get to this point. It felt like we had been to the end of the earth and back, but at long last my two girls were together.

CHAPTER 9

Speak to Me

T wo weeks before Priscilla arrived, Isabella started attending summer day camp at our local school. The camp is scheduled for eight weeks and ingeniously called *Summer Playground*, with the high schoolers recruited to entertain the younger ones with games, crafts, movies, and water play. In other words, it was just one big, long recess. All of the elementary-aged children loved it because their friends were there. We signed up Priscilla to attend Summer Playground along with Isabella as a way to meet some of the children she would see in the fall when she began second grade. She would also be hearing and reacting to English which would be a fun way for her to learn.

The next morning, we explained what Summer Playground was all about. Priscilla said, *"La escuela?"* and nodded her head in agreement. She heard the word "school" in our explanation and seemed agreeable.

The first day passed in a bit of a blur as we all just adjusted to each other. I was working a part-time schedule and planned to be with the girls in the morning. Motherhood for the second time had taken nine years, and I wanted to enjoy it, smell the roses, seize the day, and all that stuff. I had looked forward to this time as one of the few breaks in my working life. Picturing myself as happy and fulfilled in a Mother Earth sort of way, I planned to walk the girls up the hill to the school each morning, then head home to bake or garden. Like most events in my life that I would meticulously plan, I was dead wrong about the way things would unfold.

By the third day, our routine was established. My eyes would open in the morning to the sound of Priscilla softly crying. At first, I thought the crying would stop any minute, but after a few days, it was almost a constant backdrop to our family life. After a breakfast of silence and pouting, we would head out to the playground at *la escuela,* about a three-block walk. Priscilla would drag along, head down, her hand in mine like a dead fish. "What's the matter?" I would ask, pleading, "Don't be so sad." or similar things, attempting to reach her with sweet talk. Priscilla said nothing, staring at me blankly whenever I spoke.

Upon arriving at Summer Playground, Priscilla would spot her counselor, then run up and hug her. Before leaving, I tried to make eye contact, smile, and tell her to have fun. It was clear she just wanted *away* from me. When I would pick her up, Priscilla would always make a point to hug all of her playmates and then sulk over to me. It was as if to say, "Do I have to go home with you?" We would then walk back down the hill together, her shoulders almost pointing toward the ground. Isabella would be chattering while Priscilla, sullen and quiet, would have a sad scowl on her face for the rest of the day.

Of course, the counselors thought she was the sweetest thing ever and approached me enthusiastically at the end of that first week.

"Oh, we LOVE Priscilla. She is just so fun and gets along with all of the children."

"Really?"

"Yes, she's terrific."

Her actions always seemed like a deliberate and exaggerated snub and I remember being miffed but challenged to show her how much we cared and could love her.

Meanwhile, Priscilla was also getting used to living in a home. When she wanted something, she would crawl up the counter to get it. Looking for snacks, she would go to the fridge and stand there with both doors open, just staring. The ice and water dispenser on the door of the refrigerator fascinated her and when she would walk by, she couldn't resist pushing them. Every time I came into the kitchen, there were puddles on the floor.

In the living room or family room, she climbed over chairs and tables creating the fastest route to wherever she was going. Priscilla was in a rush to move away from all of us as quickly as she could. She also had a habit of crashing into things and dropping whatever was in her hand. I began to think that it was on purpose. As soon as I would hear a noise of some household object breaking or Priscilla falling, I was there in a second. But I would arrive too late, getting there just in time to see a door slammed in my face.

The Post-it Notes were also a smashing success. Despite our efforts, Priscilla had not spoken a word of English since arriving in our home. The reason for this was simple: when not at Summer Playground, she was crying or getting ready to cry. That first week, it began at dinner with Priscilla saying "No" and pushing food around on her plate. Some meals were to her liking and others were not. If one of us attempted to communicate with her, ask a question, or try to get her to talk about her day, she would shake her little head back and forth furiously, not really saying anything, eyes watering over. Eventually something would send her over the edge and she would start to sob.

I had never seen any child cry so much in my life, with her shoulders moving up and down as she sobbed. Sometimes she would just wail uncontrollably, shaking off any consoling moves from us. Other times she would try to explain to us in Spanish that she wanted to go back to Mexico. Sometimes she would bring the phone to us, asking to call Luisa or Ceci. The buildup that began at dinner would be full-blown by bedtime, when she would sniffle in the bathroom as she showered or brushed her teeth. Once in bed, she would continue to mutter softly to herself *"Deseo regresar."* (I want to go back.)

As much as I wanted support from Luisa or Ceci as this was happening, I was afraid to initiate contact because we were failing so spectacularly. All of the good intentions and pre-adoption visits felt like a waste of time at this point. What did it matter what happened in Mexico? This was new territory—my territory—and it felt like I was screwing it up. I didn't want Ceci or Luisa to know that.

I am sometimes unusually critical of myself and have a tendency to second-guess my decisions. Nothing was going as planned, yet everything we did was motivated by love for this new child. We felt so strongly that this was right for us, and when she did not agree, my world was off-kilter. I tried to tell myself that this was all to be expected and would take time to work itself out. My past success had nothing to do with my future success, and that was a tough pill to swallow at the time.

One night when she had worked herself up into a fit of tears and Spanish mutterings, she grabbed the Raggedy Ann doll off the shelf and thrust it at me, defiant eyes blazing. I took the doll and put it back telling her again that I made it for her and that I loved her.

Our carefully constructed new family was now in danger of falling apart. By the third night of crying and wailing, Isabella said to us, "Why did we go to Mexico to adopt? Why didn't we adopt a baby?" Richard and I had included Isabella in our plans from the beginning and from her perspective, things were not working out in the sister department either. We encouraged her to keep at it.

The weekend approached with the neighborhood looking forward to the Fourth of July holiday and our classic small town parade. During this celebration, block by block, everyone turns out to see bagpipers, girl and boy scout troops, a few antique cars, and lots of fire engines. Bringing up the end of the parade is the twelve-and-under section, on bikes or scooters decorated with assorted streamers and balloons. After a nice walk around the block in searing heat, the town converges on the local football field for the judging of the decorations, a few games, and lots of hot dogs and soda. It's old world charm and a chance to greet your neighbor before heading to the Jersey Shore for a couple of weeks.

Priscilla accompanied us again in silence and stuck pretty close to Isabella and her friends during the parade and hot dog time. Most of our neighbors were curious about her and wanted to try and speak some Spanish to her—"*¿Cómo estás?*" If I had to describe now what her expression said in those initial encounters, it was, "Go away. Get out of my face."

That would have bugged me, too, so no wonder by the end of the afternoon she started to flit away from us as we began our walk down the hill toward home. I guess it was hard not to feel like a specimen of some sort. She had gone from being the leader in her group of many friends, to a child alone among strangers. Not knowing the language must have been the worst sort of punishment for such a social being. She couldn't really speak to us or share her emotions or feelings. It was summer and time to be carefree. Yet her life had changed in a blink and, no matter how much we wanted to convince ourselves that she was prepared or that she wanted a family, how could anyone explain international adoption to a seven-year-old?

My feelings bounced in a crazy way from being impatient for Priscilla to get with the family program to a deep sadness at what she had lost. This was especially true when I thought of the before-and-after Priscilla. I don't think I had a realistic appreciation of a child's perspective of time. To her, every day must have been like prison—long stretches of time in solitary but with all of us poking and prodding her and waiting for some positive reaction. It was probably even worse than solitary. She wasn't alone but felt alone. All of her love and support had been taken away. We were talking at her constantly.

The Mexican children she came here with were still in summer camp. I know she was counting the days and hoping to return to Mexico with them. She mentioned the name of the camp a few times in the form of a question. I think she was asking to go there. We wanted to be honest and did not respond positively, explaining that she would be staying with us and not attending the camp. Those conversations usually ended in tears. Who is to say if the camp would have helped or hurt our cause? To see all of the Mexican children again struck me as a step in the wrong direction.

We trudged toward the house together in silence and unlocked the front door to much cooler temperatures. I was lost in my own thoughts of summer and our expectations. Walking into the kitchen, I spotted a small puddle in front of the fridge. "Humpff," I muttered to myself as I ripped a paper towel from the holder. I bent down on one knee to wipe up the water. From the dining room, Priscilla darted into the kitchen and grabbed me by my shoulders, thrusting her face close to mine and saying loudly, *"DONNE DOO THAD."*

What? Priscilla just attempted an English sentence and I almost missed it—what did she say? Releasing her grip on my shoulders, she backed up slightly and extended the index finger on her right hand, waving it along with her head in a back and forth rhythm repeating, *"Donne dooo thad, donne doo thad."*

Suddenly, I got it. Priscilla was saying, "Don't do that." Gee, for a split-second, I was super glad she had said something. But when I realized she was imitating me, mocking me, I didn't know whether to laugh or cry. That was what SHE was hearing during the last week. All this time I had been waiting for her words, but acting like my predictable, anal self, interjecting a directive at every noise or disruption. So much for smelling the roses.

How could I have missed this most obvious lesson in communication? I should have been spending more one-on-one time with Priscilla to gain her trust and reassure her about the future. It was not what was said, but how it was said. I could communicate more by the tone of my voice and body language more than anything else. That's what I told many a corporate training class, yet somehow I skipped that lesson for my home audience.

Priscilla stood there staring at me, enjoying the shock on my face and processing the whole scene. Out of the corner of my eye, I detected a hint of a smile as she ran for the door. I had to smile, too, as I mopped up the water. Priscilla had my number for sure.

CHAPTER 10

Summer Fun

W e have a small stone wall by the porch near the front of the house. During those first few weeks, Priscilla often sat there as if in detention, head in her hands, looking out into space. Her dark eyes just stared dully when we asked a question. If we attempted Spanish, her face changed into almost a smirk. Most of the time, I think she knew what we were attempting to ask or tell her, but she would not give us the satisfaction of a response. There was no trace of the chatty and gregarious girl we saw in Mexico.

When she wasn't sitting on the outside wall, as if waiting for someone to rescue her, Pris was in the house pacing by the telephone. Like a trapped animal, she analyzed her options for escape. When the phone rang, she would rush to answer, asking for Luisa, speaking furiously in Spanish. It was apparent that she was asking the caller for help to get back to Mexico. *I started to worry that someone would think we had kidnapped her and that this was her only hope for freedom.*

The afternoons stretched out in front of us and Priscilla was not to be entertained by any of the activities we had planned. She was content to wander the house from room to room looking out windows. There was not an aspect of mothering that I did not like, and I enjoyed every moment of it with Isabella. My competitive side started to emerge as I began to think, I can top whatever is going on at summer playground! Wait till you get home!

Isabella didn't know what to make of the situation. While all of her friends were congratulating her about how adorable her new sister was, Isabella was hurt because Priscilla ignored her, too. By this time, Priscilla had stopped sleeping in Isabella's room and relied on her only for snacks and the occasional game. Isabella was tolerated only if both of them were watching TV. They would play on the swing set together—but mostly separately. At first, I wondered if there was a language barrier or if she was just determined to show us all that she could live without us. Maybe she thought that if she did not speak to us, we would get tired of it all and send her home.

Richard and I talked softly one night after the girls had tussled in the family room in a struggle for the remote control. The altercation ended with Priscilla biting Isabella, who was now fully initiated into the world of having a sibling. We whispered, desperately, in our bedroom later that evening. "Was this going to work out? Is this the right thing for our family?" We never dreamed that life with us would make Priscilla so unhappy. Thankfully, Richard and I were in agreement. For as much as Priscilla was trying to tell us how unhappy she was, both of us believed that eventually we would find the way to her heart.

After all of the meetings, readings, counseling sessions, and prayers, I was being a mom in as honest and authentic a way as I knew how. Yet, Pris kept changing the rules. What the hell was going on? Just saying that we were in doubt allowed us to hear it out loud and realize that there was no way we were giving up. We resolved to get Isabella more involved as a sister and not tolerate any bad behavior. It was about that time that Richard nicknamed Priscilla "Stitch."

"What?" I said. "The little blue monster in the *Lilo and Stitch* movie?"

"Yes," he responded. "She is a monster now, all prickly and destructive, but eventually she will turn lovable. You'll see." Richard hugged me and now it was my turn to cry. I wanted to believe that it would work, but Priscilla was intent on letting us know that she did not want to be part of our family. Thinking of her as Stitch made me laugh. Everything seemed possible when Richard and I combined forces. He was always able to defuse an issue with his quick wit or dry sarcasm. He is one of the funniest people I know. The nickname Stitch has stuck to this day. There is a huge Stitch stuffed animal in Priscilla's room where it has had a place of honor on her bed. Over the years, this one-syllable nickname has been extraordinarily effective whether I am saying it to be funny or I'm mad as the devil.

In the beginning though, everything was a battle — especially her clothes. I had saved Isabella's hardly-worn pants, tops and dresses and was excited to see them get additional use. As the only grandchild in many years and the only granddaughter on my side of the family, Isabella had quite the wardrobe. Priscilla's bureau was also packed with Grammy's and Nana's additional shopping efforts. Except that Priscilla didn't want to wear any of them. Each day she would choose the clothes she brought with her from Mexico, some of which were well-worn—the elastic shot or torn. Once, wearing a pair of denim shorts, she came to me as they began to rip apart down the side seam. When I ran them through the sewing machine, I could see that they were actually shorts for a much larger child, cut down and stitched together *by hand*.

One evening, Priscilla refused to change into her pajamas. Something had distracted her, and we were not sure what it was. We kept a Spanish dictionary handy and tried to look up the words she was saying over and over. Our understanding of spoken Spanish had improved somewhat but was no match for Priscilla when she started speaking rapidly. She was asking me something, pointing and talking especially fast. Eventually, her teary request escalated into sobs and we frantically called Karen on the phone. Priscilla just poured out her heart through the receiver, explaining her question while gesturing dramatically for emphasis.

Karen provided the much-needed interpretation. Priscilla had looked through her drawers and did not see the corduroy outfit that she had worn on the plane. Because those clothes were more appropriate for the colder weather, I had put them in the closet for later. Immediately, I went to the closet and showed them to her. Everything in her world was changing and she was looking for something familiar. She grabbed the corduroy vest with the dancing teddy bears, held them close to her face, then wiped her eyes with it. I wanted to hold her and comfort her. But when I reached out, Priscilla backed up and ran into the bathroom to change, still clutching the clothes. I turned out the light that night to the same crying and pleading to go back, feeling more defeated than ever. Was there something wrong with my mothering gene?

In anticipation of long, hot summer days, we joined a local swim club. July did not disappoint with temperatures staying in the nineties for days in a row. In the early summer, when the eighteen-inch-thick stone walls of our house were still cool, the inside of the house was like a little cave. This "natural" air conditioning was then supplemented by ceiling fans and evening cross breezes. But after a few of those ninety-degree days hung around awhile, the stones would heat up and with no real air conditioning, the house felt like a really big oven.

"Maybe next year I'll bite the bullet and get air conditioning," I said to Richard, pouring a glass of water from the fridge.

"Are you going to head over to the pool later?" he asked.

"Yes. Around one o'clock, right after lunch. Come over and meet us."

It was Saturday and our day for chores. Richard had his guy stuff to do around the house and I was still cleaning up the kitchen from breakfast. The local club dues also covered golf, fitness aerobics, spinning… OK, well, we never really participated in any of the other activities, but since Priscilla had spoken many times on our Sunday phone visits about the pool at the shelter, we thought that at least swimming would be the perfect activity for her.

"*¿El baño?*" I asked, holding up one of Isabella's old bathing suits. It was a snazzy pink one-piece with a large, blond Barbie on the front. Priscilla went wide-eyed, looking at the suit complete with see-through fuchsia mesh at the midriff. The bathing suit from her suitcase was threadbare and all stretched out. Still, she wouldn't wear the Barbie swimsuit.

We had a few hand-me-down suits courtesy of Isabella, and Priscilla rejected them all. She shook her head "no" in that familiar, vibrating, side-to-side way, backing away from me as she did so. "*Vamos a la piscina,*" I told her. We are going to the pool.

We gathered our bags of towels, sunscreen, and supplies. I herded the girls to the car, putting one of the bathing suits in the bag just in case. Priscilla, still in her shorts and sneakers, buckled herself into her car seat.

As we descended the stairs to the pool, I could see that all of the good seats (i.e. shaded) were taken. Isabella and I dropped our bags on sticky, white, hot, plastic lounge chairs and immediately jumped into the water. Priscilla sat on one of the chairs and turned her back to us. Tucking one leg under her, she intently watched the golfers on the sprawling course next to the pool, ignoring us and all the happy splashing mayhem.

We swam and played, called Priscilla's name, and begged her to come into the pool, but she continued to follow the golf action as if mesmerized. Frankly, I was surprised at her willpower. She had grown up swimming almost daily. Honestly, I thought she would crack at any moment. Priscilla had a message and she was sending it loud and clear.

Drying off, I glanced over at an exceptionally sad but determined face. I held up the bathing suit again to a withering look. Sweat trickled down from the dark wisps of hair at her temple, down her cheek, onto her neck. Her eyes squinted against the harsh sun and, when I came close, she stared at me without blinking for a good thirty seconds or so, slowly turning her head back to the greens.

Predictably, Isabella got out of the pool and asked for a popsicle, which must be a universal word. When I asked Priscilla if she wanted one, she ignored me and followed Isabella down the hot concrete path to the snack stand and came back with an orange creamsicle melting all over her hand. The treat was devoured, and she turned her back to us once more.

After another hour or so, we trooped back to the car, cooled, but not refreshed. Priscilla, resolute in her sweatiness, plopped down in the back seat and stared out the window, her perfect bow lips turned down in a perpetual pout. At home, she took her usual seat on the wall at the entrance of the house, head in hands. Drawing her knees up to her forehead, she heaved a sigh and exhaled, releasing a couple of giant tears. Richard never made it to the pool. I had totally forgotten about him. However, as Isabella and I walked across the patio toward the front door, I could hear him playing a jazzy tune on the piano. I think this was his version of cooling off. At least he looked relaxed.

"How did it go?" he asked, his fingers moving rapidly across the keyboard.

"Would you believe she wouldn't get in the pool with us?

Richard stopped playing and looked at me. "I believe it."

It all made perfect sense. "Did you think that she was going to love you, be happy, and be grateful to you immediately?" asked a friend.

"Of course not," I replied. "There has to be a period of adjustment," I said sensibly. But secretly I thought that yes, at any moment Priscilla would realize how much we would love her, could love her, and how super great it was to be a member of our family. The crying would stop, she would hug me and call me "Mommy."

"Well," my friend went on, "Priscilla probably wanted a family and wanted a mother, but not one who looked like you." Ouch.

Well, truthfully that thought had not made it to my consciousness. As I began to think it through, perhaps my friend had a point. We could not imagine what her life was like in Mexico. Pris was surrounded by love from women who did look like her and she had all the friends a child could ever want. Then one day she woke up and was transported to Pennsylvania to live in a house full of strangers who didn't speak her language. By any measure, that was a daunting situation. One of the first things Karen translated for us was Priscilla begging to go home, crying, *"No deseo hablar inglés,"* (I don't want to speak English). Translation: "I don't want anything to do with this new life."

At mealtime, Priscilla said no to whatever non-Mexican food was served. Richard or I would respond that she had to eat *"un poco"*—a little. Priscilla would take a bite and then pretend to choke or throw up. She would end up actually eating a few bites, which was all we could stand anyway. After a couple of swallows, she would clap her hand over her mouth and jerk her head forward a bit, making gurgling noises from her throat. As she pulled her hand away, a bit of the offending food would trickle out of her mouth. An alternate version included clutching the arm of the chair with both hands and leaning over as if the meal were about to hurl out of her mouth onto the porch. On other nights, she held her tummy looking sad, lips sealed shut.

Mexican meals yielded significantly fewer tears but we could not eat tacos every night. Richard asked Priscilla, *"¿Cuáles son sus alimentos preferidos?"* (What are your favorite foods?) We had her talking about food at least. Later that evening we took a drive to our local supermarket. I was pretty sure Priscilla had never seen anything like it. She took it all in, eyes wide, looking up at the gymnasium lights, walking slowly at first, then running up and down the aisles. She took off down aisle number one, which had canned goods and prepackaged products like mac 'n cheese and Rice A Roni dishes. The Mexican selections were also in this aisle and included the familiar tortillas, beans, chiles, salsa, and other favorites. Coming upon any items she recognized, she grabbed them and ran up to the cart. "Oh, oh, oh," she squealed, jumping up and down in happy recognition. We agreed to anything she touched, and she talked in excited tones. *"Me gustan estos,"* she said smiling. I like these.

Priscilla happily ate beans, tacos, rice, and bread. However, a few nights later, our Italian meal of ravioli and salad went virtually untouched. We continued to face feigned gastrointestinal distress for any meal that was not Mexican. Truthfully, food was the least of my problems, I concluded, scraping the uneaten pasta into the trash. She was eating enough to stay alive. My worry was that Ceci would be visiting from *Ministerios de Amor* at the end of the month. What would happen when she saw Priscilla's new life first-hand?

Ceci had trusted us with the care and feeding of the little Stitch, and I felt like I had let her down. Although if I am really honest, I was most disappointed in myself. Why didn't I figure all of this out, utilizing my amazing motherly instincts? Did I even have any motherly instincts left or were they all used up after Isabella?

The pool was supposed to be a no-brainer as swimming was one of her favorite activities. I was wrong, but *I can be spectacu-*

larly stubborn, too, I thought, as I boiled water for some iced tea. It was hot, and we were all cranky. I checked to see if the ice maker was on. We needed as much help as possible to keep our cool.

I thought every child wanted a family. Here we were with open arms and all I had to show for it were tears and tantrums. Priscilla had no interest in being a sister, our daughter, or in any way connected to our family. Ceci would surely doubt me as a mother and perhaps second guess the fact that she had set this adoption in motion. The worst jolt to the gut would be Ceci calling a halt to the adoption, taking Priscilla back to Mexico. *I will make damn sure that does not happen,* I thought as I started jamming ice into my water bottle.

The house was quiet, the girls in bed after our day of family drama. There was no going back in my mind. Priscilla had been chosen for us, and we would see it through no matter what. If at first you don't succeed... call in the reinforcements. But how long would all of this drama last?

CHAPTER 11

First Fiesta

S ummer Playground continued with Priscilla wearing only the clothes that traveled with her from Mexico. One of the shirts that she was particularly fond of was a faded, gold tank top with the image of a dog on the front. She wanted to wear it almost every day. Three short-sleeve shirts, two long-sleeve shirts, one green and one pink sweatshirt, pink socks, Winnie-the-Pooh socks, tiny pink ballet slippers, white tights, and a pink leotard had all traveled with her, no doubt packed with care by *Tía* Vero.

I surveyed the scene in the bathroom at night after the girls brushed their teeth. Now a purple toothbrush *and* a red one were in the silver holder by the sink. Priscilla's Mexican products were carefully displayed on the shelf: two tiny white bottles of Ricito's de Ora con manzanilla with pink tops, Crest toothpaste, a dingy gray towel with blue lettering that said *"Adagio,"* and an odd yellow sponge with the texture of a Brillo pad that Priscilla used to wash herself.

Priscilla's most prized possession was a pair of open-toe slip-on shoes, a wooden slide with about a two-inch heel. The top of the shoe was pink plastic with multi-colored beads strung together in a bunch that jangled when she walked. The heel was a bit high for her and she clattered unsteadily up and down the hardwood stairs. She would put them on in the evening after her shower, using them as a sort of slipper. I did not imagine these shoes were sensible attire in Mexico. When we asked her about them, she responded that *Tía* Vero gave them to her. All of these things from home were reassuring comfort, and I let her do her own thing.

Priscilla made friends at Summer Playground. As the new kid in town, all of the children wanted to meet her and assist with English lessons. One girl in particular, Kelsey, was the most dedicated teacher. Her cousins lived across the street from us, and when she was visiting, she would shout from across the yard, "*¿Cómo estás Priscilla?* How are you?"

Kelsey invited Priscilla to her birthday party. Her first fiesta within just a few weeks! I recalled how Luisa had told us that the children at the shelter did not have individual parties. They had monthly celebrations for all of the birthdays during that month. On our weekly phone calls, Priscilla was always asking us for a cake and a fiesta, so we were excited for her.

I was looking forward to attending as the moms were invited, too. It was important for me to see how she was interacting with her friends and this represented some prime viewing material. At the celebration a week later, she mingled when she could but seemed lost when the conversations started. I watched her look blankly as the girls explained the red light/green light game. Priscilla took her place in line but began to miss some of the directions. Within a few moments, she was "out" and stood expressionless on the sidelines watching. Her new friends were talking to her, sweetly trying to include her, but she didn't respond in English. She did, however, concede to swim in Kelsey's grandmother's pool.

Priscilla chose to wear the Barbie bathing suit and had a blast, laughing and splashing along with the other girls. When she wanted to talk to the children in the pool, she spoke in Spanish. A neighbor translated for me. Priscilla yelled out to the group, "Look, I can swim underwater." The children did not respond but it didn't matter, she was having fun. What a departure from the swimming standoff just a month ago. I couldn't help smiling as it was a relief to see that she was able to swim but I still watched her every move.

Priscilla was in the "initial phase" of learning a language, according to one of the local teachers we consulted. She could understand most of what we were saying in English but could not (or would not) speak the language. We hired a Spanish teacher who had formerly worked for a local school district. Now she gave Spanish lessons to children in their homes and did special projects for teachers in our area. This last-ditch effort was necessary since our Post-it Note experiment had not produced a single English syllable. Plus, we were highly anxious for Ceci to see that Priscilla had made some progress adjusting to her new life.

Our new language teacher helped us start to bridge that gap, visiting twice a week for sessions that were interactive, instructive, and fun. We devised a unique lesson plan whereby she taught English to Priscilla and Spanish to Isabella. The girls would help with the other's lesson, sharing time and getting to know one another. During the hour-long lesson, there was laughter and both girls participated. They were supposed to practice together in between lessons, but not much ended up happening on that score.

The day after the party, Kelsey's mother called to report that Kelsey had chicken pox, with scabby spots appearing on her back and stomach. Did we know whether Priscilla had ever had chicken pox? *Just my luck*, I thought. Now what? Richard and I agreed that the only thing to do was to have Priscilla vaccinated as soon as possible. Fortunately, I was able to get an immediate appointment at the doctor's office.

Priscilla had already left for Summer Playground and I had to interrupt her play time. Catching up with her on the jungle gym, I called her down and tried to explain that *debemos ir al doctor* - we needed to go the doctor. She left without protest.

The thought of Priscilla getting a needle with no explanation made me sad and frustrated. When the glass window slid back at the Family Medicine Center front desk, I asked the receptionist whether any of the nurses spoke Spanish. Luckily there was one, and she entered the examination room with a warm smile. When I explained our predicament, the nurse made the recommendation for the vaccine, even though Priscilla may have already been exposed. She then made sure Priscilla understood what was about to happen, showed her the needle, and asked a question. I saw Priscilla's familiar rapid "no" head shaking. Glancing over at the nurse, I waited for the explanation. The nurse shrugged her shoulders and said, "I asked her if she wanted her mother to hold her when I give her the needle. She said 'no.'"

Priscilla stood there stoically as I melted into a blue plastic chair. Looking straight ahead, she did not even react to the needle. She accepted her doggy sticker prize and we headed back to the car in silence. Glancing in the rearview mirror, I saw her vacant stare out the window. Yes, I had expected it to be so different. I was powerless against seven years of her being cared for by someone else.

Was I ever going to matter in this child's life? Priscilla was calm, facing down any fear she had of the doctor's office and needle, of being in a new country... alone. I did not understand the depth of her isolation but, at that moment, feeling her despair, I started to cry. At the playground, I kissed her forehead. She turned to run without a word, her tiny sneakers kicking up the wood chips behind her, blue shorts flapping around her knees. Alone in the car again, my throat closed and my eyes watered. I gripped the wheel tightly and knew that I had to find a way into her heart.

CHAPTER 12

Reaching Out

Through the hot, difficult days of that first summer with Priscilla, it was nice to count on friends.

After a few weeks or so of settling in, Karen invited us for dinner. Karen and Tom lived around the corner and had helped us in so many ways. Speaking for us during those many Sunday night phone calls, Karen was our voice to Priscilla, building a connection across the miles and worlds. Karen had short, blond hair that fell in wisps around her face, and smiling eyes behind tortoise shell glasses. Tucking stray strands behind her ears, she spoke impeccable Spanish with a smile. It was impossible for her to say even a few sentences without a hearty laugh ringing out. Tom took care of their two girls when we needed Karen, but tonight, it was dinner and relaxing at their home. Karen had been on the scene that first night when Priscilla arrived and was anxiously awaiting a progress report.

Also, as a surprise for Priscilla, we planned to call *Tía* Vero in Mexico. We had concluded that very little had been done to prepare Priscilla for her move to the United States. Vero was one of the most important figures in Priscilla's young life and she did not have the chance to say goodbye. Each night in the midst of her sobbing, Priscilla would mention Vero and Ceci, pleading for them. I planned to tell Vero about Priscilla's difficult adjustment and ask for suggestions and, yes, maybe even prayers.

Priscilla was weepy as soon as we arrived at the house. Hearing Karen greet her in her native Spanish seemed to send her into a deeper funk as she ate mechanically, perking up only as she attempted to play with Karen's eighteen-month-old daughter. *"Bebé,"* she said as she tried to take the baby out of the playpen. I raced over as Priscilla's grip seemed precarious. Karen was not fazed and guided Priscilla to a nearby rocker. Calmly and quietly, Priscilla rocked her to sleep, looking extra pleased with herself.

After dinner, Karen explained our plans to call Mexico and talk to *Tía* Vero. Priscilla nodded yes, her lips turned up in an almost smile. However, the phone service in Mexico would not cooperate and we could not establish a connection. Each time we dialed the number, it rang once or twice and then went to a busy signal. We were not totally surprised because something similar happened during one of our Sunday evening phone calls before Priscilla's arrival. After the third or fourth try, Karen managed to contact an operator and asked about the problem. The operator advised us to try the call a bit later. We knew the number worked as we called it many times. We would just have to wait it out.

As Karen began to explain our phone dilemma, Priscilla ran out the back door sobbing and wailing. She worked herself into a frenzy, crying out in Spanish about Vero and Ceci as she climbed to the top of the swing set that was right outside the back door. Moving from the red A-frame edge to the top of the middle connecting bar, she sat screaming and holding on for dear life. We all watched. My mouth was hanging open, dinner churning in my gut.

I caught sight of Isabella looking on at the scene, which once again had been hijacked by her one-day, someday, hope-to-be sister. She was staring expressionless at Priscilla who was having another meltdown moment. Big sis Isabella took it all in stride most days. As someone who bordered on shy, she was not one to call attention to herself. She had been so excited for a sister and now nothing was really working as planned. I had such a clear picture of the four us in my mind doing the things that we had enjoyed with Isabella. Priscilla's love for her Mexican family was so deep, but wasn't that a good sign? She was able to form attachments. Would there ever be any love for us? I saw all of this drama and resistance to us as parents as a reasonable beginning, but wondered how long it would take to achieve calm.

To say that I am impatient would be an understatement. My personality is such that if I am reading a book that is taking too long to wrap up, I jump ahead to read the last few pages, then go back to my bookmark and finish the book at an accelerated pace. Richard, who enjoys books with mind-numbing plot twists, in-depth character development, and detailed setting descriptions, was horrified when I shared this with him. It's the same thing with TV or movies. If we are watching at home, any cliff-hanger prolonged tension sends me to the remote control to move the plot along.

Those strategies were not going to work here, unfortunately. All I wanted to do was get to the last chapter or leave the room and come back when there was some good news. Were we going to be a normal family? Would Priscilla ever think of the United States as her home? Could I mother this child? The fast-forward function was definitely not available for this particular program.

Now in Karen and Tom's backyard, Richard pulled Priscilla off of the swing set with a secure hand and held her in his arms. She promptly began kicking, screaming, and punching him in the face, arms, and shoulders. Waving goodbye to Karen and Tom, Isabella and I followed Richard down the driveway and up the road to our house. *Neighbors be darned*, I thought, as the Spanish screams permeated the cool night air. We were trying our best, and no matter what we did, the night ended in tears.

Back inside the house, I told Isabella to get ready for bed. Richard put Priscilla down on her bed. At some point, I heard my own voice, loud but screechy, telling Priscilla to stop.

Sunday morning, my eyes opened to the sound of crying and soft murmuring coming from Priscilla's room. For such a tiny child, she had a surprisingly deep and raspy voice. I was getting used to it, but wondered what that same voice would sound like in normal conversation. Most of what I heard now was accompanied by deep sobbing and tearful gasps. In this early morning, Priscilla was content to keep the volume low, and for that I was grateful.

For the other dozen or so children who came to the United States with Priscilla, their thirty-day visa was about to expire. Ceci would arrive in a few days to help escort the rest of the group back to Mexico. Priscilla was still constantly begging to go back. *"Deseo regresar a México,"* was a phrase we heard night after night. Ceci was eager to see Priscilla in her new home. After the dinner scene at Karen's, I feared what we were in for.

The week passed with our same routine, and, as the weekend approached, I was a jumble of nerves. Priscilla persisted in grabbing the phone, frantically attempting to tell her story to whoever was on the other end of the line. One night, after a particularly tearful dinner as she was getting ready for bed, Priscilla ran down the stairs to the front door of the house, attempting to open it. Thankfully, all of the doors in our home are massive old wooden structures. Her tiny body did not have the strength to open the door, and she collapsed in a defeated heap.

The days leading up to Ceci's visit felt like our adoption process from years ago. I cleaned the house with tension and anxiety in my bucket, attempting to wipe and vacuum away my negative thoughts of dread. After all, Ceci was a kind Christian woman who could see that we were giving it our all. Still, I knew that Priscilla was singularly special to Ceci and there was much emotion invested in the decision for *Ministerios* to proceed with the adoption. On top of that, nothing was final yet, legally speaking. Priscilla was on a tourist visa and we had not cleared the most significant legal hurdles in Mexican court. That was the part that scared me to death and no amount of scrubbing could change it.

On the day of Ceci's visit, Priscilla took up her post on the steps at the front of the house. We were watching her carefully lest, due to her over-anxious state, she would run under the car as it came up the driveway. Ceci was traveling with her twin boys, and they were set to arrive mid-afternoon. We held out hope that this visit would be good for Priscilla and would give both of them a chance for closure. Richard and I wanted to be validated as parents and Ceci was the only woman for the job.

Ceci stepped out of the car, a regal vision in white linen. She smiled broadly and held out her arms for Pris who ran to her, already choking back tears. Ceci introduced her boys who gave kisses to us on both cheeks. We settled onto the white wicker porch furniture. It was a sweltering July summer day, but occasionally, a breeze wafted over us as Ceci summarized her trip so far. A sobbing and sweating Priscilla faced Ceci on her lap, with her legs dangling one on each side, her head resting on Ceci's chest. Her arms were wrapped tightly around Ceci's neck, which must not have been pleasant for Ceci, but she sat supremely patient, stroking Priscilla's hair, trying different calming strategies, but to no avail.

Sometimes you know when you need a good cry. I wanted Priscilla to cry it all out, hoping that it would be over. Unfortunately, Priscilla's weeping would not be wrapped up anytime soon. She began with a deep breath and let out a sob that seemed to go on forever. An endless stream of tears flowed on the porch that afternoon. Through it all, I managed a pitiful smile, crossing and uncrossing my legs.

Ceci tried to ask a few questions about life in *Estados Unidos* but Priscilla was not talking. Between loud sobs, I tried to fill in with conversation about Summer Playground, Priscilla's new friends, life with Isabella, and other assorted topics, but this only reinforced the marathon crying. When Priscilla felt like talking, she let a torrent of words flow out—almost spitting them into Ceci's face. We waited for the translation.

Ceci began almost hesitantly, "When I talked to Priscilla about leaving Mexico and coming here to live with you, I told her that she did not have to stay if she didn't want to. I told her that no one could make her stay. She is telling me now that she does not want to stay. She wants to go back to Mexico with the others."

With that, Ceci stood up and held out her hand to Priscilla and asked for a tour of the house and her room. Richard and I were left alone on the porch.

"I need a drink," I said hoarsely, drained from the drama and desperate to move around.

Lemonade was our porch drink and I poured a couple of cool ones from the pitcher in the fridge. Ceci came down the stairs alone about ten minutes later, shaken by the level of Priscilla's grief.

"How can you make her stay if she really doesn't want to?" Ceci asked us.

"She doesn't know what she wants," I said, my voice cracking. Throughout this exchange, Richard was quiet and we held hands and traded looks of support. He let me take the lead with Ceci in conversation and provided additional commentary when necessary. At that moment, he shared some of the backstory as to how hard we were working to make Priscilla feel part of our family.

Richard then added, "Priscilla already has a few friends in the neighborhood. We think she just needs more time to adjust."

Ceci's work with Mexico's most destitute children taught her many lessons about children and the time it takes to adapt to a new life. She explained, "In the beginning, the children are tired of looking for food, so they come with me to the shelter. There they are safe, and we are able to offer them a meal and a warm place to sleep. But then they miss their friends and perhaps miss the excitement of the streets. I tell them that they are free to go. Some of them leave. But the ones who return do so because they want to be there. If you let Priscilla go, she will realize that this is her chance for a family and she will come back to you and want to be with you."

I could not believe what I was hearing. This was a chance I was not willing to take. Richard and I fumbled for words. The ice cubes had melted into my lemonade and I took a watery sip. I also did not believe for a second that Priscilla would want to come back to us. Everything about Mexico was familiar to her and nothing about the United States was. There was no way I was giving up on her or on the family that I wanted. As I was thinking this through, I was fully focused on presenting a calm exterior, but my head was pounding and all I wanted to do was scream. I felt betrayed by Ceci but tried exceedingly hard not to let my anger show. After all we had been through, why did Ceci think that this was a strategy that made sense? No child should be making a decision like this about her life. Should I have seen this coming? Wasn't I supposed to be Priscilla's mother now? In providing our commitment to adopt her, did we have any say in this? Didn't all of our efforts up to this point count for anything?

As I started to deep-breathe, I could see how distressed Ceci was at witnessing Priscilla's tears. Normally I cannot stand to see any child suffer or cry. Priscilla's tears were constant. By this point, I had grown numb. If Isabella cried or was upset at any- thing no matter how small or seemingly insignificant, nothing was more important to me than solving the issue and helping my daughter. When I could not make it all better—like the time Isabella broke her arm—I was unusually distressed and felt sick to my stomach. I could only imagine how hard it was for Ceci to see Priscilla hurting this way.

I managed to shut out Priscilla's crying along the way. She wasn't giving us a chance, and I was slowly coming to the conclusion that no one could really help us get to the point of "family." I needed to take back this situation and control it. Ceci went on to tell us that Priscilla's mind was made up. In Priscilla's room, Ceci had tried to explain the importance of family to her. Afraid that Priscilla would hear her, Ceci was almost whispering now. "I told Pris, 'Haven't I always done what is right for you? I have known you since you were a baby in my arms. I know that this is best for you right now.'"

"All she can think of is going back to Mexico to see her friends. Then what?" I said and could hear my voice getting loud. Richard put his arm around me.

Priscilla, Isabella, and Ceci's boys appeared in the kitchen for a drink, then the boys went to the backyard to play on the swing set. Priscilla moved over to the corner of the room motioning to speak with Ceci. They sat down at the kitchen table with Ceci pulling in a chair close to Priscilla. Richard and I waited, the Spanish whispering making me even more anxious. Ceci then stood up to listen and grabbed the edge of the chair to lean over closer to Priscilla. Ceci had a look of astonishment on her face.

"What is going on?" my eyes pleaded with Richard.

Ceci asked Isabella to take Priscilla to the backyard with the boys. When the screen door slammed, Ceci's face was grim.

"Pris told me that she does not want to stay here with you because you have abused her."

Richard and I stood there dumbfounded. My mind flashed to a scene in a courthouse in which we were being questioned. I saw the family that we had worked for all disappearing because of lies. My chest felt like I had run around the block.

Richard, Ceci, and I returned to the porch and sat down. Ceci leaned forward in her chair. Even though the children were in the backyard, she lowered her voice as she spoke to us about what Priscilla was feeling, but I could hardly hear her. Had it come to this? Lies? We lost trust in Priscilla that day. We had crossed over into a world now where I knew that I had to let go of our precious family plan and begin to focus on the moment. My family vision was skewed by the dreams of four Christmas stockings, two girls waving to us from the Ferris wheel. I needed to shift gears. It was going to take everything we had to get through one day at a time to build this family from scratch.

Ceci looked down. Her brows knit in worry when she looked up and said softly, "It's not the first time she has made up a story."

Priscilla was a smart aleck for sure and had street smarts in spades. Did she learn about "abuse" from her friends at school, health class, or other well-meaning adults? She paid attention to the right language to use. She knew how to game the system. It was the trump card played at the eleventh hour that would be sure to get Ceci's attention.

On the verge of tears, I said, "Ceci, Priscilla will say anything to return to Mexico. You have to give us a chance to make this work. She has to know that you support us."

My mind raced ahead to the possible outcomes. Luisa had warned us that first day in the office, and now the story started coming back to me. Priscilla had been in time out for lying. The *Tías* had told us the same thing before a few of our Sunday evening telephone calls.

We poured our hearts out to Ceci. Through all of our planning, we knew this would take time. This is where she belongs. We are a family now. Priscilla has a Grammy, a Nana, friends, and so many opportunities here. I was shaking. It was time to say what I knew to be the difficult truth. I looked directly at Ceci, "If she leaves she won't come back to us. I am not willing to take that chance."

Ceci sighed heavily and rose to go, taking my hand. "I want you to know that I think this is the best for Pris. I see that you love her... " Her voice trailed off. "It's just that it is so hard for me. I have known her since she was a baby, and it's so difficult for me to see her unhappy." Choking back tears and wiping at her eyes, she hugged us. Ceci summoned her boys and then reluctantly agreed to leave while Priscilla was distracted visiting a neighbor's new pet across the street.

The light snack and pleasant visit had turned into a four-hour crying jag. Ceci reiterated her support for us as she lowered herself into the car. Thankfully, she did not mention "setting Priscilla free" again.

"I have spoken my piece. Pris knows that you are her family now. Please tell her that I love her and that I will keep all of you in my prayers."

Priscilla came back to the house and was surprised that Ceci had left. The wailing and crying had stopped. I pretended everything was normal and sent the girls back to the swing set. Priscilla was standing on the teeter-totter, flinging herself back and forth, hair flying and looking like a kid with not a care in the world. Who knew that she had a heart of steel which was proving to be stupendously difficult to pry open? My definition of success as a family began to change that day, and I became more focused on winning smaller victories. Since it was not possible to turn the pages to the end of the book, we would focus on the present.

The fact that Ceci left without Priscilla told me all that I needed to know. I felt her support and her love. Our family was what was best for Priscilla now and anyone could see that —except Priscilla—which made me bite the edge of the plastic cup I had been holding. I stood at the kitchen window, staring out and unable to move.

I was still shaken from the events of the day when our babysitter arrived. Richard had left with Ceci and her boys to drive them to where they were staying and he would meet me at a neighborhood party later. As I showed the sitter what dinner to prepare for the girls, I felt sad for the way the day had gone. Everything felt wrong and out of place. I left the house without much of a goodbye as I didn't have the energy for a single word. Walking up the street, the air had started to cool. I realized that I was still wearing the same clothes from earlier in the day and looked like a hot mess. Changing would have required energy and a decision on my part, and I did not have the capacity for either. It felt good to have something else to do and, for three blocks, I put one foot in front of the other.

It was difficult to start mingling at first, but gradually I relaxed. Wine helped. When Richard appeared, we hugged and hung on for dear life, then began to tell friends about our roller coaster of a day. Ceci was that rare woman who was strong enough to show her feelings at a deep and tender level. She was responsible for changing the way Mexico cared for its children. After adopting two children of her own, she knew a thing or two about love and loss. Priscilla and Ceci had entered into this adoption arrangement with the thought that if it was not to Priscilla's liking, she could change course. I don't think either of them anticipated an equally determined force from her new mother and father. We didn't have all of the answers, but we showed our cards to Ceci and it was clear she believed in us as parents.

I also became a bit wiser to Priscilla's maneuvering after her astonishing revelations that day. It was easy to be angry, but it was also evident that she was hurting, and I knew we had to tread carefully but lovingly. The abuse story downright scared me. Who knew when and where it would be repeated? Should we share that with anyone now as our own pre-emptive strike? Did I even have the street smarts to compete with her?

It was one of those days where nothing could be unsaid. Richard and I walked home holding hands, quiet and totally spent. My outlook up to that point had been stubbornly optimistic, but now everything felt like it had seeped out onto the floor, and we were left to build the relationship with our new daughter one day at a time.

CHAPTER 13

The Rocks

In the early days of our courtship, Richard and I did the usual "where did you grow up?" and other sharing activities, discovering that we were raised just miles from each other. He was one of the lucky ones I always envied because he spent summers at the beach. When Richard was a child, his parents rented various homes in the Atlantic City area. His fondest memories were sitting on the porch listening to Phillies baseball games with his dad and cooking pasta and clam sauce with his grandmother. After a few years of renting, his parents purchased a home in Margate, New Jersey. As a teen, he worked in a salt water taffy plant and held other glamorous jobs like towel boy at a boardwalk hotel. His father, a dentist, would arrive each weekend to be with the family which also included his mom, and younger brother and sister. "The shore" as all Philadelphians called the beach, had been an important part of his life for over thirty years.

The shore had not been a big part of my girlhood. Our family vacations were few and far between, so when we were dating and Richard first suggested a visit to his family's beach house, I agreed immediately. As the weekend approached with a stormy forecast, I was second-guessing our plans.

"Is this a good idea?" I asked as we pulled out of the driveway. The rain was already misting, barely visible against the gloomy, late-winter sky.

"It will be fine. Besides, when will we have the chance to go again? Summer is too far away."

"That's true." I was still skeptical.

"And there won't be any crowds. Plus, I really want to show you my favorite place in the world."

We drove, talked, and listened to music. As Atlantic City came into view across the vast marshland, a fishy ocean smell enveloped the car as we drove down the deserted streets. The sky was brighter here as the sun peeked through tiny openings in the thick cloud cover, casting a violet glow over the island. We drove along Atlantic Avenue and parked at the narrow tip, the blue-gray waters rippling in the distance. Walking down 11th Street holding hands, the waves churned, rising up to meet the sun on its final descent. The sky was almost purple in color now as we stood at the end of the giant jetty of rocks and concrete that separated the ocean and the bay. We made our way carefully along the rocks, silently stepping over puddles and feeling the spray of the waves. The ocean waves pounded the black mass of rock with angry whitecaps on our left, and the calmer bay waters stretched out endlessly on our right, the lights of Ocean City flickering across the gentle swells.

More than halfway down the jetty, I spotted an odd rock shaped like a lounge chair for two. One side of the rock curved up, while the "seat" was flat and wide enough for us to sit together. Climbing carefully, we made our way to this front row chaise on the ocean. Sitting close, we laughed as the ocean water continued to spray us. From the house, we had borrowed some old rain jackets that smelled a bit musty and looked ridiculous, but we were laughing and didn't really have a care except for being together.

Years later, we told Isabella that we fell in love on those rocks. As our lives filled up together, the jetty was our family place. Most of the time we rode our bikes to the end of the island in the early morning when there was still a low cloud of fog over the bay. Depending on the tides, our rock chair could be underwater. When the moon was aligned with our shore trips, we brought breakfast, oblivious to the men fishing farther out toward the bay.

When Isabella was a baby, Richard and I had to take solo bike rides to the rocks while the other stayed at home. Isabella grew to love the shore, first from the baby seat clamped to Richard's bike, then from her tricycle that she rode endlessly up and down the driveway, and finally, a big-girl bike pedaling along the boardwalk and all the way up to rocks. When we put our adoption materials together, the books and videos included photos of us at the rocks. "What better place for family bonding with our newest member?" we said, as we made plans to introduce Priscilla to our special spot.

"Let's go, girls," Richard shouted from the bottom of the stairs.

"Maybe the change of scenery will be just what Priscilla needs," I said to Richard as we carried bags of groceries out to the car.

When we explained our plans to Priscilla, she gave us a bit of a smile. I saw it! *"Nosotros vamos a la playa,"* (we are going to the beach) I told her. Last year, the shelter arranged for a holiday weekend to a local beach near Veracruz. We heard from Ceci that the children had a wonderful time. Now as we crossed the bridge into New Jersey, I hoped that the ocean would be a calming influence. The crying had stopped, her attention diverted by our field trip. As we pulled up to the shore house, I announced that it was still early enough for a swim. The girls jumped out of the car.

Our rule was plenty of sunscreen, but we almost didn't make it to the beach because Priscilla decided to have a tantrum about it.

"No," she cried running into another room as I squeezed on the tube and that familiar smell filled the room.

Sunscreen was not the practice in Mexico, and she made no secret of being grossed out by the goop. Isabella grabbed her purple boogie board while Priscilla watched cautiously. "Boogie board," Isabella shouted as if Priscilla were deaf. I noticed our tendency to increase the volume with new words. No translation needed as Pris grabbed the green board out of the shed and followed us down the block and to the beach.

Parked under an umbrella near the water, Richard and I watched the girls play. They drifted from one activity to another. The bell of the ice cream cart signaled time for Choco Taco — a waffle cone material folded to resemble a taco shell filled with ice cream, fudge and peanuts. The week before, a storm had shifted the sand, creating a large sand bar. Isabella and Priscilla waded, splashed, and swam in the shallow water, then ducked under the bigger waves. With sisterly collaboration, Priscilla sat on her boogie-board while Isabella pulled her through the shallowest part of the sandbar. They both collapsed in the water, laughing. I couldn't keep from smiling as I read my book, feeling relaxed for the first time in weeks.

We had our fill of the beach by late afternoon and soon our conversation turned to thoughts of dinner. Isabella and Priscilla were coated with sand from head to toe. After washing off in the ocean, we walked back to the house, as Isabella talked about Priscilla's first experience in the Atlantic. As we hosed off at the curb, I could see that I had a problem. Upstairs in the bathroom, I knelt down to talk to Priscilla face to face.

When Pris first arrived from Mexico, her hair was parted in the middle with three tiny ponytails on either side, held in place by six miniature red rubber bands. The hair was pulled flat and tight, keeping the strands off of her face. Sari had told us that the *Tía* Vero delighted in doing her hair, and this style was Priscilla's favorite.

During the last month, Priscilla had not allowed me to touch her hair. *Tía* Vero had lovingly crafted this "do" and Priscilla could not bear to part with it. After a few weeks however, stray hairs were escaping from the ponytails and sticking straight out of her head. It looked like she had just rolled out of bed, but she didn't seem to care. She shook her head vigorously when I approached her with a brush, spray, or comb. "No," came the familiar refrain as she pushed me away, her hand springing up protectively to hide her head.

Now the sand and sea were embedded in her hair and scalp. The only solution was to cut the rubber bands and give her head a good washing. I showed Priscilla the manicure scissors and touched her hair lightly. She nodded, and I began to pull the hair out of each elastic band. Her sad face reflected back at me in the mirror as I loosened her hair. I kissed her cheek and gave her a towel. The bathroom smelled of strawberry as Pris showered and shampooed.

Later, after she dried and dressed, I peeked into the bath-room to see her brushing her hair in a trance-like state. I smiled at her, but she did not smile back. Priscilla looked different to me somehow. The loose black hair falling around her face made her look suddenly older, her big brown eyes stared sullenly back at her in the mirror, her lips in a pout. I wondered what she was thinking. As I came into the room, she dropped the brush and turned away.

Determined to keep whatever positive energy we had going, we set off for the boardwalk in a nearby beach town. My Spanish may have been halting, and I was all thumbs attempting to braid hair, but I had one thing going for me in the battle for her heart: carnival rides and junk food. After buying our tickets, the girls huddled and, with much finger-pointing and nodding, decided that the huge carousel of swings would be the first ride. About one hundred chairs hung from long chains. Priscilla and Isabella kicked off their flip-flops and buckled in. As the carousel spun around, the swings extended out, creating a giant merry-go-round of lights and flying legs. The girls laughed and waved as they spun on the ride, ponytails swinging in the breeze.

A visit to the Boardwalk is not complete without ice cream and popcorn. Kohr Brothers orange-vanilla swirl covered in chocolate jimmies and Johnson's candy corn and cotton candy filled us up. Priscilla's face and hands were covered with melted ice cream and popcorn as she dipped, sometimes with both hands, into the popcorn bag. We all had a good laugh at her enthusiasm for the treats.

That was pretty much how the week went. Blessed with brilliant days and cool nights, we concentrated on swimming and relaxing. One night, after soft vanilla cones dipped in hard chocolate and a walk on the beach, Isabella asked to go to the rocks. We had been at the shore a few days, and she wanted to share this important family place. Piling in the car, we chatted about the day, but fell suddenly silent when the bay came into view.

As we made our way over the long jumble of rocks the ocean's spray hit us and sent the girls into surprised squeals. Suddenly, Priscilla gestured excitedly, talking in Spanish. She recognized the place as the setting of a picture from the photo-album family history we had prepared for our Mexican application. Arms around each other, Richard and I had posed on the rocks together the summer before. I was surprised and happy that she remembered.

Walking down the jetty toward the ocean, Priscilla and Isabella were holding hands. When we reached the tip of the rocks we all hugged, a little awkwardly at first, and ended with a strong squeeze. I finally felt that we were a complete family, joined together as one, rocks that bridged the sky and water, merged together in darkness in front of us.

The lights from the beach homes lit up our faces as we walked back along the jetty. I held Priscilla's hand as she gazed up at us, her look shifting from scared cat to contented child back to scared cat. When I squeezed, she squeezed back. Something was beginning to happen and this diversion trip to the beach started it. It was also one of the first positive experiences that the sisters had together. They had fun.

One of Ceci's throwaway comments when she was translating Priscilla's state of mind to us was that Priscilla said she was "bored" in our home. Initially, I was insulted and quite put out that all of the fun summer activities we planned resulted in boredom. What did she expect? Was I supposed to entertain her around the clock? When I calmed down a bit, I realized that her day-to-day existence involved playing with a crowd of children (and perfecting ways to get away with mischief). Everything was a group activity, and if one friend was not available there were at least twenty to thirty other children to hang out with. Now, there was only Isabella, who definitely "played by the rules." We were a family unit of three and Isabella had no problem with us as parents. She had plenty of time with friends, but our family time was also special.

Priscilla had a different style and always seemed to be pushing the envelope. If I said one popsicle, she always wanted two. If the two girls played a game together, Priscilla never wanted to hear the instructions, which was probably because she didn't understand them. Isabella would explain patiently, but Pris did not stick around long enough to hear. Sometimes, she would just quit the game saying it was "stupid," or profess not to care about the rules and proceed her own way.

Games like *Twister* or *Operation*—where the rules were simple and also involved physical activity—got them laughing and playing more often than not. Games were Richard's department, though. He loved going to the toy store and getting something that was fun and interactive. He loved to play, and I usually joined in for a few rounds.

So now for maybe the first time since she arrived, Pris had a bit of fun, and I think it surprised her. It opened the door a crack for me. But it was a crack that would open and close a thousand times. For every positive experience, the negative ones stung and managed to shake my confidence.

Today, though, we were just like any family *down the shore* and that was something to hold on to.

CHAPTER 14

Phone Home

A t home after our trip to the shore to wait out the summer, with the Summer Playground over, we tried to fill our days with fun activities for the girls. Our Spanish/English lessons were still taking place. Dora cookies were the prize, and I could hear the laughter coming in from the porch as the girls traded answers for sweets. Priscilla was especially excited because we had arranged a playdate for her after the lesson. One of our neighbors was bringing his daughter Therese to meet Priscilla. This was a special playdate because Therese spoke Spanish!

Therese arrived promptly that afternoon. It was a rare treat for me to observe Priscilla at play. I could hear snippets of Spanish through the kitchen windows. After a while, Therese came inside for a drink and told us that Priscilla was outside on the lawn. As she was sipping her juice, Therese announced matter-of-factly, "Priscilla says that you are not her mother and she doesn't really live here." She put her plastic cup on the counter and turned to go back outside.

"We have to give her time," I said to Richard, trying to convince myself, but the disappointment was back. Would it ever really disappear? Richard was a little angry, I think because the comment made me sad. He was protective and Priscilla had upset our family rhythm in a big way. Normally, Richard was pretty stoic and stayed a bit in the background to let me handle things, but today's comment, directed at me specifically, got to him. I guess he saw my face at the proclamation "You are not her mother" and reacted to that.

I found myself in a perpetual state of anxiety about everything. Things had certainly been taken down a notch from the days of incessant crying. However, during the moments when Priscilla did not acknowledge us as her family, the wound was opened all over again. I couldn't shake a general feeling of hopelessness with our family dynamic. It was disconcerting and upsetting in a way that we had never experienced before. We had been such a tight three-person unit for so long. The fact that the newest person invited into our space did not want to be there threw us all off kilter. There was nothing to do but wage each battle as presented. This was our challenge today and Richard decided that we would talk to Priscilla after her playdate ended and Therese went home.

We had been told by *Ministerios* that the children did not have much contact with males and that it may be difficult for Priscilla to relate to Richard. Mostly, she ignored him, but I think it was more the case where she was a little bit afraid of him and a little bit unsure as to what would follow if she did engage him.

By this time, Richard had developed quite a robust Spanish vocabulary and was able to piece together sentences. In her room that night we told her that she did live with us and that we loved her. We were sad that she did not respect us. We were her parents and she would continue to live with us.

Priscilla did not react until Richard added emphatically, *"Tú vas a comenzar la escuela en septiembre."* You are going to start school in September. After all, it was less than two weeks away. Did she think a return trip to Mexico was imminent?

At this news, Priscilla wailed loudly and fell into a heap on the floor, her palms pounding on the carpet. She was always yelling about not learning English and this was what I heard first. She wrenched her arms away from me as I reached to console her. It was clear that we needed to leave her alone, and we stepped out of the room. Taking up my usual position in the hallway, I paced and peeked in. I could look at the mirror on the far wall and see her lying motionless on the bed, sighing, crying, and talking to herself.

I couldn't imagine how she had processed the events of the last few weeks. Like most children, she lived in the present. Any gain we made as a family seemed to disappear if Priscilla was reminded that she was stuck with us. It was time for all of us to go to sleep, but I tossed and turned restlessly through the night, still wondering if she would ever accept her new life.

In the midst of all this Priscilla's eighth birthday was coming up. Isabella's birthday had been the month before and mine would follow Priscilla's. We decided to have a neighborhood get-together to celebrate all the family birthdays. Our small town was quite supportive and caring, showing up, offering encouragement to us and the occasional glass of wine. However, in preparation for the party, one event stood out.

At some point before the big day, our neighbor, Maria, presented us with two lovely gifts for the girls. They were matching white dresses with their names stenciled across the bottom. The top of the dress was a simple white tank style, with a skirt that was gathered at the waist. The girls' names were written in a decorative script lavender color with green vines and flowers along the bottom hem of the dress. Maria had done all this work by hand and I absolutely loved them. I noticed that on Priscilla's dress, her name was spelled with two "L"s. I happened to mention that Priscilla's Spanish name had only one "L" but we planned to change it to the English two "L" version that was now on the dress. Up to that point, I had changed the name, informally anyway, when I needed to write it down. I had never seen the name Priscilla spelled with one "L" and thought it only logical that we would change it officially when we returned from Mexico. Maria gently took the dress from my hands and insisted on making it over.

I protested. Why change it when Priscilla's birth certificate would be spelled out the English way? Then I told Maria matter-of-factly, "Priscilla is actually her middle name. Her full name is Pamela Priscilla and she wants to be called Priscilla, which will be with two "L"s when we have the birth certificate." We had asked Priscilla specifically about this.

I told Maria, "I have already ordered her birthday cake with the two-L version." Plus, we had also similarly filled out every form, including doctor appointments and school registration.

However, Maria felt strongly that her roots should be honored. I did not disagree, but my mind was distracted and my heart full of resentment. It seemed like a lot of work for a girl who did not want to be here, but honestly, I was too exhausted to talk about it further. Tired and overwhelmed, I left it up to Maria, who made a new dress in time for the party.

After all that had happened that summer so far, I fully expected Priscilla to make another scene when she saw the birthday cake and her new two-"L" name. It turned out my worrying was for nothing. Priscilla did not react to either. In their new, white handmade dresses, the girls floated easily among the guests, looking charming and sweet.

I was so appreciative of this lovely gesture, but felt guilty at how easily I threw away her birth name. Maria had taken the time to make a new dress. However, I had made the decision to Americanize Priscilla's name because I thought it was time to move on. This was my practical nature taking over. Looking back now, I can see how some may say I rushed this decision. But it was a coping mechanism for me—a small victory. Priscilla set the tone of our household that entire first summer, and for the next many years afterward. Nothing else was working, and as I sifted through all of my thoughts, it was a time of survival for me. I had to keep moving to the next hurdle. Our house had shifted from happy to sad, and I was looking to control what I could.

In the years that followed, Priscilla wondered aloud a few times if she should change her name. When I asked her what she was talking about, she said that we had picked her name and she might change it one day. I reminded her that we specifically asked her what she wanted to be called and she had said *"Priscilla."*

"Oh no, Mommy, I meant my last name."

"Really?" I said, giving her a quizzical look. I told her, "When you are eighteen, you may proceed with changing your name legally, if that's what you want to do." I never heard about it again.

Another time, during a playdate years later when she was more comfortable with her English, Priscilla told a friend that one of her (original) names was Lopez and that she could possibly be related to Jennifer Lopez. Now that made me smile.

But during the days of crying and screaming, my mind was a dark cloud and I just wanted it to end. As with any trauma victim, I thought that I was the only one in the world who was going through such a thing. The birthday party had been a pleasant distraction for which I was grateful.

Richard and I leaned on each other during those times. We rarely talked about all of our family difficulties with friends. One time, during a multi-family gathering in the neighborhood, the kids were running around, the husbands were drinking beer, and the wives were getting the food ready. Someone asked me how things were going, and I just started to cry. It seemed to come out of nowhere. The days were so disappointing, one after another, and I was feeling so all-around crappy, but I tried to put on the best face I could. In answer to the question, though, no words came out, just the tears. All the women stopped bustling around the table and did their best to comfort me, but it was awkward, and I felt silly. The whole adoption experience was something that I felt like I should keep to myself. The one exception was my sister, Kathy, who always listened and offered encouragement, although, since she didn't have children, she struggled to understand my feelings.

One neighbor told me that Priscilla was perfect karma for our family. She explained that Isabella was not even low maintenance — she was no maintenance, and the fact that Priscilla was a whirling dervish of a child who needed our constant attention was nature's balancing act for our family. The problem was the two of them did not balance out so well together and our family never seemed to get into a harmonious rhythm. As soon as I heard myself talking to anyone about our struggles, the noise in my head was a big yawn. Who wanted to hear me drone on about how difficult my life was when in fact there were so many positives? I had a great career, wonderful husband, dream house, and blessings too numerous to count. Sometimes when I did share, friends would offer advice that was not helpful or practical. I had grown up thinking that what happens in the family stays in the family. Our angst was a private family matter and maybe that influenced me to keep mum. For all of those reasons, as time went on, I kept things pretty close to the vest.

Isabella was also experiencing her own pain at being a rejected sister. My daughter, sensitive and sweet, loved any type of game, was exceptionally active, and wanted to do just about anything with Priscilla. However, Priscilla would often retreat to her room and did not interact much at that point with any of us. Isabella stopped waiting for Priscilla to want to do things together and went back to playing with her friends in the neighborhood. It broke my heart not to see them together. At home during our family time, Priscilla engaged in an endless game of contrary girl. Whatever Isabella wanted to do, or said she liked,

Priscilla would not want to do it or would do something completely different or opposite. It was comical sometimes. Priscilla would want to play a board game only after Isabella put it back on the shelf. Priscilla would leave the room if Isabella played her favorite music, then go to her room and play Spanish music that we had given her. If Isabella was eating ice cream, Priscilla would say that she did not like it and did not want any, then ask for it later. Whatever sports team we watched, Priscilla would cheer for the other team. The girls rarely agreed on a TV show and there was constant bickering over the remote.

After one of Priscilla's scenes at a family dinner the grandparents had attended, I was getting Isabella ready for bed when she tearfully sniffled, "She's … getting … all of the attention." It was hard for her to accept this new life and a sister that did not play nice. Individual time with Isabella was in short supply and I should have tried to balance the attention a bit more. It was a huge change for her and, because she was so positive about it in the beginning, I mistakenly thought she would persevere as I was doing. When all of her efforts yielded zero, her heart and mind gave up.

But while I was working hard to make us a family, Priscilla would disagree or take the opposing stance with whatever the rest of us were doing. Priscilla's behavior as uncooperative, stubborn, and willful prevailed for years and was a constant source of frustrating fascination for me. We could not force the girls to be sisters, but as the years have passed, we've experienced glimpses of a loving and harmonious relationship, and I have treasured those times. Ultimately though, I blamed myself for failing in this sisterly bonding task. When I asked myself what could I have done differently, I have come up with a perfect response: everything and nothing. Because our two girls were so close in age, the original assumption was that they would become thick as thieves and would be thrilled to have a sister. The truth was that they were both so jealous of one another that baking cookies together required Middle East peace treaty skills. Who would mix the dry ingredients? Who would shape the cookies? Who would do the icing? I was constantly trying to set the rules up front and God help us if we deviated.

I tried to get to the bottom of these feelings and thought that they would dissipate over time and, in large part, they have. When people who don't know our story learn about Priscilla's background, one of the questions I frequently hear is, "Oh, are the girls close?" Sadly, even to this day, I have to say, "No." They are so close in age with perfectly opposite personalities. Priscilla craved and needed attention, which was the fuel for her existence. Isabella, as more of an introvert, was completely confident in her sense of self and did not need outside validation.

~

With school just around the corner, I was still looking for closure with Mexico. I had post-traumatic stress from Ceci's visit the month previous. Ceci's exit was so sudden. I am sure Priscilla did not understand the impact of her behavior and why Ceci left without her. Also, due to the faulty phone line, when we tried to call Vero at Karen's house, Priscilla didn't have the chance to say goodbye.

"We have to make this right," I told Karen one afternoon when she stopped in to check on us.

"Yes, let's try another call to *Tía* Vero," Karen said. As I played out the last call in my mind, for a second I wanted to chicken out, close the door, and forge ahead. Even in my battered mindset, I knew that I could not deny Priscilla's connection to the only mother figure she had ever known. It was hard for me to admit, but deep down I knew I was jealous and afraid. Priscilla wanted to be with *Tía* Vero, not me. There was just no way around the fact that she needed to hear from this woman who meant so much to her.

"Yes, let's do it tonight."

Karen arrived after dinner. We consulted in the living room while Priscilla waited in the kitchen to pick up the extension.

I whispered anxiously to Karen, "I want to talk to *Tía* Vero first." Karen nodded as I dialed the phone and then held it up so that we could both hear it. We shared the phone out in the hallway while watching Priscilla in the kitchen. Someone soon answered at the shelter and Karen asked for Vero.

I spoke softly, not wanting Priscilla to hear me. "Ceci may have told you that we are having a tough time," I began. The words spilled out in a hurried jumble. Karen's translation was so rapid that I almost felt that I was speaking directly to *Tía* Vero.

"Yes, I spoke to Ceci," *Tía* Vero responded.

"We love her. We want to be a family. Will you tell her that?"

Vero was silent for a long moment on the other end. I knew Pris meant a great deal to her. I was asking for her blessing.

Karen looked straight into my eyes as she translated Vero's response. "I will tell her."

I stepped back past the door frame so that I could see Priscilla in the kitchen, and I nodded to her to pick up the extension. I leaned into Karen as she pushed up her glasses in concentration, holding my breath as her translation allowed me to eavesdrop on my daughter's despair.

Tía Vero began quietly, "Hello Pris." Priscilla didn't say anything but started to cry quietly. "*¿Como estás, Priscilla?*" In this simple "How are you" that Karen did not have to translate for me, I could hear the care in Vero's voice as she reached for Priscilla across the distance that now separated them.

"*Deseo regresar,*" Priscilla sputtered. I want to go back.

Vero reacted calmly, talking to Priscilla as only someone who truly loved her could. "Do you have a grandmother now?"

"*Sí,*" Priscilla choked. In fact, Nana and Grammy had both been to the house to welcome her soon after her arrival from Mexico.

Vero went on, "Well, I never had a grandmother. I grew up without one. You know, Pris, it's a precious gift to have a family."

Priscilla whimpered as Vero continued.

"Why are you crying? You have a family who loves you and will take care of you for the rest of your life."

Priscilla's cries became louder. "I want to come back to Mexico. I don't want to learn English."

Vero spoke loudly now through Priscilla's wails, cutting her off abruptly. "There is nothing for you here."

Suddenly sensing our intrusion on her grief, Priscilla turned her back on Karen and me. Taking a deep breath, she said, "I want to come back to you."

This time Vero was even more forceful. "Pris, I am not always going to be here. Besides, I am needed to take care of other children." Vero sounded almost angry at Priscilla, admonishing. "Your parents have made sacrifices for you and will continue to make them. Don't call me again until you are happy. Don't call me again until you will tell me that you want to stay with your new family."

There was a long pause as Priscilla absorbed the news and continued to cry in short, breathy sobs.

Vero implored quietly from thousands of miles away, "Pray with me now."

Karen was looking at me now as I gave silent thanks to this woman who was helping us create our family. We looked around the doorway into the kitchen to see Priscilla clutching the phone, her face scrunched up, tears spilling down her cheeks.

Karen silently disconnected, and we walked out to the porch. I closed the screen door quietly as Priscilla murmured her prayers and goodbyes to *Tía* Vero. Dusk was falling, and I could feel a slight chill in the air as the cicadas began their evening chorus.

I am sure that Vero's responses were not quite what Priscilla had anticipated. That night was a big step for all of us. *Tía* Vero's strong statements about family left no doubt where she stood on the subject and her immediate support was a tremendous relief, especially given Ceci's reaction just a few weeks earlier.

I hugged Karen. "Thank you again for being our voice. We could not have done this without you."

Karen smiled and hugged back and then said softly, "She'll be fine."

I came back inside to see Priscilla trudging up the stairs as if she has just been given a life sentence.

"Time to get ready for bed," I said. Stopping at the landing on the stairs, she turned to look at me. Her face was tear-streaked, her eyes lined and puffy. Later, when she stepped out of the shower, I hugged her with a big towel and then dried her hair. I coaxed a slight smile, kissing her perfectly tanned cheek. Tucking her in, I spoke what was on my mind. Who cared whether or not she could understand? What I wanted to convey, I could do with my voice and tone. Kneeling at the side of her bed, I pushed her hair out of her face and leaned in. She let me hug her, and we cuddled inches apart.

"*Te amo*," I whispered. "I want to tell you something. You did it! You came from Mexico to a strange country to live a whole new life and it was scary. You are meeting new people and making friends. I am so proud of you. We are your family. I promise you, we will never forget *Tía* Vero and Ceci. You will always be able to talk with them."

When I pulled away, she looked at me silently as I blew her a kiss.

I lingered in the hallway and listened for any sound. It was blissfully quiet and within minutes, Priscilla was asleep.

Love at the Border

CHAPTER 15

School Days

T he first day of school inched closer and I began to take stock of our progress. Two steps forward and one step back was still movement in the right direction. It was still too soon to call us a family. Settling into the car one evening for a run to the grocery store, Priscilla buckled her seatbelt and said in a clear voice, "Where are we going?" It was her first English sentence, so unexpected and spontaneous. Up to this point, it had been one word here (mostly NO!) and two words there. But the fact that she was able to pull it all together in a sentence was amazing. More often than not, Pris was quiet. We didn't know what she was thinking and she wasn't saying anything, so I had no barometer for each day. This was really a milestone moment.

"Wow," I said turning around from the front seat. "Our little girl is starting to speak. That was cool." Priscilla smiled at me and I squeezed Richard's hand. We stopped for Rita's Water Ice to celebrate.

~

We knew that all of the children at the shelter had chores. Ceci was positively beaming when she told us of the tasks the children did to contribute. Priscilla was always eager to help around the house. Chores were a habit that she kept doing, whereas Isabella could not be bribed, cajoled, or otherwise convinced to do anything that was considered "work." Ok, so that was sort of my fault. Why should she do anything with two parents catering to her every whim?

In the morning, when I walked into Priscilla's room, she would wake instantly, and immediately begin to make her bed. The double bed was bigger than her reach and she crawled around the mattress, smoothing the covers and tucking them in. The finished product looked like a bed in a military barracks, with blanket and bedspread pulled tight, pillows fluffed and in place.

In the coming months, Priscilla would tell me stories of sleeping at the shelter. The twin bunk bed was not large enough for two little girls. One of them would eventually be kicked out before the night was over. Priscilla said that she slept many a night with just her blanket on the floor. Now in a full-size bed all to herself, sleep did not come easily. We were single-minded about enhancing her communication skills during the day, and I knew she was trying to learn English. Maybe she just could not turn everything off at night. Whenever I listened outside her room, I heard tossing and turning as she was muttering to herself. Most nights, there seemed to be something that she was complaining about.

It usually began at dinner time with comments about the food, then ending with her leaving the porch whining about the "flies" which were anything that buzzed around her: mosquitos, fireflies, bees, and of course flies. She hated them all and would run inside.

In thinking over what to do about all of our issues, I did what any normal American parent would do—I called a therapist. "Phyllis" had been referred to us as a specialist for families with adopted children. "Have you tried bedtime stories or singing to her?" Well, no—most nights ended with some type of drama, after which I felt like screaming or crying myself, so we were not singing and reading at night.

Phyllis used play therapy as a way to encourage Priscilla's communication with the family. I remember at one of the appointments all four of us were asked to select mini toys from a shelf. Phyllis had thousands of miniature plastic figurines on shelves along one wall of her office. We took turns placing the little toys in a sandbox and telling a story about the toy. After a few lines of the story, another family member would put their toy in the sandbox and continue the story. It forced our interaction around a story that we made silly and fun. It eased a bit of the tension and had us all taking part. I don't remember our story. Most of the sessions were with just Priscilla and Phyllis. It was an important outlet for Priscilla to say things to someone else that she was not willing to say to me.

The biggest benefit of our time with Phyllis was that she got me thinking about my routine with Isabella when she was a baby. The nighttime bed ritual would last a good hour because it included a bath, a story, cuddling play, and ended with the "Barney" song we all sang together. Her music box then played "Twinkle Twinkle Little Star" over and over again until she fell asleep.

I tried a nursery rhyme one night with Priscilla who recognized the tune. *"Estrellita,"* she exclaimed when I began to sing to her.

> *Twinkle twinkle little star, how I wonder what you are*
> *Up above the world so high like a diamond in the sky*
> *Twinkle twinkle little star, how I wonder what you are?*

The words and music burned into my head, the tinny music box playing it over and over. But now as I sang the words, Priscilla sat on her bed looking at me, shaking her head and repeating them back to me in Spanish. I smiled at her as she sunk back into the pillow. As I bent down to give her a hug, she turned away. With a new school, new friends, new everything, Priscilla was proving to be resilient and strong, but it was a tough sell to let me in. I used to tell her that when I would get frustrated. She probably had no idea what I was talking about. After a bad day, I would try to sum it all up: *"Let love in. That's all you have to do. We are here for you. Just let love in."*

I didn't know if Pris understood a bit of what I was trying to say but it felt good to say something positive. Our success as a family would hinge on love and acceptance. We did not want to blame her for not having feelings for us.

On the first day of school, with Isabella in fourth grade, and Priscilla in second, the girls posed on the porch with four and two fingers extended respectively. Priscilla was assigned to Mrs. Cindy Burnett's second-grade class. Mrs. Burnett, an African-American teaching in a mostly white suburb, knew a little bit about being different.

"Priscilla, welcome!" Mrs. Burnett's twinkling eyes and smiling enthusiasm lit up the room. She reached out to hug a surprised Priscilla who hugged her back.

Priscilla came home each day and struggled with homework. Reading and comprehension during class time were not easy for her. We met with the school guidance counselor in August after Richard had a chance to review Priscilla's homework notebooks that were in her bag from Mexico. The notebooks showed basic lessons in letters and numbers and together we decided that second grade was appropriate. This would be only one year back from her age group. It would be two years behind Isabella which we also thought was best in terms of giving them both a bit of space at such a small school.

Pris had stopped working with our English home tutor as her new school schedule included two hours on a daily basis with an ESL teacher. Priscilla seemed to really look forward to working with both teachers, and her English was improving each day. Unfortunately, she was still crying herself to sleep at night or talking to herself about I didn't know what. We had finally been given our date for our family court hearing in Mexico City in a few weeks and I was anxious to have her somewhat settled.

We kept tabs on the school progress and checked in with the principal and teachers each week. A few weeks after school started, Mrs. Burnett had a unique story of her own to tell us. On "Back to School Night," she explained one of her special class activities. "The afternoon circle time is an opportunity for us to share a story," she said. On this particular day, Mrs. Burnett gave Priscilla a story to read to the class—in Spanish. Seeing her native tongue and saying the words aloud must have been a joy for her.

"Priscilla read it beautifully," Mrs. Burnett continued. "Then one of the boys said, why do we have to listen to this? We can't even understand any of the story." Mrs. Burnett imitated the second grader's impatient voice and put her hands on her hips. I smiled back at her.

"I had their attention now," Mrs. Burnett said as she poked her finger in the air. "Then I said, 'Well, that's what it's been like for Priscilla these last couple of weeks. She has been listening to our English language and doesn't understand it. Let's try to be patient and learn a little bit from her as she learns from us.'"

Mrs. Burnett then had Pris repeat some of the more familiar phrases in Spanish for the class. Second grade Room 2-B just had their first foreign language lesson. Richard and I were grateful and felt lucky that Priscilla landed in Mrs. Burnett's class.

Even though school had started, we continued our routine of eating dinner on the porch. It was a way to extend summer and have a more relaxing meal. Sometimes it worked and sometimes it didn't. One night, Priscilla was particularly fussy at dinner. She refused to eat some part of the meal and sulked until it was time for bed. After her shower when both girls were tucked in, I hovered outside Priscilla's room and could hear her talking softly. I went out to the porch for some fresh air but soon felt like it was time to check on the girls again. Isabella was still settling in, but Priscilla was grousing, "The flies, the flies, I don't like flies." I sighed (heavily) and went into her room.

"What now?" I said. "The flies are flying," she said. The hallway light was on so I did not need to turn on her bedroom light. When I sat down at the edge of her bed and tried to comfort her, I was right about one thing—there was no fly in her room. As I leaned in to assure her, something flew too close to my ear instilling instant panic. It was a bat!

I shoved Priscilla under the covers and began screaming for Richard who came bounding up the stairs. He ran in the room and I ran out, slamming the door behind me. He yelled for me to get a broom which I did, handing it to him through the cracked bedroom door. Meanwhile, Isabella and I were extremely helpful holding on to each other just outside the door, screaming, "Kill it, kill it!"

I could hear Richard dashing about the room. He must have been swinging the broom as I heard a lamp crash to the floor. After a few minutes of thumps and grunts, it was quiet. When Richard announced that all was clear, I went back in and peeled the covers off of Priscilla. We both were sweating and I was thinking that if Priscilla didn't already have nightmares, she surely would have them tonight. She looked to be somewhat in shock as I pulled her out of bed and into the bathroom. After I applied a cool washcloth to her face, we went back to her room where Isabella was also waiting. When we came into the room, Isabella screamed, "Do you believe what just happened?" Then we all started laughing and talking at once. Richard came back upstairs and said that everything was taken care of. Priscilla seemed to take the excitement pretty well and had transitioned to laughing and talking with the rest of us. Thankfully, the bat struggle did not last too long, but now it was time to try and get Priscilla back in bed. If there ever was a time to try a bedtime routine, this was it. After I turned out the lights and leaned in for a hug, I took a few deep breaths sang softly:

Estrellita, ¿dónde estás?
Me pregunto qué serás.
En el cielo y en el mar,
Un diamante de verdad.
Estrellita, ¿dónde estás?
Me pregunto qué serás.

Priscilla's breathing slowed and I could see she mouthed a few of the phrases as I repeated the nursery rhyme again and again, with probably the worst Spanish accent ever heard. It was not long before she was asleep.

~

On the day before our departure to Mexico to finalize the adoption, Priscilla came home from school very excited, showing us a colorful book, a camera, and a teddy bear. Each class member had written a letter to Priscilla wishing her luck. We sat together as she paged through each message, reciting the names of her classmates aloud. She could not quite read each letter, but we did it together slowly as I sounded out and pointed to the words.

The book also had blank pages for Priscilla to write her own story. Mrs. Burnett had personally given her a small, milk-chocolate-colored teddy bear and wrote her own message:

Dear Priscilla,
I look forward to hearing about your trip to Mexico. Please use your journal to record all the fun things you will get to do.

I will really miss you! I will really miss your bright smile and warm hugs. Love, Mrs. Cindy Burnett

It was evident that Priscilla was feeling more comfortable in her new classroom. She smiled and was so glad for the gifts. It's not clear what she thought about our Mexico visit, but she was eager for the trip. I was looking forward to the next step toward closure.

I wished desperately for these transactions to be done electronically. To bring Priscilla back after such a heart-wrenching separation would be a struggle, and as much as we tried to prepare her, I knew it would not be easy. Priscilla said that she understood the purpose of our trip, but I don't think that was the case.

However, I had a few reasons to be optimistic. With so many people now in our support circle, I was growing stronger each day. Doctors, therapists, school teachers, and neighbors had all lent a helping hand. This most recent victory felt the best. After the weeks of tears in anticipation of school days, Priscilla was going to school each day with a smile on her face. We made it work so far with a little help from a wise teacher, a teddy bear, a bat, and a nursery rhyme.

CHAPTER 16

Family Court

B efore Priscilla arrived earlier that summer, she had been declared legally free for adoption. Still, under Mexican adoption law, we had to wait an additional six months to see whether
her birth parents would respond to advertisements in Mexican
papers. Once we made it through this tense half-year, our attorney petitioned the Mexican court for a hearing that would
officially designate Priscilla as a member of our family. The date
for Family Court had finally been scheduled. Priscilla, Richard,
and I flew off to Mexico City in an anxious state, leaving Isabella
to stay with neighbors so that she would not miss any school. If
all went as planned, we would return to Mexico a third and final
time to secure her birth certificate and new passport.

We were concerned that something would go wrong at the
court hearing. The worst possible thing that could happen was
that Priscilla would have a meltdown in court and not be allowed to return with us or possibly create a scene at the airport
on the return trip. Priscilla would now be back in Mexico again
for the first time since the emotional upheaval of her arrival.
All of these thoughts weighed heavily on us when we passed
through immigration to meet the always-smiling Sari and her
driver Hector.

As our car sped along through the unrelenting traffic of
Mexico City, Priscilla grew quiet. Once again, I explained the
details of our trip. Sari interjected and translated at various

149

points because we were not sure at this point if Priscilla was most comfortable in English or Spanish as she had been living with us for only three months.

I turned to Pris and held her hand. "Honey, as you know we are back in Mexico to finish the paperwork for your adoption. Ceci will go with us to the courthouse where we will meet a judge."

At the mention of Ceci's name, Priscilla began to cry quiet, drippy tears. From the back seat of the car, she watched all of the familiar sights whisk by. It must have looked like a cruel joke to her. Knowing that Priscilla would not take much comfort from me on this difficult trip, I made sure that the teddy bear from Mrs. Burnett was tucked into our suitcase. Priscilla needed something to hold on to.

Instead of the agency apartment where we stayed on our first trip, we booked a hotel room in *Zona Rosa*—the Pink Zone—a trendy, tourist section of Mexico City. The hotel was lovely and included fragrant flowers everywhere. A rooftop pool allowed me to imagine that we were on vacation.

We rose early for our court appearance. After a quick breakfast, we waited outside for Sari, who was driving solo today. Priscilla wore a denim dress and a matching jacket with red, white, and blue trim, black patent shoes with white lace-top socks. With her cute teddy bear in tow, she looked beautiful with her long dark hair pulled back into a simple ponytail, the top hairs anchored with clips.

In addition to driving in the bustling rush hour, this time without incident, Sari was also an expert at parking, pulling quickly into a spot that opened in front of the Family Court. We made our way through a large crowd and up the steps leading to a courtyard that fronted the lobby, which was already packed with people talking and gesturing. We joined a long line to wait our turn for the elevator to the third floor.

The judge's final decision would come after reviewing our adoption paperwork and Ceci's statement. Sari drove the stress level up a notch when she mentioned that she had seen this particular judge delay an adoption when the child cried during the proceeding. This news confused me a bit. What judge in his right mind would delay a family coming together?

After witnessing Priscilla's teary reaction in the car ride from the airport, Sari suggested that Ceci should give her statement on the fourth floor to a deputy, while the actual hearing would take place on the third floor. At the appropriate time, I was summoned upstairs to see Ceci, with Richard staying behind with Priscilla.

Tall and elegant in a camel-colored wrap, Ceci hugged me warmly. "Tell me everything," she said, leaning forward eagerly as we sat in a corner of the bustling office.

Trying to pick up the story from the traumatic scene in our kitchen back home, I blurted out, "We just love her to pieces." I began to describe the strides we had made, pulling assorted family pictures out of my purse. I told Ceci honestly that Priscilla was getting used to us and that we were coming together as a family.

Priscilla, of course, would not be saying or thinking any such thing. There were moments of family togetherness that I treasured. Sometimes she would completely forget that she was supposed to be sullen and unhappy and I could hear her laughing and dancing to music. One time we decided to film her dancing and singing in Spanish. Pris was quite the ham and I wanted to bottle the moment and keep it for the next year. The next day she was back to her disagreeable self.

Thinking back on it now, maybe I oversold our happy family story a bit. I knew that Priscilla still didn't trust us, didn't think of us as mother and father, and still was in a sour mood most of the time. If I had X-ray thought vision, I would bet she planned her escape nightly. But, seeing those precious moments of light and laughter, I had so much hope and certainty of what we would become as a family. When I spoke to Ceci about our progress, I focused on that.

Before we ever traveled south of the border, one activity that initially occupied my free time was my fixation with the news and media stories related to Mexico—the drug violence, endless cartel wars, and the dismal economy. I saved these items in a folder that I could have called, "See How Right I Was About Everything." It's amazing how anger and disappointment affected my thinking. This would be my "proof" to Priscilla that she won the lottery of parents, and that she should love us and appreciate our efforts. Priscilla carried around her hurts with such a heavy heart and, of course, they became my hurts, too. I didn't want to hurt or think that I should be hurting at all. After all, wasn't I right about everything? For my new daughter, losing her two other "mothers" in a blink was a serious wound that I did not take the time to fully process. I was focused on how great it was to be part of our family and thought it would only be a matter of time until Pris realized her good fortune. It felt extremely satisfying to grab the scissors and clip a story about how easy it was to get killed in the Mexican border town of Juarez, or how difficult it was for most Mexicans to earn a decent living.

See Priscilla? Why aren't you happier here with us? I knew that those thoughts did not reflect why I began this journey in the first place, and I felt small and petty whenever I drifted to that place. I wanted a sibling for Isabella, but we were also providing a life for this child that she would not otherwise have. It was pointless to shove that in her face. Maybe that's why I never showed her the folder. The good news is that my anger melted away to the point where I stopped clipping resentment coupons. Years later when I cleaned out my closet, I found all of the newspaper articles in a mailing envelope under a pile of clothes and threw them out.

As I sat inches away from Ceci in that tiny back office that day, our heads pressed together looking at photos and smiling, I could say truthfully that first, we loved her, and second, we would go to the ends of the earth to be a family. It would be a struggle that would take years. Maybe Ceci knew that. I don't know. For the moment, however, we were committed to building our family day by day and that was the most important thing. She hugged me, looking relieved that she did not have to see Priscilla.

Weaving my way down to the third floor once again, I signaled to Richard that all had gone well. Sari kept Priscilla entertained with questions and stories. Our attorney, Elaine, appeared and motioned us down another corridor. With her close-cropped hair and pointed features, Elaine was professional and serious. Pleasant and matter of fact, she knew the law. In her plain black suit and sensible heels, she led the way into a crowded room, a sort of records repository. Women sat at long tables typing, not on computers, but word processing machines not seen in the United States since the 1980s. Along one wall, printed documents were being bound together by hand as women with long needles and sturdy thread, sewed booklets together that were the size of small phone books. I did a double take, watching the stitching technique! Stacks and stacks of these booklets were piled almost to the ceiling and covered every bit of available floor space.

We sat down at a table across from a small woman who looked dwarfed by the monster terminal. She wore long, gold, dangling earrings, which swung back and forth as she typed the answers dictated by Elaine. Once in a while, Sari helped with an answer. What does Priscilla weigh? How tall is she? Does she have any identifying marks? We described Pris physically and filled in the blanks of what looked to be a boilerplate form. Richard and I signed something official looking. Elaine smiled and said, "That is it."

Confused, I asked for an explanation. When and where would the hearing be? Did the judge not want to see Priscilla? Elaine answered that there would not be a hearing. The Judge was busy with other cases and had accepted Ceci's statement as soon as it was presented to him. There would be no need for further questions.

I didn't know whether to be happy or sad. It was frustrating not to have the sense of closure that we had anticipated. We had jumped through many hoops to get to Mexico. Why couldn't we have just signed the documents and then faxed or sent them overnight to the courthouse? Naturally, we never received any answers.

Because we were staying in Mexico for less than five days, we needed a special addendum to our visa. I am not sure why— we had not been told about it before our trip. Our court hearing was on the first day and we had planned to leave only three days later. Since the adoption ended up being so simple, we decided to leave a day earlier than planned. The net result was that we needed special permission from the Mexican government to depart early.

Once again fuzzy on the rules, we followed Elaine to the Immigration Bureau. It was a low-slung, white, stucco, nondescript structure where lots of official papers were dispensed, stamped, inspected, and notarized--a lot like the U.S. DMV office. Elaine waited with us, as the line snaked up to the counter, and helped us fill out the paperwork. We would have to return the next day to pick up the final documents for our departure from Mexico.

Papers signed, we all walked out to the parking lot where we would pay Elaine her fee. This being Mexico, however, we were careful about how we handed over the money. Elaine pretended to be looking for something in the trunk of Sari's car. Richard then attempted to help her, sticking his upper body as far into the trunk as he could. There he handed Elaine a brown paper bag that contained a sizable amount—for all of the legal expenses. We had been told that the cash payment was a requirement but not the reason for it. Just moments before, Richard had been in the men's room where he had taken the money from inside his belt.

The maneuver unnerved me a bit. Was all this really necessary? After thanking Elaine, we drove off with Sari to return to the hotel. We deserved a little rest and wanted a chance to enjoy the glorious Mexican sun. The hotel pool provided the perfect oasis of calm. We changed into our bathing suits and excitedly pressed the "ROOF" elevator button.

Dark blue tiles held the warmth. Potted palms blew in the soft breeze as we threw towels down on the white lounge chairs. Swimming in this bathtub was liquid heaven. I jumped in first, while Priscilla cautiously surveyed the scene. I splashed her when she came close to the edge and she laughed. Priscilla jumped in, touched bottom, and bobbed up through the surface. The afternoon sun bathed her face and made her brown eyes sparkle. She smiled, splashed me, and laughed again when I swam after her. It had been a long day and I was happy to have it behind us.

The next morning, Sari was unusually late for our appointment to return to the Immigration Bureau. Elaine was supposed to meet us there to verify the finished paperwork. We were pacing up and down the walkway outside of the hotel, trying to enjoy the sun and balmy breeze when Richard's phone rang. It was Sari. Elaine would not be able to meet us until later. A scary thing had happened. After she had returned home the previous afternoon, a man dressed in the uniform of the local water company showed up at Elaine's door, asking to read the water meter. Elaine allowed him into her home, but he was not there to read the water meter. Instead, he pulled a gun and demanded cash. Elaine was sure that if not for the cash we had given to her earlier in the day she would have been killed. Richard and I were speechless. I wondered if Elaine had been followed after our "transaction" in the trunk of the car.

When Sari pulled up to the hotel, her usual smile and carefree air were gone. She confessed that kidnappings, armed robbery, and murder were all too common in and around Mexico City. It was chilling to experience this sort of thing firsthand as we had all been thinking of it recently. Elaine's family had been targeted before, so she probably had not been followed home. Sari matter-of-factly said that Elaine's neighborhood was not safe and that she had told her so.

It was all so unnerving, but at the same time frustrating, as there was nothing to be done about it. We spent the next two days touring Mexico City. Our first stop was Frida Kahlo's house, which was pure inspiration. On the second day, we arranged a special trip to *Papalote Museo Del Niño*, a popular children's museum in Mexico City. When we stepped out of the hotel to wait for a cab, I became tongue-tied and could not think of the name, but Priscilla blurted it out loudly and everyone smiled. For the ride home, the hotel concierge warned us not to accept any alternate transportation. He gave us a card with a cab company and telephone number.

The *Papalote* museum was the largest children's playground I had ever seen. It reminded me of the Franklin Institute in our native Philadelphia. Similarly, it was a favorite destination for school field trips. There were hundreds of children playing joyfully on the exhibits, the girls in bright-colored jumpers and the boys in dark pants with white shirts.

We were one of the few families there and there was no mistaking the strange looks we received as Priscilla's parents. Two white adults, one curly-haired and freckled, trailing a sullen and reluctant Mexican child. It was as if we were forcing her to play. In one of her moods, she moped around to the different activities, taking pains to play away from other children. Her memories of playing with the children from the shelter were too fresh and the experience was definitely not fun for her.

When it came time to go, we called the cab company and told them where we were waiting, gave our names and a general description of our clothes. When the cab arrived, the driver called us by name, and we gladly slid into our seats. I noticed that there were no seat belts and instinctively hugged Priscilla to my side. Pulling her onto my lap I told her how proud I was of her for coming back to Mexico, and that we loved her.

We were at a funny stage in our communication with Priscilla. She was beginning to understand many English words and phrases, yet as I tried to talk to her about feelings or our family, I would start to ramble and use expressions that probably didn't make a bit of sense. In the cab, my tone was soft. I kissed her cheek and she let me.

Turning around to face me she asked a question that had the word Cuernavaca in it and then, "my friends." Richard and I were prepared for this. Given the tears we had seen up to this point we decided that the time was not right for a visit to the shelter to see any of the *Tías* or the other children. The mere thought of going back there and saying goodbye to all of the children, then watching Priscilla's reaction, would be traumatizing for all of us.

Luisa had actually advocated for making the trip to the shelter when we discussed our final travel arrangements. She urged us to think about it as Priscilla had no closure. Yes, but I had no sleep the entire summer, and I didn't want to throw away all of the precious and fragile headway we had made. I felt bad and wrestled with the decision for a while prior to our departure but, in the end, Richard and I were in agreement. Luisa had not been in attendance with Ceci at our house during the porch visit. I was physically unable to take a repeat of that. Vero was able to communicate her goodbye on the phone and that is where we decided to leave it.

"No", I almost whispered to Priscilla. "We won't be able to go to Cuernavaca." She must have been expecting this answer. Maybe she was relieved. I had no way of knowing what she was really thinking. Up in our room at the hotel, she found her teddy bear and slouched on the sofa in front of the TV.

On the day of our departure, I rose early to take one last dip in the pool. Alone on the roof, I gazed out onto Mexico City, shrouded in the smoggy morning clouds. In thinking about our journey thus far, I had a small glimpse of Priscilla getting used to us— and felt like her mother for the first time. I was convinced that the distraction of the trip—coming back to Mexico and not seeing Vero or Ceci—was the right decision and good for us as a family.

The city was so quiet at this time of day and I slipped into the water with hardly a ripple. The effect was immediately womb-like and I floated, weightless, empty—nothing more to give—but my spirit renewed. It was time to return home.

On the sofa: Isabella (l) and Priscilla (r) moments after meeting
at the shelter in Cuernavaca, Mexico, August 2002.

From left to right, Priscilla, Isabella, Richard and Anna Maria saying good-bye to Priscilla after our first day together August 2002

Family Dinner in Mexico City January 2004. Left to right: Ceci Blanchet Pezet, Priscilla, Richard, Isabella and Anna Maria

Priscilla ready to play soccer at eight years' old

Priscilla in her Brownie uniform in 2006

*Tia Vero and Priscilla at the end of the day of
their reunion in Mexico City July 2013*

Priscilla and "Mommy" Ceci during their
Cuernavaca reunion visit in 2013

Priscilla and Anna Maria during a college visit in October 2015

CHAPTER 17

The Letter

S chool, homework, and family activities became the norm again. Our next and final Mexican trip to complete the adoption and secure Priscilla's new visa, passport, and birth certificate was many weeks away and we put it out of our minds. Priscilla was settling in and this would be our first holiday season together.

Thanksgiving was a frenzy of activity as my brother was getting married on Saturday of that weekend. Isabella was to be the flower girl which had been arranged far in advance of Priscilla joining our family. After careful consideration, we decided that Priscilla should not be added to the wedding party. Both girls wore lovely party dresses, but it was a tall order to expect Priscilla to walk down the aisle throwing rose petals. There were just too many unknowns. If, halfway into the ceremony, she decided that she would go no further, I didn't want a meltdown to ruin the wedding. Priscilla was the queen of disruption, and I could not do that to my brother.

Priscilla and Isabella danced together at the reception and had a fun time. We stayed the weekend at a lovely old hotel in Manhattan. Richard and I even snuck out one evening for a romantic drink while Grammy babysat the two girls in her room. Priscilla was really bonding with my mother. She was always compliant when Grammy was around, and my mother adored both girls.

A month later at Christmas dinner, it was my turn to host. I made many of our favorite foods, including my traditional anise-flavored pizzelle cookies. The anise flavoring can be quite strong, but as soon as Priscilla took one bite and smiled, I think she became part Italian. Thank goodness for that—Isabella took the same bite at about two years old and has been eating them ever since!

Grammy helped me get the family to the table for the Christmas feast. As soon as we were settled, Priscilla spilled her juice, the dark grape liquid running all the way up the white table cloth. I had worked so hard on the dinner and decorations, and I gave her a look to gently reprimand her for fussing and complaining. Grammy jumped to the rescue, grabbing a dish towel to soak it up. When I looked at Priscilla's face and saw her head down, dejected and upset, I stopped my nitpicking self and smiled at her.

My mother and I were not particularly close as mother-daughter relationships go. But, with the arrival of Priscilla, Grammy was having fun as a grandmother all over again. At the time, my brother Sam's two boys were grown and it had been a while since she had grandmotherly things to do. On Sundays after attending mass, she loved to drive to our house. In good weather, we hung out on the porch, drank iced tea, and talked about anything. Sometimes she would stay for dinner. Grammy loved to ask the girls about school and see any update to the American Girl Collection or Build-A-Bear wardrobe.

As time passed, we included Grammy in significant family events such as school plays, ballet recitals, and science fairs. Grammy's company created a sense of normalcy for us as a forming family. At school, Priscilla was constantly reminded that we were different. There seemed to be never-ending assignments for children to explore their family tree, and it was all so new and confusing to her. With Grammy in her life, she had something to contribute to these stories—another person who fussed over her and cared about her as we waited for the next phase of the adoption.

This last trip to Mexico City was scheduled to begin on Martin Luther King Day. Isabella was excited to be with us, but we knew it would be the most difficult of them all. As a result of our visit in October, Mexican Family Court had designated Priscilla as a member of our family. In order to complete the adoption, she now needed a new birth certificate, new Mexican passport, and visa. We could do all of those things in Mexico City except obtain the visa, which could only be acquired in Ciudad Juarez—a town on the Texas border.

Almost every movie ever made in Mexico seemed to have a plot focus of drugs and murder, with Juarez as the setting. I read stories about a serial killer targeting women, terrifying the local population for almost a dozen years. Another article revealed that fifteen bodies were found buried in a shallow hillside grave. It was a mystery to us as to why this was the destination for families who needed to complete an adoption.

Luckily, only one of us needed to go to Juarez with Priscilla, which would obviously be Richard. This meant that we would all travel together for the first week in Mexico City. Then, Isabella and I would return home to wait for our family to be together.

As we readied for the trip, I was reminded of our fragile connections to Priscilla and her past. The books she received as Christmas gifts needed to be organized in the corner cabinet in her room. When I pulled a mess of papers from the top shelf, a white letter-sized sheet drifted out of one of Priscilla's story books. It was a single sheet of paper, not in an envelope, but folded in thirds. Priscilla was watching me as she sat on her bed. However, when she saw the letter, she jumped up and grabbed it, but then, after thinking a moment, handed it back to me. Pouting, her lower lip quivering in a pre-crying pose, she crossed her arms and waited for my questions.

"Where did this letter come from, honey?" I asked.

"*Tía* Vero gave it to me," Priscilla was almost mumbling.

"What?" I asked. "When?"

"*Tía* Vero helped me pack and gave me the blue bag with the flowers on it. She said she wanted me to have it, so I would never forget her. She also gave me a letter for you, but I was too scared..." Her voice trailed off and she began to cry.

Several months after our fall trip to Mexico, Priscilla could now form all of her sentences in English. Her grammar was not always on point and sarcasm was completely lost on her. As I glanced down at the Spanish on the paper, I wondered if Priscilla could read the words.

I pulled her to me and just held her for a moment. It was so hectic getting ready for the upcoming trip and we were all so preoccupied. As I held Priscilla and looked into her eyes, I felt protective of her feelings and then kissed her forehead, happy to be able to communicate with her.

"It's OK. We love you and so does *Tía* Vero."

I couldn't believe what I now held in my hands. What would I learn from the lost *Tía* Vero letter? With our final trip to Mexico just a few days away, would it help provide some closure for us all? Or would it re-open overwhelming feelings of loss and pain for Priscilla, and for me?

Richard scanned the letter and emailed it to Karen for translation.

I could not focus at work the next morning as I finished up some last-minute projects. I was shaken alert, though, when I saw Karen's incredibly quick reply forwarded by Richard. I anxiously clicked on my future, unable to breathe as I read Karen's words.

The Letter

"What a heartbreakingly beautiful letter," Karen wrote in her email above the following translation:

Dear Richard and Anna Maria,

I am grateful to God for the kindness he has spilled over with regard to you, and I hope also that the blessings of the Creator are in your family.

I am the Aunt of Priscila. She is an enchanting child who has stolen my heart — that is to say that of the sixteen girls for whom I am responsible, she is the one who has taught me to love. I am a little sad that she is going, but at the same time I know that our Lord has provided her with the most beautiful gift: a family that loves her and waits for her with all the love in the world.

It is difficult for me to say goodbye after many years of being with her, and the only thing I can do is ask you that you love her, care for her and more than anything have patience. I know that God has put much love in your hearts and that you will do more than a thousand things for her, and I thank you.

I don't know if these words are good or bad; I only want to give thanks to you for accepting her. She has lived at the shelter for almost seven years and today there are many people who will miss her.

I will be asking God to spill his blessing over each one of you at the same time so that she can be completely happy in her new family.

Thank you for the gift of having a family; at the same time, I hope that you will permit her to receive letters or telephone calls. Also, Priscila knows how to do many domestic chores: sweeping, mopping, cleaning, folding clothes and washing soiled clothes.

With love in Christ,
Vero

I read the letter several times, re-living the anguish and heart-ache of those first few months together. Getting ready for this final trip to Mexico, I didn't know what Priscilla had been feeling. I stared at the letter taking it all in, visualizing them together doing the most mundane tasks, but sharing a life. *Tía* Vero was not just doing her job, she loved Priscilla and, in turn, Priscilla was missing the only mother she had ever known. I had foolishly thought that an international adoption would be the fastest route to the family I wanted. With no one in my way, I could be her mother, love her, and care for her. Ridiculous as it sounds, that was the plan.

Tía Vero also could have had a plan. She had loved Priscilla since she was a baby, taught her about the warmth and affection that a mother could give. Priscilla returned that love unconditionally and then her heart was broken. Would I get the chance to give my daughter this precious gift?

The last sentence in the letter made me smile as I reached for the mouse to print before shutting down the computer. A mother's proudest moment—Priscilla had learned all of her housekeeping duties to perfection!

It was past five o'clock and the office was quiet. Luisa had told us how Priscilla and *Tía* Vero were inseparable. Here was a written testament to their relationship, to their mutual love and loss. After folding the letter into my bag, I was overwhelmed with gratitude. What precious insight to gain on the eve of what was to be our final trip to Mexico! On the train ride home, I re-read the letter again, making a promise to myself to reunite them in the future.

CHAPTER 18

Paperwork

O ur last, and longest, trip to Mexico took place in January. Despite our nervousness, average temperatures of seventy-five degrees south of the border was a wonderful break from a frigid Philadelphia.

We were less cheerful ten hours later after the madhouse scene at Mexico City airport where—surprise—some of our luggage was missing. Richard was beside himself because one of the missing pieces was his. Luckily, he had carried all of the important adoption documents (which had taken us since October to produce) in a shoulder bag.

After being assured that the luggage would eventually show up, we left the baggage claim area and walked outside into an unusually clear, late Mexican afternoon. This was the first time we landed in Mexico City alone. With no Sari or Hector to greet us, we took a cab to the hotel. Soon we could see the famous *El Ángel* statue, shining in the fading sun on top of the *Monumento a la Independencia* welcoming us—and a good omen for our own angel. Our driver confidently joined the pack of cars on *Paseo de la Reforma* careening by the base of the statue.

Although much smaller than where we had stayed in October, our hotel was still quite lovely, and in a much quieter part of *Zona Rosa*. After a quick meal, a slow coffee for us, and an ice cream dessert for the girls, we decided to rest up for the next day's activities. Richard couldn't sleep because of the lost luggage and stayed up until three in the morning, when a knock on the door signaled that the bags had finally arrived.

We ate an early breakfast the next morning in order to get on the road to *Magdalena Contreras*, one of the sixteen *delegaciones* (boroughs) of Mexico City. Even though it was just on the western edge of the city, it would still take us an hour to get there. Outside the hotel, Sari was smiling, already holding the car door open for us, while Elaine was in her own car. Luisa was inside Sari's car, which was now crowded as we all squeezed in. Priscilla had to sit on my lap.

Everyone was in a great mood, especially the girls, who were already laughing probably because they were going to miss at least a week of school. We marveled at how the temperature would reach the mid-70's on this beautiful January day. Even though it was only slightly chilly that morning, the Mexican men and women on their way to work were wearing gloves and scarves. Luisa smiled, sighing, "We have to wear them sometimes. It's cold to us."

As with our earlier trips, navigating the unseen obstacles of a Mexican adoption, it was never really clear why we did what we did in the order we did it. We were told that the purpose of the trip this morning was to obtain a new birth certificate for Priscilla. This document would list us as her parents, and her last name would be changed to ours. In the strange world of foreign adoptions, the birth certificate is no longer an accurate record of a child's background, if it ever was in the first place. Now if this weren't odd enough, we wondered why we had to leave the huge, bustling urban center of the Mexican universe to go to a dusty outlying borough. This was easier to answer: Elaine, our attorney, knew the local authorities and Priscilla's birth certificate could be processed with no waiting and—best of all—no questions.

When we arrived at *Magdalena Contreras*, I was thankful for the strange paths we had been forced to take. We found ourselves in a storybook Mexican town with a sun-drenched central plaza surrounded by shops. Everything looked old, but clean and quaint. At one end of the plaza sat a large mission-style building, clearly the main governmental office. As I took in the sights on this beautiful, crisp morning, I could see small pockets of adults and children talking animatedly. No one seemed to be in a hurry to go anywhere.

Walking through the well-worn, carved wooden doors into the government building, we entered a small room with clerks busily typing away. In a scene with which we were now very familiar, a noisy crowd of at least two dozen people were talking and jostling, waiting their turn in another bureaucratic nightmare. Elaine's connections did the trick and we were led forward past the suddenly silent group. I could feel all of the eyes in the room looking at us, wondering who we were to get this special treatment.

We crossed over to the clerks' side of the counter and were handed several forms to fill out. I noticed that the application asked specifically for the father's information: name, address, date of birth, occupation, address of work, etc., but there wasn't even a line for mother! The only request was for a "name" on a line that simply said "other."

"It does not matter," Sari said, putting a hand on my arm. *Well, precisely*, I sighed to myself. I signed my name with a flourish at the bottom of the application.

As we stood together in the office completing forms on old clipboards, Sari and Elaine seemed unusually particular about how careful we needed to be in our answers. They explained that the slightest inconsistency among all the forms that we would be filling out over the next several days would be spotted and could derail everything. This should have raised a flag. Little

175

did we know at that point that no matter how careful we were in filling out forms, "errors" were just part of the dance.

When the paperwork was finished, we finally had what we came for: a new birth certificate for Priscilla, printed on a long piece of official-looking parchment. It was a strange feeling to see all of Priscilla's information (her name now officially with two "L"s!) written in Spanish, only with our names and address in the U.S. listed for her. We couldn't stop and congratulate ourselves, though, because we had many more stops to make, starting with making multiple copies of the papers we had just been issued. Sari explained that we would be dropping off copies everywhere we went that day. What would we do without Sari there to navigate this sea of government offices?

Making copies seemed impossible in a town that felt like it was from a different millennium. Elaine knew just what to do, though, and we followed her across a tiny street just at the edge of the plaza. We stopped at a neighborhood coffee and candy stand, the kind of place you would hurry to at lunch to buy a lottery ticket. Elaine handed over all of our precious documents to a tall, mustached man behind the counter who carried them to the copier on the other side of the store. As he lifted the lid of the copy machine, Elaine explained what she needed: two of this page, three of that, and make sure they're dark enough to read. The girls couldn't take their eyes off all the candy at the stand, and we chose a treat from Priscilla's childhood—watermelon candy smothered in chili pepper.

After stapling the copies, Elaine carried them back to the office. While we waited for her in the plaza, Isabella was approached by a stooped man with a scruffy beard. His clothes were stained with streaks of brown and black and I could see that he was carrying a wooden basket of sorts with brushes, rags, and different colors of shoe polish. With a few encouraging words from Sari, he went to work on Isabella's tiny leather Mary

Jane's. Without glancing over at his basket his hands grabbed a brush and some polish. He finished the job with a vigorous side-to-side pulling of his long, narrow rag. Barely looking at us, he accepted our change—two pesos (approx. twenty cents U.S.)—and walked away. We marveled at how inexpensive the shoe shine was, a reminder of the deep poverty in which so many Mexicans live.

When Elaine returned, we made our way to the cars for the ride back to Mexico City. This time Luisa rode back with Elaine, giving us all some much-needed space in Sari's car. Sari was an even faster driver than Hector, and we soon became separated from Elaine. Our first stop was a large government building where we would apply for a new Mexican passport for Priscilla, one that would now include her new last name.

Making Richard envious, Sari found an empty parking spot in no time that appeared to be guarded by a one-legged man with a cane and a bucket of brushes and rags. A quick exchange of words and money between Sari and the "parking attendant" ended up giving us both a prime parking spot *and* a car wash for only two dollars. (Sari explained that many war veterans in Mexico could only survive by squatting over a length of side-walk and tending to cars that parked there.)

The passport requirement was relatively painless, although there was one glitch. The passport photo that Richard had taken of Priscilla with his new digital camera was not the appropriate size, even though he had followed the directions from the Mexican website exactly. Leaving Isabella and me waiting at the counter, Sari took Priscilla and Richard across the street to a little photo shop. Ten dollars later, they appeared with the revised passport picture. We filled out the passport paperwork and left for the next stage of our journey.

Our next stop was crucial. Maya, the translator with whom we had met briefly on our October trip to Children's Court in

Mexico City, would translate the new documents we had acquired that morning. She needed to get the Spanish copies ASAP because we would need them early the next morning, when we would present all of our documents at the American Embassy.

With Sari driving and talking animatedly we always worried about an accident, especially through the worst Mexico City traffic. She seemed to know every side street, though, and would turn into them at high speed if there was the slightest indication of any delay ahead of us. After being so sick on our first trip to Cuernavaca the year before, I had become accustomed to Mexican driving and could somewhat relax in the back seat. Okay, well, relax may be a little strong, but I did not feel nauseous and could concentrate on the task at hand.

Turning off onto a quiet street, Sari pulled up quickly into a small parking area on the first floor of a nondescript, four-story apartment building (of which there seemed to be thousands in Mexico City). We walked up two flights of stairs to a small landing with brightly-colored walls where Maya, a petite woman about sixty years of age welcomed us warmly. The paperwork required for international adoption has been essentially the same for decades. She told us that everything would be completed by 8:00 a.m. the following morning, in plenty of time for our interview.

Through all of this, we naturally assumed that notarization was a routine transaction—bring in the forms, show our passports, and receive a set of official-looking documents. We thanked her profusely, glad that out of all the crazy turns in our Mexican adoption, translating documents was the least of our worries.

Once again, we were naive. We would soon re-discover the danger of making assumptions in Mexico.

CHAPTER 19

Reunion

A fter a long day of traffic and paperwork, we returned to the hotel to change clothes. Luisa was waiting for us downstairs to take us to dinner with Ceci. We had to make it fast. I asked the girls to quickly change into their "dinner wear." The pants with matching jackets were probably a gift from Nana and they looked positively sisterly as they watched TV while they waited for us to finish pulling it all together. I changed into my standard no-fail black pants and a silk blouse with a flow-ered print. That night, I wanted all to go well, and I had fussed over everyone's appearance—except Richard. He was wearing his usual khaki pants and a long-sleeved shirt.

This dinner would be a reunion of sorts for Priscilla, as she would be seeing Ceci for the first time since the crying and lying scene on our porch the previous summer. I was nervous about Priscilla breaking down again. Would it be hard for her to be with these women? Her old family and her new family would be trying desperately to have a normal dinner and conversation. I was counting on her to get through it.

"Do you want to take your teddy bear?" I asked, wanting her to be comforted in what had to be a confusing time for her. Pris shook her head no and sat next to Isabella on the bed. We took the elevator down to the lobby in silence.

Luisa navigated the rush hour traffic. We were all lost in our own thoughts as dusk fell on Mexico City. The air was cool and the lights flickered invitingly. I turned and gave a reassuring smile to the girls as we pulled into the restaurant parking lot. Once inside we were seated right away. As we waited for Ceci, I looked around at the beautiful setting. Golden yellow walls with creamy white molding provided a warm atmosphere, but, with super high ceilings and crystal chandeliers, the restaurant was also elegant.

The girls were sipping sodas when Ceci entered with the larger-than-life flourish that defined her. We all got up to hug and kiss, Ceci and Priscilla squeezing each other especially tightly.

The dinner passed leisurely as we lingered over the many courses, trying new and flavorful dishes. Ceci and Luisa spoke to us in English, of course, and Priscilla and Isabella listened intently. At some point, when Priscilla piped in on the conversation, Ceci was surprised.

"Oh, your English is so good," she exclaimed smiling. "Do you remember your Spanish?" she asked, then asked the same question in Spanish. Priscilla just stared at her blankly and my heart sunk. Ceci then looked at Priscilla and implored, "Please don't forget your Spanish. You have to speak to your sister, teach her, and then you will not forget." Priscilla just shook her head. She had been quiet but totally in control of her feelings. How difficult it must have been for her to acknowledge, even to herself, that the language tide had already turned.

It was not clear if Priscilla realized how rapidly her Spanish was disappearing. One of her most heartfelt pleas those first few weeks with us was that she did not want to learn English. Now with English being spoken at school and at home, Priscilla did not have command of Spanish anymore, and we spoke to her freely and one hundred percent in English. At the same time, her English was not perfect and she struggled with her reading. Her comprehension and ability to interact with friends was good. For a brief moment, Richard and I considered more intensive tutoring aimed at preserving her native tongue. However, with no one to practice with in between lessons, we dismissed the idea as impractical.

It was another loss for Priscilla that I carried around in my grab bag of guilty feelings. Most of the time, the bag could be pulled shut very easily with the drawstring of good intentions as I rationalized all that it took to get our family to this point. This effort was made even easier as friends and relatives acknowledged and applauded our struggle, encouraging us with accolades like, "You have done so much for her" or "She is such a lucky girl to have you as parents now." The savior line of logic was a popular reaction among our friends and family, but Richard and I did not enter into this adoption to save the world or to win a prize. We wanted a sibling for Isabella and I wanted another chance to be a mother. No one understood that we felt awful inflicting hurt on this child. It was true that she would have advantages that other *Ministerios de Amor* children would never have, so every time I was reminded of all that I had taken from Priscilla, I told myself that we were also giving a great deal in return. Given time, I hoped she would come to appreciate that.

Ceci was eager to hear about our adventure earlier in the day to complete our paperwork at Magdalena Contreras. Excitedly, we also shared our plans for sightseeing later in the week. I watched Ceci and Luisa talk to Priscilla, pride and happiness on their faces at their first successful foreign adoption. Yet traces of sadness lingered in their voices as they spoke to her. I could see them exchanging glances as Pris spoke in English about school, ballet, and her friends.

When dessert was served, Ceci asked about our families. Because Grammy's Sunday afternoon visits had already started, I expected Priscilla to say something about that. Thinking about the two of them made me smile a bit as I could picture Priscilla setting her place next to Grammy at the dinner table or following her around the house. I think she also loved the idea of having a grandmother. She would frequently repeat the word "Grammy" over and over again when they were together.

But at the table that night, when Ceci asked if Priscilla had seen her grandmother at Christmas, Priscilla looked up from her ice cream with a puzzled look on her face. Ceci asked how often Priscilla saw her grandparents. Priscilla still didn't respond.

"Did you have Christmas dinner together?" she asked.

"No," Priscilla said, shaking her head.

"Did you exchange gifts?" Ceci persisted.

"No," Priscilla responded, shaking her head. "I don't know what you are talking about."

Jumping into the conversation, I corrected Priscilla, "We spent Christmas day with both of our families at our house." I went on to describe the holiday events, and gave Pris a look. She was stirring her dessert into soup, her nose almost inside the bowl, avoiding acknowledging her family or anything good that was happening to her. Perhaps it felt like some sort of betrayal to those who had raised her. But after the attempts at "normal" family interactions up to that point and seeing a bit of progress, it felt like a kick in the gut to have it all denied as if her new life did not exist.

The evening drew to a quiet close. We took some pictures and, of course, vowed to email and send newsy updates of the girls' activities. Priscilla had managed to keep it together. We didn't have the drama that I feared, but Priscilla let us know where she stood. She was not ready to own us as a family. While I wanted to understand, I was hurt and sad that there was no recognition of us as her parents.

Back in the room, I told Priscilla that I was disappointed that she did not want to talk about Grammy. Why did she tell Ceci that she did not remember that we spent the holidays together?

Priscilla turned away from me to go to sleep. Her teddy bear had fallen on the floor beside her bed. I picked it up and gave it to her. Tonight was not the night for explanations. I kissed both girls and turned out the lights.

CHAPTER 20

No Habla Inglés

The next morning was the day of our dreaded trip to the American Embassy. Luisa and Sari were not permitted to accompany us into the building. The Embassy visit was necessary to certify to American officials that legally, Priscilla was an orphan and that our adoption was final in the eyes of Mexico. There we would obtain written confirmation from the United States that Priscilla was our daughter. These certification papers would be produced by the Embassy as a result of all the documents secured at the family courthouse during the previous visit back in October. Feeling vulnerable and somewhat nervous, we got in the car for the short ride from our hotel across the bustling traffic on *Reforma*. Just a few blocks away, the imposing Embassy building structure was hard to miss as hundreds of Mexicans lined up each morning behind the security barricades to apply for visas and citizenship papers.

Sari was her characteristically buoyant self, talking nonstop as we rounded the last corner, the Embassy looming up ahead. The person we needed to see was Jorge, the head of the department that approved US-Mexican adoptions. He was pleasant enough, Sari explained, however she went on to tell us that his senior clerk, Juanita, took perverse pleasure in making couples jump through hoops to get paperwork approved. She would be the one to review our information first, and then pass it on to Jorge for approval.

"Don't worry," Sari said, smiling and looking in the rear-view mirror. "Everything will be fine."

Where had I heard that before?

"And remember," Sari continued, turning around to face us after she stopped the car by the curb, "Priscilla should not speak English to Juanita."

At this point, Priscilla's tourist visa, which had only been good for six months, had expired. However, the court date from a few months ago had jump-started her immigration status change for a new visa. Priscilla was technically a participant in the summer hosting program sponsored by our Pennsylvania agency, arriving in the United States the previous June, along with twenty other children. These children all stayed with families that had agreed to host them for four weeks, after which they would return to Mexico. The idea behind Priscilla staying with us made perfect sense, but we did not want to highlight that fact to the authorities. We would all begin bonding together as a family, taking care of the paperwork later. It amazed us that the folks at *Ministerios de Amor* were willing to do this and convinced us even more of their deep love and concern for the children. They believed it was to the benefit of the entire family that we all should live together as soon as possible.

After checking our translated documents, we would be interviewed as a family, then given another document to take to the U.S. Consulate in Juarez, which would be used to produce Priscilla's U.S. visa. The visa was the crucial piece: without it, she couldn't re-enter the United States; with it, she automatically became a citizen upon her re-entry into the U.S.

We were not looking forward to the interview. Since the beginning of our Mexican adoption odyssey, we had received several mailings from this same Embassy. The letters were very official, and forbidding. In so many words, they warned us of the dangers of a Mexican adoption because many children weren't really available for adoption, i.e. they hadn't been legally declared as orphans. We were never really worried about the embassy warnings, confident about *Ministerios* and Elaine's attention to detail.

Of course, given Sari's admonition, Priscilla learning English was the last thing that we wanted Juanita to realize during the interview. Luisa added her advice to Sari's warning, "Just say that you met Priscilla through the hosting program. That's all. Don't give any other details."

Yikes—now I was approaching panic. I felt sick as we got out of the car to stand on the sidewalk in front of the Embassy. The line at the entrance gate extended for over a block. With Isabella and Priscilla holding hands, we walked boldly up to the guard at the front of the line. Sari worked her magic once again as we were given the okay to enter through the elaborate black iron gate which led into a windowless security area. Heavily-armed personnel asked to see our passports. To our surprise, they demanded that we leave our cell phones and any other electronic devices with them. Priscilla immediately started talking about Isabella's CD player in her backpack. I shushed her with a deadly look as the guards in the security booth suddenly looked up at us. Her English was too good. If Juanita spoke to her in Spanish, I was sure that Priscilla would not know how to respond. Priscilla certainly knew selected Spanish vocabulary words but, without everyday use, she could not string sentences together anymore.

Security personnel pointed the way and we started up a steep set of stairs that led from the entrance up to the second floor of the embassy. We were relieved to see Maya, our translator, leaving the Notary office as soon as we reached the landing. She wished us well and pointed the way toward the office where our interview would be held.

Our steps echoed down the empty corridor as we approached an office with a sign that read "Homeland Security and Passports." Entering, it appeared that we were the first ones there. We signed in at the window and were told that the wait would be "just a minute." When we sat down on leather chairs in the tiny waiting room, we could look just past the receptionist into an enormous room with women busy at computers or on phones. An hour and a half later, it did not matter that we were first in line; now there was standing room only with at least a dozen more in line down the hall. We were the only ones there with children, who were now extremely bored and getting fidgety. Isabella and Priscilla would leave the office every few minutes, walking up and down the hallway. When they wanted a piece of candy or needed a hug, they came back to find me.

"Remember," I whispered in Priscilla's ear. "DON'T answer any questions. We will answer all of the questions."

"Okay," she said.

Finally, we were called. Taking our seats at the long conference table, Juanita introduced herself and began to ask general questions about our adoption application. Juanita was all about the work and she dressed the part by wearing nondescript navy pants and a white blouse, her dark hair pulled back into a ponytail. Occasionally, she looked down at our translated documents, which she must have retrieved from the notary office. She began by asking Priscilla a question in Spanish and then repeating the question in English for us. Juanita looked directly at Priscilla and asked something about "enjoying her stay." Presumably this meant the hosting program. Priscilla sat up a little straighter then looked over at me as if to ask for permission to respond.

I jumped right in with a chatty answer, and Priscilla smiled and shook her head up and down. Juanita then asked Isabella if she was ready for a sister. We all smiled again and agreed in unison. Juanita glanced down at the paperwork again and asked Isabella what grade she was going into. Isabella responded, "Fourth grade."

Juanita asked Priscilla the same question in Spanish. The silence was deafening for a moment, and then Priscilla answered with a definitive, "I am in the second grade."

We all laughed together as Juanita looked at Priscilla in surprise. "Well, you have learned quite a bit of English in your short time there."

"Yes," I added. "She has really picked it up."

While Juanita looked down at her folder, I put my lips together and at the same time gave Pris a wide-eyed glance. My eyes telegraphed, "Quiet!" She read it instantly and sat back in her chair.

After a few more questions about our knowledge of the required adoption steps (Yes, we have made arrangements to go to Juarez), Juanita smiled and said that our papers were "in order" and our application should be "no problem." The interview had lasted no more than ten minutes. I was relieved to get this most difficult part of our day over and reached out to squeeze Priscilla's hand as we walked back down the long hallway together.

We needed to wait in the notary office at the other end of the corridor. Just like any tired old government office in any U.S. city, we took a number and sank into some uncomfortable chairs. Isabella and Priscilla began to play cards. Like clockwork, only Mexican style, Juanita appeared about an hour later still holding our documents. She appeared angry. Seeing us, she told us that the papers could not be processed because now there was "a problem." Richard and I did a double-take.

Juanita's face was grave as she shook the papers—our translated papers—and said in a clipped voice, "This is unacceptable." We stood up, conscious of the others waiting in the notary office staring at us. "Look at this," she commanded. She had our attention as we looked at her hands holding the same papers that an hour ago were "no problem." The problem? It seems that our papers were in the wrong order.

I strained to hear Juanita's English, trying to understand how this grave sin could be remedied. "I am so sorry," she began in a somewhat calmer tone. *No, you're not*, I thought to myself. "I have tried to get your papers through, but they are not in the right order. Instead of a Spanish page followed by its English translation, you need all the Spanish documents in the front, followed by all of the English translations."

So, we were talking about a simple re-shuffling of only FOUR Spanish and English documents? This can't be happening! I could see Richard struggling to stay calm. He began in a soft, measured tone, "The translator has been doing this for many years. She said that this was the required order."

"And why can't we just re-order the documents ourselves?" I sputtered. That last question came out a bit louder than I intended.

"No," Juanita said, turning her head in an official-looking way. "The documents are now stapled and notarized. The seal will be broken if you remove the staple, and the translator must be present when this is done."

At that point, Juanita began to complain fiercely about Maya, saying that she was unprofessional, and that she would never allow her to submit translated documents again. Looking at us coldly, Juanita reminded us that the office would close for the day in a little over one hour. Maya was already gone! Was she trying to derail the process because of a grudge against Maya?

We left the notary office in a daze. By now it was early afternoon. The girls were starving. Richard and I were incensed at what had happened. Because our cell phones had been taken by the security guards, we had to use an always-erratic Mexican payphone to call Sari. After several tries, we finally got through and tried to stay calm as we described what had just happened.

"I was afraid of something like this," Sari lamented. "I will call Maya."

We agreed to meet Sari and Luisa at a coffee shop around the corner. At least the girls could eat while we tried to regroup. Richard and I had no appetite. We would lose a full day if the documents were not returned to the Embassy before it closed. If we waited at the Embassy again the next day, would Juanita find another "problem" then?

Amazingly, Maya was able to catch a taxi and make it back through the Mexico City traffic to the embassy by 2:30 p.m. We hurried into the security area where Sari and Maya pressed a bored guard at the entrance. To our surprise, he opened the gate with little or no protest. Richard, Maya, and I rushed up the stairs, leaving the now panicky Isabella and Priscilla with Sari and Luisa.

At the passport office, Juanita told us again, rather testily, that the order of the documents was incorrect. She didn't even acknowledge Maya's existence, and Maya did not speak up. We hurried to the Notary office. Maya, who had known the head notary clerk for many years, began talking animatedly with her about what had transpired. After what seemed like an argument between them, Maya turned to us and explained that the papers were in the CORRECT order! In other words, Juanita demanded them in an order different from what the notary herself wanted. We didn't know what to think at that point. Was this some sort of power struggle?

We explained to the notary that we needed the papers then, or all of our other official visits and travel plans would be jeopardized. The notary grudgingly removed the staple, re-ordered the documents, and had Maya sign a new cover sheet before re-stapling them. We thanked her profusely, and ran back to Juanita's office where she was just about to lock the door. We handed her the newly re-ordered documents. She seemed both surprised and annoyed at this turn of events. I'm sure that she had not anticipated that we could complete this goose chase all in one day.

In a flat, emotionless voice, Juanita told us that she would call us the next day with the news that we needed to hear—that Priscilla would get the approval for a visa. This was crucial for us because our travel arrangements had already been confirmed. Isabella and I were due to leave early Saturday morning, leaving Richard and Priscilla to go on to Juarez to get the visa. If we did not get the visa confirmation, we would need to change our trip home, which would be difficult and costly. We left the Embassy relieved and anxious, but extremely puzzled at what had happened. As we drove back to our hotel, Sari explained the history between Maya and Juanita. There had been some arguments in the past, and now there was really bad blood between them.

"Why weren't we told about this?" Richard asked, sipping on a water bottle. We were drained from the day's activity. I was planning on wine with dinner.

"I didn't want to worry you," Sari replied.

Would it have been worse to worry than to be blindsided by Juanita's actions? Who can say? At least we had gotten through this hoop. The reality was that although we were supremely annoyed by Juanita's antics, our girls desperately needed attention and food. We decided not to speak of the day's events, which helped our mood. Eating, talking, and laughing together felt so good. Exhausted, we walked back to the hotel under a beautiful moon and starlit sky.

After the girls had brushed their teeth and were in bed, Richard and I whispered what-if for an hour. What would happen tomorrow or the next day? As much as Sari and Luisa tried to help us navigate the requirements, there was always some roadblock being thrown in our way. Even from the beginning, the Mexican adoption application had more hurdles, more reference checks, more questions, and more detours than any of the other countries that we researched. Nothing made sense to us that evening as we readied for bed and then tossed and turned the rest of the night.

CHAPTER 21

The Pyramid
of the Sun

W ith nothing official to do the next day, Luisa and Adolfo, her friend and tour guide, drove us out to Teotihuacan— the Aztec pyramids just outside Mexico City. The weather was gloriously clear in Mexico City and we enjoyed being tourists for the day, investigating the ruins of this ancient civilization. Adolfo led us down the *Calle de las Muertos*, which sounded much more romantic than its English translation *Street of the Dead*. We posed for pictures, squinting and smiling in front of the Pyramid of the Sun.

Richard, Adolfo, and the girls climbed to the top of the pyramid while Luisa and I stayed below. It was one of the few opportunities I had to speak with her alone and I decided to take advantage of it. Proceeding cautiously, I asked Luisa if she or Ceci had any information about Priscilla's biological mother. Luisa was quick to respond that she did not. I pressed her. The feeling that I had from *Tía* Vero's letter was that perhaps this was a local woman. It was just a feeling though. Luisa assured me that she and Ceci knew nothing and I was left alone with my thoughts. I didn't feel comfortable going any further at that point. Honestly, it was also a bit of relief as I was afraid of the questions Priscilla might ask me. Now I could truthfully say that I knew nothing, but it could be something that we could sort out later together. The sun was beating down, and when I shielded my eyes to look up, I could see the girls still climbing the stairs to the top of the pyramid.

Luisa had been a trusted partner for Ceci and for us, and I knew that she only wanted what was best for Priscilla. She had visited the United States just a few months earlier while we waited for Priscilla's paperwork to clear. *Ministerios* had sent Luisa in order to familiarize her with the laws regarding foreign adoption. It had been a cold and rainy weekend when we met for dinner in Philadelphia. As we'd shown her the sights around town, I'd decided to ask her about her calling. How had she known that she wanted to minister to others in this way?

We'd been sitting in Marra's, one of our favorite South Philly restaurants. The pasta with marinara sauce arrived steaming. Luisa bowed her head and with eyes closed prayed intently for about fifteen seconds. Lifting her head and picking up her fork, she almost glowed as she said, "The Lord came into my life like a whirlwind, changing my priorities, aligning my desires to His, changing my patterns, healing me and moving me in directions I never would have thought possible." Luisa's eloquent response, describing her relationship with God, was delivered in hushed, reverent tones. She paused to twirl spaghetti, "He made everything inside me new and I allowed Him to do it."

"But what about Ceci?" I'd asked her. "How did you know you wanted to work together?"

"I can tell you I was attracted to Ceci's work at *Ministerios* because of the passion that she has for the Lord. I could never have imagined myself working with children and never thought I would be involved with the adoption process."

"Why?" I persisted. "You seem so confident, so comfortable with children."

"Years ago, I worked for a bank and insurance broker before *Ministerios*, and I always thought that I would work in those areas and then take care of my own children."

Luisa was the prototypical insurance employee. Her clothes were professional, tailored. She walked with a casual elegance, black hair against porcelain skin. When she talked, her voice was low, her brown eyes intently focused on me, radiating caring and compassion with an intensity that no one can teach. Luisa had found a more deserving goal. She leaned over toward me as if telling me a secret.

"I am beginning to realize something that I heard for so long...that I am really His hands, His mouth, and His eyes. He needs my hands to touch others with his love to bring hope, freedom, and truth."

I'd marveled at the force of her faith as well as the beautiful and articulate way she verbalized her love for God. How did she feel the love of the Lord on such a deep level? We ate in silence for a while as I took it all in, feeling grateful that my family was in such good hands. Luisa played in the spiritual big leagues, while I felt like an amateur. My mind pondered all of this as I ate my own feast of lasagna stuffed with cheese and sausage and wondered how to characterize Luisa. Fundamentalist? Evangelist? Born again? I wondered if my inferior praying skills and faith struggles were evident as I sat there—not sure if I would ever be able to connect with Luisa on a spiritual level.

Now, as I sat in the Mexican sun, remembering and thinking, I looked up to see Richard, Adolfo, and the girls making their way down the pyramid steps. For our next stop, we headed to Chapultepec Park. As we walked through the beautiful gardens and castle building that had been the residence of Emperor Maximilian, Adolfo again provided the expert commentary. He was a certified tour guide, which meant that he had taken a set of required courses in Mexican history, art, literature, and architecture. The park surrounding the castle was filled with street vendors selling things like roasted chorizo tacos, salads, and fruits. One woman, dressed in a colorful, swirly-type skirt and white peasant style blouse, was selling fresh fruit slices in clear plastic bags. It was the end-of-the-day-tourist prices—just a few pesos. Handing the bag to Priscilla, she motioned toward a tub of red chili pepper and Priscilla nodded. With a coffee-like scoop, she proceeded to generously sprinkle the spicy pepper over the fruit. Priscilla plopped the fruit in her mouth, smiling broadly, while Isabella and I just stared. It was obvious that she was eating a slice of heaven that also reminded her of her past life in Mexico. She chomped on the orange, cantaloupe, and honeydew excitedly, offering them to us. Richard, Isabella, and I each tried a slice. We all had to recover with our water bottles while Priscilla laughed.

Richard became increasingly quiet because we had not yet heard from Juanita at the embassy. Luisa was reassuring, doing her best to convince us that everything would be all right. It wasn't clear if she would call that day or tomorrow, but I was able to put it out of my mind as we enjoyed the remarkable scenery visible from the veranda of Chapultepec. The sky was a deeper blue than we had ever seen in Mexico City, home of the worst smog on the planet.

Later that night, we went to the *Ballet Folklórico de México*. I was not sure what to expect, but Richard and I both thought it was important to show Priscilla some aspects of Mexico that she had not experienced before. The dancers were not performing ballet in the classic sense that we are used to seeing, but instead moved in beautiful coordination to amazingly intricate pounding steps and rhythms. The brilliant women's costumes were an especially mesmerizing display of swirling and twirling skirts.

I kept glancing over at Priscilla who was taking it all in as if in a trance. I wondered, did she see herself as one of these dancers? Because ballet had been a part of Priscilla's life for many years, we arranged for her to continue to dance as soon as she began to live with us. Her dingy well-worn pink flats were at the bottom of her carry-on when we unpacked it together. She grabbed at the shoes, holding them up to show me repeating, "ballet, ballet" pronouncing the "t" at the end of the word. After the performance, however, she was quiet and looked tired.

The next morning was another day of sightseeing as we waited for Juanita's call.

We began the day in a cab to the *Zócalo*, the largest public square in the Western Hemisphere, and the third largest in the world after *Tía*nanmen Square in Beijing and Red Square in Moscow. The square is the ceremonial center of Mexico. Its formal name is *Plaza de la Constitución*, and it has been the heart of the city ever since the days of Aztec rule. The word *zócalo*, though, means base or plinth. During the 19th century, the Mexican leader Antonio Lopez de Santa Anna ordered a sculpture commemorating Mexican independence for the middle of the town square. The statue was never finished. The only remnant of the work was the plinth, which no longer exists, but its name remains.

We wandered around the square and into the Metropolitan Cathedral and National Palace. The vendors, musicians, and performers in the square provided some of the best people-watching of the trip. We were fascinated by the diverse activity. Looking for food, we ended up at McDonald's because we all needed to use the bathroom. I saved a table while Richard stood outside the bathroom waiting for the girls. After a quick bite, we left the crowded restaurant. Making our way through the crowds, I noticed a woman trying to catch up to us as we crossed the street. She was extremely animated and started to shake her finger at me. I backed away and at the same time attempted to tell her that I did not speak Spanish. She was intent on saying something to me. When she left, Priscilla translated. The woman had been irritated that I did not accompany the girls into the bathroom because it was not safe to leave children alone in a public place. The fact that Richard was waiting just outside the door obviously did not count.

I marveled at Priscilla's language skills. It certainly was impressive that she could still understand her native language, but spoke English most of the time now. Like any other child on vacation with parents, she held my hand, stuck close if we were in a crowd, and still tried to get my attention if my eyes were elsewhere. I cherished these moments when everything felt normal, and it was possible to imagine that we would be a family.

At the edge of the square, Sari met us and took over as tour guide, driving to the Shrine of Guadalupe, about three miles northeast of Mexico City. This most holy place, second only to the Vatican for pilgrimages of the faithful, had been on our must-see list from our first trip. It seemed fitting that we would visit today.

The sky had turned gray and our anxiety started to build a bit as it was almost 2:00 p.m. and we had still not heard from Juanita. From the backseat of Sari's car, Richard called the Embassy office, only to reach Jorge. Juanita was still not back from lunch. Jorge explained that he would complete the final approval once instructed by Juanita, but he had not heard anything from her about our case.

As it was Friday, the embassy would soon be closing for the weekend. Two days earlier when we had handed her our re-ordered papers, she had told us that she would approve them "first thing in the morning." What the heck did that mean? I guess we forgot to ask which morning.

Richard decided to take matters in his own hands and called the Director of Foreign Students at De La Salle University in Mexico City. De La Salle is a sister school of La Salle University in Philadelphia where Richard worked. He had been in email contact when we were planning our trip. The Director worked regularly with embassy staff and had offered assistance with any issues there. Richard provided the short version of how difficult it had been to get this last set of papers approved and nodded his head as he listened, then put the phone back in his pocket. "We've done all we can now," he sighed.

"That Juanita, she gets everyone excited, but it will all work out," Sari said matter-of-factly as she navigated traffic once more. I was relieved that Richard had contacted someone else. Who knows? This may just be the push we needed. Still in the car driving toward the shrine, Richard's phone rang about fifteen minutes later.

"Hello," he said with urgency. I looked at his forehead creased in worry. Suddenly, his whole face relaxed and I could tell it was Juanita. "Thank you," he said as he hung up. "She said that our papers were in order, and that we could pick them up first thing Monday morning." Richard exhaled, leaning back in his seat.

As we drove through a part of the city we had not seen before, I started to relax. Isabella and I could return to Philadelphia the next day, as we had planned, and Richard and Priscilla would stay the extra week to take care of the Juarez visit. As if on cue, Sari then turned a corner to reveal the massive dome of the Shrine of Guadalupe in the distance.

We pulled into an underground parking lot and passed through a maze of dimly lit souvenir shops. Climbing up the stairs to the plaza, we walked by women and children huddled together asking for change, their eyes desperate and sad. I looked up to take in the imposing Basilica, feeling the presence of thousands who come to worship and pray. It was cloudy and overcast now, with just a few groups of visitors spread out over the vast expanse leading up to the entrance.

We walked into the enormous, rounded interior space of the Basilica. Mass was being offered at the main altar in hushed tones, the pews sparsely filled. Sari had begun to tell us the story of Juan Diego as we walked to the church, and now she continued in a whisper. Pointing to Mary's likeness framed in gold above the main altar, Sari explained the visitation of the Blessed Virgin to Juan Diego, an Aztec Indian farmer. Mary implored him to build a church on that very spot and Juan Diego visited the bishop twice to give him the message but was twice turned away. Juan Diego was asked to bring proof of his vision. On his third visit from the Holy Mother, he found white roses on a frozen hilltop. He placed them under his cloak and upon returning to the bishop the image of Mary appeared on his cloak. This preserved image is framed and is visible from virtually anywhere in the church. Beneath the main altar is a moving walkway for viewing the likeness even as mass is celebrated.

I lit a candle to pray and gave thanks for this holy place and our own little miracles of Priscilla and paperwork. We climbed to the top of the building behind the original dome, looking out on the city skyline. Just then the sun broke through the clouds, which we took as a sign that good things were happening for our family.

In the car, weaving our way back to the hotel, I reached inside my brown paper souvenir bag and held the holy card image of Our Lady of Guadalupe. I felt a connection to her from that first visit with Juan at the agency in Pennsylvania over two years ago. She was so beautiful and serene. Her image was everywhere in Mexico and today she had smiled down on us. How did I ever doubt Her?

CHAPTER 22

Reunited

A t the airport, we ran into the frustratingly long lines — the universal signature of life in Mexico City. Given everything that had happened on our quest so far, we knew that we couldn't leave without incident. Sure enough, there was an acid reflux moment at the airline check-in because we didn't have the appropriate notarized papers permitting Isabella to leave a country with just one parent. Airline personnel ultimately relented and made a notation on Richard's return ticket, so any additional paperwork would not be necessary.

Richard's patience was put to the test on Monday. Packed and ready to leave the hotel, he received a call from Juanita at the embassy announcing that the documents she had promised would not be ready after all and would need an extra day. Richard then spent the rest of the day changing all of the travel arrangements for the rest of the trip.

Of course, on Tuesday morning when Richard and Priscilla arrived at the embassy, they waited over two hours for the documents to be handed to them. With a flight to Juarez scheduled for late afternoon, the clock was ticking. Juanita appeared with an envelope only after many of the Mexican citizens in the waiting room joined in Richard's pleas for the timely delivery of the papers.

Documents safely in hand, Richard and Priscilla checked out of the hotel where a waiting Sari drove them to the airport.

After landing in Juarez, Pris and Richard checked in to the local Holiday Inn. The next day at the American Consulate, the visa would be approved. Easier said than done.

Arriving at the Consulate before seven in the morning, Richard and Priscilla joined—you guessed it—another long line. Only this time it was a line of several hundred from all across Mexico waiting for an entrance visa to the U.S. by way of El Paso, which was visible just across the Rio Grande.

After inquiring a number of times as to whether or not they were supposed to be in the immigration line, Richard and Priscilla were led to another entrance. They then proceeded to wait almost ten hours before Priscilla's petition for a visa was approved. Richard swore that each time he asked the status of his application, he was moved to the last place in line.

When all paperwork had been stamped and approved, Richard returned to the locker location in the shopping area across from the Consulate where he had been required to store his cell phone, but everything was all locked up with no attendant in sight. Richard went door to door asking for the owner and eventually found someone with a key. He and Priscilla then raced back to the hotel and grabbed a taxi to the airport, flying back to Mexico City.

Richard and Priscilla spent one more morning in Mexico, then caught an afternoon flight home to Philadelphia. Isabella and I were ecstatic. As the airport train pulled into the station, we spotted them through the frosty windows and jumped up and down, waving our hands. The four of us hugged right there on the train platform. What a huge, overwhelming relief it was to be back together!

That night, I sat at my computer looking over my email response letter to *Tía* Vero—the woman who loved Priscilla enough to let her go. I don't know why I waited so long to respond to her, but now that the trips to Mexico were over, the time seemed right. As difficult and lengthy as the adoption process had been, it paled in comparison to the separation struggles of Vero and Priscilla. It was only because Vero had the courage to let go that we were able to become a family, and I wanted to say thank you.

I clicked on the document file to read it over again.

Dear Tía Vero,

Would you believe that we have just now discovered your letter amidst all of Priscilla's things? I was so moved to read your heartfelt and loving words and it made me happy to know that Priscilla was cared for by someone as warm-hearted as you. When we called you this past summer, you gave Priscilla the message that a family is important and that we loved her very much. Those were trying times and I will always be grateful to you for believing in us and telling Priscilla that our love was the best thing for her.

As you know, Priscilla was not happy when she first arrived in the United States. She cried for months, constantly saying that she wanted to return to Mexico. She missed you and her friends so much. One weekend, Ceci came to visit and Priscilla cried and clung to her for hours. Priscilla told her things that were not true, perhaps in the hope that she would be allowed to return to Mexico. We were scared that Pris would never love us.

Gradually, she has begun to have fun with her sister Isabella and meet some other little girls in the neighborhood. Priscilla has quite an appetite and has enjoyed our food, especially candy and ice cream! With each passing week, her English has improved and her comfort level has increased. She enjoys school and calls it "fun." Priscilla received a terrific report card. All of the teachers are just crazy about her and in turn, Priscilla is doing her best in school. She wants to learn and participates in many other activities like ballet.

Priscilla has just captivated everyone she meets. At one neighborhood gathering not too long ago, one friend said that she just has a "sparkle" about her. She laughs easily and now makes us laugh during our family time together. We love her, squeeze her and kiss her all of the time. Isabella is learning how to be a sister as well as adjusting to not getting all of the attention.

Christmas was a dream come true for me. After so many years of wanting another child, I have the most adorable girl in the world and so much to be thankful for. We tell Priscilla almost every night how lucky we are that she came to us from Mexico. I tease her that I have "the cutest girl in all of Mexico." I ask her if she knows this? She says that she is not cute but laughs anyway.

When Priscilla is a little older, I would like to bring her back to Cuernavaca and to see you again. Please let's stay in touch. Thank you again for your prayers and your help in our time of need. We will never forget your kind and supportive words as we struggled to become a family. We are so grateful that you influenced Priscilla so positively. We are also sending family pictures that I hope you enjoy.

Much Love,
Anna Maria

~

Two months after returning from our final trip to Mexico, Priscilla announced that George W. Bush was her favorite president. This sudden allegiance was due to the fact that she had just received her own important letter from Washington DC:

Dear Fellow American:

I am pleased to congratulate you on becoming a United States Citizen. You are now a part of a great and blessed

Nation. I know your family and friends are proud of you on this special day.

As you begin to participate fully in our democracy, remember that what you do is as important as anything government does. I ask you to serve your new Nation, beginning with your neighbor. I ask you to be citizens building communities of service and a Nation of character. Americans are generous and strong and decent not because we believe in ourselves, but because we hold beliefs beyond ourselves. When this spirit of citizenship is missing, no government program can replace it. When this spirit is present, no wrong can stand against it.

Welcome to the joy, responsibility, and freedom of American citizenship. God bless you, and God bless America.

Sincerely,

George W. Bush

As a way to celebrate and share the event with Priscilla's second-grade classmates, we found a large red, white, and blue star piñata at Target. We loaded it with every type of candy, and tied ribbons, one for each classmate, around the bottom opening of the piñata. This was the peaceful alternative to beating it with a bat, which I am sure her teacher, Mrs. Burnett appreciated. Priscilla helped me count and cut the ribbons, then supervised the candy loading.

A little bit before school ended for the day, Mrs. Burnett told the class all about the President's letter and the process of becoming a citizen. They didn't have to think about it, but for Priscilla, this was a big change and time to celebrate. When the second graders formed a circle in the front of the room, Mrs. Burnett counted, "One... two...three!" and the class pulled on the ribbons.

It was the symbolic end of our long adoption road but just the beginning of Priscilla's journey.

CHAPTER 23

One Year Later

I t's been a little over a year," I said to Richard after the girls had gone to bed. "Do you think we are ready for Luisa?"

It had been a tough year to say the least. We were sipping hot chocolate, enjoying the quiet. Richard shook his head and I knew what he was thinking. Last October was the date of our Mexican court hearing, which wasn't really a hearing at all, but it did grant us custody of Priscilla. We were now looking toward our second Thanksgiving and Luisa would be in Philadelphia again to continue her training on international adoption law and to formally close out our adoption. We made arrangements with her to visit us on a cold night in November.

The girls finished up their homework early in preparation for Luisa's arrival. *The suburbs must be just as daunting to Luisa as Mexico City traffic was to us,* I thought, as I washed the dinner dishes. Priscilla was getting ready for bed when the doorbell rang, and she rushed downstairs. Luisa immediately hugged Priscilla, pulling back smiling as she admired her pink-flowered fleece robe and Pooh slippers.

We traded kisses all around. Initially, Priscilla hung back, uncharacteristically quiet. Soon, though, as Luisa asked questions, about her new life, she began to put on quite a show. Priscilla was making progress in school, had many friends and, in general, seemed like a normal kid. Luisa asked Priscilla, "Are you happy?"

Priscilla looked down and fidgeted and mumbled for about fifteen seconds. The questions had been posed in English, and Priscilla knew exactly what was being asked despite the long pause. Meeting Luisa's gaze, she put her thumb and index finger close together, separated by an inch or two and responded, "A leeetle." Then she cuddled up to Luisa, hugging her. She did not let go for the rest of the evening.

As I sat there and watched Priscilla struggle between two worlds, I couldn't help but think, well at least I get "a leeetle" credit. Once again, the best gift we could give Priscilla was time. I resolved for about the one-millionth time… to be patient.

We went into the dining room to complete the needed agency paperwork and sign the post-adoption assessment. Luisa asked a number of questions about Priscilla's assimilation into school, her activities, and overall health. A social worker who accompanied Luisa for the visit took notes as we spoke of the school year and life in the United States. At the end of the visit, the hugs were tight and long. We promised more pictures and emails.

When Luisa returned to Mexico, she emailed the following:

Dear Anna Maria and Richard,

Thank you very much for letting me visit you last week. I was pleased to see that Priscilla and all of you are doing well.

I would like to talk to you about the "homesickness" that Pris expressed while I was there. She seems to be very adjusted and happy with the new life she has with you, but there is also in her heart all the good memories she has from Ministerios de Amor and from the home where she used to live, the people who used to take care of her and her little friends. All of that is normal and shows that her time here in Mexico was somehow good for her. That does not mean that she would rather be there or that she wants to go back, but probably she needs to know that they still care for her. What could be is that she does not want to lose all that she had before.

I think that you should not be afraid because of her need of having contact with her past, but it would be positive for her to be encouraged by you to write to the people at Cuernavaca, to make a phone call or to write emails.

It is just part of her process. We really want to help you through her total adjustment so that it is as smooth as possible. Please feel free to be in contact with me. I will be pleased to help.

Have a wonderful Christmas time and a flourishing year.

Sincerely,

Luisa

Yes, I was disappointed that Priscilla did not confirm to Luisa that we were a smashing success as a family. The truth is we were not... yet. Sometimes it all felt so right, but other times I was still wondering what we had gotten ourselves into. There was the ever-present resentment that Isabella was the first daughter. Everything was a competition, and from Priscilla's vantage point, Isabella always won. They seemed to fight over the smallest thing, with Priscilla as the instigator more often than not. If Priscilla did not do well on a school assignment, did not like what we were having for dinner, or just woke up on the wrong side of the bed, the anger was leveled at Isabella first. Then we would spiral downward from there. I wanted her to feel these things and work them out in her head, understanding that family trust would build over time. But my attempts to reason with her went nowhere and, after the night with Luisa, I began to wonder—would she ever think of us as her parents?

Our altered family dynamic was a new feeling for me. I was adapting to the fact that our household focus had shifted from the administrative headaches to Priscilla's assimilation into the family. It was easy to focus on things to do, but now that the adoption checklist had come to an end, I was running in place, trying to balance all that was expected, thinking I would get the hang of it at any moment. We wanted to tread carefully with the goal of positively affirming her previous life yet still moving forward with new family activities and challenges.

Most of the time the sisters fought over nothing and that made me crazy. Things like who got the last cookie, who got the best seat on the couch, the favorite blanket, the remote control were all sparks. Later, when they could ride in the front seat of the car, it was whoever called shotgun. There were endless fights about clothes—primarily with Priscilla "borrowing" clothes from Isabella. Years later, when they both had phones, Priscilla would take clothes that belonged to Isabella, then post a picture of herself wearing the outfit. When Isabella noticed the posting on Facebook, Instagram, or whatever, the fireworks would start. Once, Pris took one of Isabella's favorite sweatshirts, left it at a friend's house, and then pretty much never accepted responsibility for getting it back. Clothing that was lost or destroyed was fair game for arguments for years.

It was so hard to make things even when Isabella had such an advantage. By second grade, Isabella had been designated as gifted and participated in a program at the elementary school level with extra coursework and challenges in reading and math. Isabella was so good at both, but when she tried to be helpful to Priscilla with homework, Priscilla would interpret any assistance as bossiness and wave her away. Priscilla would do or say anything to get under Isabella's skin, including playing her music too loudly or agreeing to play a game then quitting when things would not go her way.

When the arguments surfaced, I made an effort to allow them to work out their differences like any pair of siblings. Yet, as time went on, things kept escalating, with me totally underestimating the jealousy factor. As Priscilla's communication skills increased, so did her ability to express her pain. She was totally fluent in English now—and didn't understand Spanish at all. Although it made me sad that she no longer had her birth language, I balanced it with the loss and disappointment that we were all feeling. The whole family was hurting as a result of our transition, and I was in a *no pain, no gain* frame of mind. Our local school had a small class size that was a tremendous benefit to Priscilla. With Spanish instruction to start in a few years, it would be up to her to see if she could become proficient once more. We had stopped her tutoring because an ESL teacher had been assigned to Priscilla at school, providing support and instruction for the next three years.

We all worked hard to include Priscilla in family discussions and encouraged her to share her culture and childhood memories. Both worlds needed to be fully tossed around in the proverbial salad. Her heritage was important to us and the key to our success as a family. We took Luisa's advice and began to send an occasional email with pictures to Vero and Ceci, keeping them up to date on Priscilla's activities—like Brownies and soccer.

When Priscilla would begin a sentence with the words "In Mexico... ," I knew that she had a story to share with us about her prior life. I would stop what I was doing and focus on listening. These stories frequently relayed tales of food or fun, and I wanted her to cherish those memories. It was entertaining to hear explanations of how the children at the shelter helped with chores, meal prep, or whatever she was trying to tell me.

As Priscilla watched me slicing into a cantaloupe melon one Saturday morning, she began with the familiar "In Mexico..." and proceeded to tell me about being called down to the kitchen at the shelter where fruit salad was being prepared. *Tía* Vero always gave her fresh slices to eat, which she did down to the rind, adding chili pepper with each bite. She smiled as I gave her pieces of fruit that I was cutting. She took a large bite of cantaloupe and the juice ran down her chin.

However, as the new family routine took hold, the acting out increased. To make matters worse, Isabella's ability to give her sister the benefit of the doubt decreased. When Pris would launch into a story about the shelter or tell of tales of Mexico, Isabella would roll her eyes or leave the room. It was tough on her now eleven-year-old self to see the family disrupted in this way.

And so began a lifetime effort of trying to equalize the two in terms of my time and motherly tasks. Whose favorite meal would I make? How much homework time would I spend? It was never even because Pris needed so much more. Their arguments were constant and as much as I wanted the sisterly bonds to form, they could not be forced. Isabella was in transition mode herself—from only child to a sister with a younger sibling. The patterns of Priscilla seeking attention were predictable, incessant, and had convinced Isabella that Priscilla just wanted to take me away from her.

Our home had a large staircase and when she was in full tantrum mode, Priscilla would stomp out of her room and throw things down the stairs. Sometimes it was a doll or pillow, but sometimes it was plastic or something breakable, which made a racket and was extremely disruptive or destructive. Whenever I entered Priscilla's room to calm the storm, she would be crying on the bed or packing her suitcase. Things erupted this way routinely for years. I kept thinking that Priscilla would grow out of these testing-types of behaviors, but, we were constantly living on the edge. Isabella began to cope with this new normal by spending more nights at her friends' houses.

One day, I heard Priscilla say more to herself than anyone else, "Isabella looks like Mommy and I look like Daddy." While Priscilla was struggling with how she fit in, I was right there with her, anxious in a high-maintenance way, wondering if she would ever accept me as her mother. During Priscilla's first weeks in our home, she called me... nothing. She wanted zero to do with us. One night, as she was filling the bathtub, the hot water faucet was stuck in the ON position and she could not turn it off. Priscilla came running into my bedroom and screamed, "Anna Maria!" and ran back into the bathroom. I followed her and took care of the water. But with that, Priscilla started to call me Anna Maria all the time. At first it bothered me, but then I got used to it.

Isabella asked, "Why is she calling you that?"

"Because she is not ready to say anything else and it does not feel like I am her mom yet."

Those first few months, if Priscilla needed me, she would yell, "Anna Maria," or would tap me on the shoulder. There were moments that I thought she would call me "Mom" at any second, but that moment never came. The tapping became more incessant. When we were shopping, running errands, cooking, cleaning—if Priscilla wanted something, she would tap to get my attention and it was getting on my nerves. In the day-to-day rhythm of life, I reasoned that it was her way of staying connected to me but not committing to owning me as her mother.

One night, I was helping her to get ready for bed and putting away clean clothes in her bureau. Because I was kneeling down to fold the clothes, we were at the same height and Priscilla came over and tapped me on the shoulder. I looked up to see her holding a shirt that she wanted to wear the next day.

I don't recall if we were having a good day or bad day, but I was tired of the tapping, tired of being reminded that we were not what I wanted to be. Folding the shirt by her bed for the next morning, I said to her, "I am your mom now and I would like you to call me Mom from now on. Okay?" It felt like cheating to orchestrate motherhood this way, but it also felt like she was never going to get there on her own.

Priscilla nodded in agreement and that was that. In forcing the issue, I was putting the theory, "act happy, be happy" to the test and it felt satisfying. We had invested so much, and I was always waiting on the edge of my chair for that validation. I reasoned that it couldn't hurt to give our family a nudge in the right direction. Were we doing all the right things? We managed to network with a few other families who adopted from Mexico, and their stories were not much more encouraging than ours.

As part of our previous domestic adoption efforts, we were required to read books and take training classes. I sorted through countless other books and articles, and actively encouraged regular contact with the other families who had adopted older children. All of our experiences were so different and none of the stories were encouraging anyway. There was one book, *Primal Wound, Understanding the Adopted Child** that provided a lightbulb of recognition and understanding—but I would not discover it for several years.

Meanwhile, I struggled with the process one (sometimes painful, sometimes gratifying) moment at a time. During the spring of her first year at school (which was second grade), I remember a Back to School night for the annual art and science show. Parents strolled through the halls and gym to view the projects and paintings. Priscilla's class exhibited portraits with the theme: *People Who Are the Most Important to Us*. I was practically skipping down the hallway, looking for Priscilla's portrait, naturally expecting to see myself hanging on a 16x20 poster board. I stopped flat-footed staring at a picture of a blond woman holding an infant as I checked and rechecked the tiny scrawl of "Priscilla" in the bottom right-hand corner of the paper.

"Who the heck is that?" I ask Pris who was hanging back.

"It's Mrs. Schwartz who just had a baby. She teaches in another classroom and she let me hold her daughter when she came to school to visit."

"How is she important to you?"

"She knows I love to hold babies, and she let me hold her."

"Oh."

These small denials were a big part of Priscilla's transition, a continuation of those first few weeks in summer camp. She was cute, outgoing and naturally formed relationships with people. However, the ambivalence toward us, her new family, played out in subtle, but always visible ways when we were out and about. At home, Priscilla gave any excuse to retreat from a family function and was frequently angry at someone in the house. We tried many times to break down these events and understand what had occurred. But that only seemed to make things worse as she loudly and vigorously defended her actions. Later, a tearful, repentant Priscilla would be at my door apologizing for the disruption. My bureau drawer already contained a stash of notes beginning with "I'm sorry." I think she wanted to love us, but still felt disloyal to Mexico.

At least that was my theory initially. Although it may simply be part of who Priscilla is. Priscilla's behavior has been frighteningly consistent over the years. To this day, family events continue to have an element of drama.

Back then, I looked for ways to make Priscilla feel special and came up with "Family Day," which was June 30—the anniversary of when she came to live with us. I had read that birthdays can sometimes be painful for adopted children. It is a day that reminds them of losing their biological connection—the loss of a birth mother and family. The recommendation was that adoptive parents come up with other days for celebration that have a different and more positive connotation. That first year we went to a baseball game, and the next few years, we would try to plan a special dinner or other treat. Sometimes I surprised Priscilla with a small gift and she liked the attention.

As the years passed, it never failed that as Family Day approached, Priscilla would do or say something to disrupt the event. By the time the day arrived, we would be too exhausted or mad to all be together. Priscilla's anger or tantrum pushed us to the point where the event had to be cancelled or made it impossible to enjoy the function that we planned. We didn't need to wait for Family Day for that to happen either. It was a familiar pattern and I was always blaming myself for not being better prepared. Was all of this anger directed at us—or was it internal because she felt unlovable? This type of transition behavior persisted, and as I learned through the years, was a natural coping mechanism.

Richard had his own story about making progress. Priscilla spent a lot less time with Richard so there was no tapping for attention or information. Priscilla used his name as she did mine. Calling us by our first names bothered Richard just as much as it bothered me, but we never discussed how to change it.

At the end of our first summer together, Richard took Priscilla shopping for a clock radio so that she could set an alarm for school days. It was probably their first concentrated time together and perhaps he heard her calling him "Richard" one too many times that day. He told me later that after the purchase of the radio, she was excited about having it in her room, but before he helped her to set it up, he told her, "I am your father and you need to call me Dad." She shook her head up and down.

Was it the right time to do these things? Who knows? In that first year, I was so proud of what we had accomplished. Priscilla called us Mom and Dad from then on, she was succeeding at school, was socially well-adjusted, and loved by her teachers. Yet we had only scratched the surface of understanding the complex emotions inside her. Sometimes it was a full-blown tantrum. Other times it was a line in the sand or passive aggressive type behavior at maximum volume: No, I am not eating ravioli for dinner tonight; I do not want to go shopping with you and Isabella and will pout and hide in the clothes racks so you will have to continually look for me; I will go to Isabella's band concert, but will face opposite the stage and then crawl under my seat and stay there; I will play board games with the family, but then will pretend not to understand the rules or will quit playing if I am losing; I will not let anyone touch me to apply sunscreen; I will not tell the truth to any question that I am asked.

Sadly, the light was dawning that a mother's love was not always enough.

CHAPTER 24

Blessings... Pero

P riscilla's personality continued to evolve. Some days she was indescribably funny and full of life and other days—look out. You did not want to be in the way of her wrath. Her tantrums and general nastiness had two themes: food and Isabella. I tried desperately to get ahead of both. One night at dinner, I announced the end of the food-related arguments.

Drawing my own line in the sand, a calm came over me when I said, "Priscilla, we will not hear ONE MORE WORD about the food that is being served for dinner. If I hear any grumbling, objections, complaints, questions, or refusal to eat—you will be excused immediately." When she complained about the vegetables a few nights later, I pulled out her chair and pointed up the stairs.

Kicking, screaming, and throwing things were normal. I would try to reach for her and comfort her with a hug. Just as I held Isabella as a baby when she cried, I reasoned that at some point, my hug would squeeze the bad out and let the good in. Some days, magically, that worked. On other days, nothing could break through and a dark cloud hung over the house. We frequently sent her to her room to quiet herself. But that only worked if she was fighting with Isabella. It was a way to divide and conquer. I tried other strategies to defuse her anger—go to the bathroom and splash cold water, count to ten, take a walk.

The stubborn unwillingness to be a part of the family just wore us down. This was her way of asserting her feelings. Life in the United States was not her decision. Pris did not choose to be a part of our family and she made that known at every opportunity. It was all about control.

In one maneuver that I called "the slowdown," Priscilla would take forever to get ready to leave the house or come downstairs for dinner. I stood at the bottom of the stairs countless times screaming like a lunatic, which sounded something like, "You have been getting ready for over an hour! What the hell are you doing up there? Come DOWN here!"

Pris would saunter down the steps at a frustratingly slow pace, not acknowledging my angst in any way. In another version, she could be standing just a few feet away from me and would pretend not to hear when I spoke to her or asked her to do something. Maddening.

"Sibling spat time," which was any time, was when Priscilla and Isabella would argue on any topic no matter how small or insignificant. All they had to do was cross paths in the bathroom they shared—which was every night.

Isabella: "Why did you use my brush?"

Priscilla: "You used my hairdryer yesterday."

Isabella: "Who cares, it was in the bathroom."

Priscilla: "I hate you, stay away from my stuff."

Isabella: "You stay away from MY stuff."

They were not above smacking each other, which I ruled as crossing the line. In breaking up a fight one night, I grabbed Priscilla's arm and brought back my other hand to smack her butt. But she blocked my hand with hers and when I went to smack her, my hand must have hit her hand. The next day a huge black and blue welt covered my palm. Glancing at that bruise for the next week depressed me. I had lost my temper and felt about as inadequate a mother as ever. It was a lesson for me to slow it down and calm myself. I was the one apologizing now.

There was no doubt that Priscilla liked to entertain us with her goofiness. My sister Kathy said, "Priscilla says the same things we all say, but they just come out in a way that makes you laugh." With her deep and husky voice, words were drawn out in a way that exaggerated her delivery. It was not the sound of a child. Her accent lingered and playing catch-up English was not easy after speaking Spanish for her first seven years. Richard says it was like living with Antonio Banderas. Except that when you looked up, this little kid was talking to you.

Sometimes in the midst of it all, Priscilla would say something unexpected which had the effect of stopping the fight or whatever was happening. When that didn't work, she would fart ("Oh, I am sorry, I didn't see that coming") or burp, which she could conjure at will... an effective conversation-ender.

One evening, when I forcefully suggested that the girls watch TV in a more harmonious and loving way (read: screaming, "Why can't you two stop the arguing?"), Priscilla shouted back, "Mom, you are putting a hard time on me." Pris had a habit of taking an everyday phrase and mixing it up and spitting it out with amusing results.

Priscilla had one volume level: loud. I could hear her voice even if she was down the hall, and sometimes even down the block. When she was excited, I noticed that she had a habit of thrusting both arms straight up from her elbow. Fingers spread apart, she would bend her head down and mess her hair as she began to giggle, then she would throw her arms down as her head shot back and she would finish with a hearty laugh all in one quick motion. Knowing how my gestures and laugh are the exact copy of my sisters and mother—it made me think about Priscilla's family connections. Yes, those gestures were odd, but there were other things that got my attention.

One day when we went shopping at Target, Priscilla got out of the car, cleared her throat, and spit a huge amount of phlegm on the ground. I turned to look, not sure that I heard correctly.

"Did you just spit?"

"Oh, I have always done that," she said.

"Really, since when?" I responded.

"I used to do it all the time in Mexico."

"Well, that is the last time you will ever do it. A lady doesn't spit. If you have something in your mouth, please use a tissue." She just stood there staring at me and I sighed, "Priscilla, will I ever figure you out?"

"Yes, you will, Mom."

"When?"

"In a few days."

Priscilla played soccer and softball during her elementary school years. Soccer games were a chance for her to burn off energy and she followed the ball like a demon. She was tenacious on the field and this more than any other sport put all her energy to use. In softball, there was more sitting and waiting, which was trouble. She was frequently distracted on the bench and did not hesitate to make a comment about the skill level of other team members or mouth off to the coach or umpire. "This game is stupid" or "When do I get to play?" Those were just a few of the things I heard from my seat in the parents' section of the stands.

It was extra fun when we shopped together. One Saturday at the produce market, Priscilla yelled, "Mom, you didn't pay for that!" All of the customers turned around to stare at the lettuce thief. Because the store is bulk produce, receipts are not provided but the veggies are bagged and I showed Priscilla the evidence in my hand. At a gift store in the mall, Priscilla shouted to me over in the next aisle, "Why is everything in here really expensive?" Or an alternate question that I have heard while I have waited in line is, "Do you have enough money to buy that?"

But just when I thought Priscilla didn't "get it" or a particular cultural nuance was lost on her, she would surprise me. On another weekend shopping trip, when leaving that same bulk produce store and after putting the bags in the back of the car, she said, "Is everything in there really cheap because all of the help is Mexican?" Well, now that you mention it, yes.

Two significant things happened around that time period. First, Priscilla reported that she was unable to see the board at school. Sure enough, she needed glasses. Her first pair were wire rims that gave her a studious look. Second, after many months of struggling with her hair, we had it cut Dora-style. Her straight dark hair was blunt cut to her chin with bangs that framed her face. She didn't like either of the changes, particularly her hair, and she frequently said so. Whenever she saw a picture of herself, she would say, "I look like a little boy." Most of the time, Priscilla could not be bothered with her hair, which was the main reason for the shorter style. When I think back on it now, the shorter cut style did not last long. As Priscilla grew, so did her interest in her appearance and she took care of her long black hair by the time she was in middle school.

As her English improved each day, I still noticed the lingering Spanish patterns. When Priscilla searched for the appropriate word to answer a question or explain her day, she would often add the word *pero* (which means *but*) into the sentence to bring it all together. For example, "My friend was showing me the homework lesson, *pero* I was having trouble understanding."

Other Spanish words also hung around, like *donde* (where) and *cuando* (what), and then there were occasional vowel issues in words like daycare, which became *daycaro*. Opposites were also tough concepts to remember as were the word order of things. The *"control remote"* was essential for TV watching, and one morning, Priscilla mentioned that she could not sleep because she had a *"marenight"* about bugs. In addition, the "t"

225

in ballet continued to be pronounced. Whenever I heard these things, they always made me stop and listen—amazed at how quickly English had taken hold and how much she had grown. By the end of second grade, she was now reading and mastering the language in her new country. During her daily routine, I wondered how often she thought of her life in Mexico.

One night after dinner, I sat at the dining room table sorting out pictures of the recently completed school year and vacation. I selected one of Priscilla in her Brownie uniform and one with sister Isabella at the beach. Isabella stood a good eight inches above Priscilla with one foot slightly ahead of the other looking like the confident older sister that she was. Priscilla in her blue Brownie ensemble smiled with her chin upturned. If she could have been on tiptoes, she would have done it. I gave the photos to Richard and said, "Will you send them to *Tía* Vero, Luisa, and Ceci?"

I knew it was important for all of our Mexican contacts to see progress. It took a week or two, but *Tía* Vero responded with her usual kind and sweet words. She had been thinking of us as well. We received the translated version from Karen within a day:

Dear Anna Maria and Richard,

I am very grateful to you for the chance to know about Priscilla. I imagine that it is a little difficult for you as her parents to have her not forget me, but I believe that our God has permitted it. I give thanks to the Heavenly Father for the chance that you have given me and for your good heart and that you understand that she was someone very loved by me.

The moment of her leaving was difficult and more than anything, it was difficult to spend days without her. It continued to be hard with the other girls asking each day where she was and me telling them that she had gone with her family and we had to pray for her that they would love her. Time has passed and although I have not forgotten her, I believe that the love you gave her was the best for her. I give thanks to God for each one of you and for the love that you have for Priscilla.

Please give the following letter to Priscilla for me.

Tía Vero

~

Dear Priscilla,

Hello, how are you? I hope that you are well and that your vacations have been super fun. I hope that you behave well and that you don't do the mischief that you used to do here. Tell me if you continue with ballet or if you changed to another activity.

I want to make you laugh a little and I hope you don't get mad but do you continue with your wild hair? I used to call them tropical explosions of hair… ha ha ha. Do you remember that it was very difficult to fix your hair? Well, the photos that your parents have sent to me, I see that you have grown a lot and that you are becoming very pretty.

I would also like to know if you continue speaking Spanish. It's important that you don't forget and that you teach your parents and your sister. I suppose that English already dominates to perfection and that you understand what everyone says to you.

It's important that you behave well and that you be a good girl now that your parents love you. Do you understand? I have to go, but I ask that you pray for your friends still here. The girls and I do each day. One of the boys already has a family that loves him and he went with them and now his sister is a little sad because she says that her little brother already left, but I hope that God sends a family to her too.

I hope that God continues blessing you and that everything you do is a blessing to your life. Remember that in obedience is the blessing. I love you.

Tía Vero

That night after dinner, I gave Priscilla the letter and she smiled when she read the comment about her hair. I waited for a reaction to the advice Vero gave regarding speaking Spanish, but there was none.

It was clear that Vero loved her immensely, and still supported us as parents. To have learned about love from such a woman was the greatest blessing for all of us.

CHAPTER 25

The Orphan Chronicles

I snapped up the paper from the kitchen counter, tsked, rolled my eyes, and heaved an enormous sigh all at once. It was a letter from our elementary school music teacher, Mrs. Bobbie Leiter, announcing this year's drama production of *Annie Jr.* Eleven-year-old Isabella in sixth grade and ten-year-old Priscilla in the fourth grade eagerly awaited tryouts.

> *Dear All,*
>
> *Well, it has finally arrived—the Spring Elementary Drama Club production. I am happy to announce that the show we will be doing is Annie Jr. As you probably know, the music and story are absolutely fabulous and there are many parts available. I am looking forward to many fifth and sixth graders auditioning for parts and signing up for stage crew, and fourth graders joining chorus. This is going to be a great show to work on and to perform. We are looking forward to your being involved!!!!!*
>
> *Love, Mrs. Bobbie Leiter*

"But why *Annie*?" I moaned. I have nothing against the optimistic redhead. But, ever since Priscilla came into our lives, I have been desperate to make sense of the entertainment industry's most popular obsession—orphans.

Orphan. There is no other word that pulls on heartstrings and purse strings the way that one does. As the foundation of countless children's tales, orphans are irresistible to parents and children alike, or at least Disney thinks so. The orphan theme isn't omnipresent just in movies or TV, though. One of the girls' favorite pastimes was playing with their American Girl Dolls. These dolls, about eighteen inches high and sporting a range of complexions, hairstyles, and clothing, represent various periods of American history. Each doll has a backstory that provides a mini history of that time period. Priscilla's Hispanic doll was named "Josefina." Her Mexican family settled in New Mexico in 1824 and we soon learned that Josefina's mother passed away the year before.

Similarly, the girls could not wait for the American Girl movie, which was the story of "Samantha" set in 1904 New York. Samantha's parents died when she was just a baby, so she lives with her extremely wealthy grandmother in the rolling New York countryside. At their spacious and luxurious home, Samantha is friendly with the caretaker's three daughters who are a sympathetic bunch as they are not only the maids of the house, but they *also lost their mother* several years ago. I watched Priscilla stare expressionless at the screen all through the movie. It was a topic I didn't have the nerve to discuss with her. Would it be like poking a hornet's nest?

At dinner, Isabella announced that her tryout song would be *"Do-Re-Mi."* Would I listen after dinner? Meanwhile, Priscilla confirmed aspirations for her chorus part with a shrug. Isabella did not belt out her song but did not fade away either. *"Do-Re-Mi"* was clear and sweet. We practiced reading a scene. I played Annie while Isabella, as Daddy Warbucks, intoned with great seriousness, "What good is money if you have no one to share it with?" At the end of the scene, I/Annie replied, "My parents are coming for me, I just know it." I looked to Priscilla after this line, but she was not paying attention.

The next evening, Isabella said that her tryout went smoothly. My hints for acting as Daddy Warbucks (timely and brilliant hand gestures) came in handy.

Sixteen weeks until the performance...

Reading was always difficult for Priscilla. It had been a challenge to get her to read anything—but one series of books held her interest: *Lemony Snicket's Series of Unfortunate Events*. Guess which "unfortunate event" happens first? Shocker... the children lose their parents in a fire and spend the rest of the twelve-book series being shuffled from one uncaring relative to another while smarmy Uncle Olaf tries to adopt them. Orphans seem to be consistently at the forefront of many captivating children's stories. We only have to wait until page twenty-seven to find out that Harry Potter is an orphan. Losing a parent is daunting at any age. We all seem to love watching children as they try to fill the gaping hole created by such loss.

Friday was the big decision day. The roles for the play would be posted, ending the suspense. As Isabella hoisted her backpack to leave for school, I told her, "Just be happy with whatever happens. You will do a great job no matter what part you get." The phone rang later that afternoon. "Mom... guess what? I'm Annie," Isabella said breathlessly into the phone.

Both girls arrived home in a jumble of laughter and excited conversation. Isabella explained the schedule for rehearsals, with special lessons for those with solo songs. Priscilla, in the chorus, would be one of the "orphans." The girls had already signed contracts, promising that they would attend designated rehearsals and be willing to take direction. Clearly Mrs. Leiter had done this before.

I immediately started to worry. What would Priscilla think as her sister sang of orphan woes on stage? How would she cope when Isabella became the guaranteed center of attention for the next three months? Priscilla would be investing considerable time and energy to memorize the songs and dance numbers. I desperately hoped that she wouldn't think about the plot in a deep and meaningful way.

Fourteen weeks until the performance...

The *Annie Jr.* CD played endlessly in the kitchen and both girls sang along. Initially indifferent, Priscilla was reading every word of the script when Isabella did not have it in her hands. She promised to help Isabella with her lines. Her deep gruff voice and staccato delivery of Daddy Warbucks' lines sent us into fits of laughter. Sometimes though, I had to pause as the words sunk in. One evening, I heard Priscilla read through a scene in the kitchen.

"No one cares for you a smidge when you're in an orphanage," she said haltingly. I cringed a little as I saw her ponder the words in her head. She stopped reading. "Sometimes, it makes me cry," she said. When I asked her why, she answered, "I don't know, it's happy and sad all at once."

Then unexpectedly, a few nights later as Priscilla was doing her homework, she said, "Mommy, guess what? I am so happy that we are doing *Annie*."

"How come?" I asked.

"Because all of the kids are in an orphanage and it reminds me of you and Daddy coming to Mexico to find me. Now I have a family."

This exchange came out of the blue one evening as we were preparing for dinner. Totally spontaneous and not prompted by my usual hovering questions and concerns, it made me smile. I was relieved that her reaction was positive, as I had stressed about her response to lines such as, "Why would anyone want to be an orphan, anyway?" Now, like most observations delivered simply from the mouths of babes, Priscilla's reasoning came without further explanation or questions. I just had to accept the fact that she was going to be okay through it all. Let the show go on!

Twelve weeks until the performance...

I took my turn as parent chaperone, assisting Mrs. Leiter during rehearsal one cold February afternoon after school.

Bobbie Leiter, a tall, thin presence with boundless energy, wore a loose-fitting brown jumper. Her straight, blond, no-nonsense hair, blunt cut to her chin, swung side to side as she flitted around the gym. She was all business as she corralled the choral cast members in for a scene. Each child was assigned a number and letter, with the designated song mapped out on a large poster board that she propped up on a stand at the foot of the stage.

"NYC, NYC... line up for NYC." Her announcement immediately created a rush of ten and eleven-year-olds to the stage.

"Every year, I lose my voice, so my doctor told me to get one of these," Mrs. Leiter announced to no one in particular as she adjusted a microphone around her neck attached to a purple ribbon. She proceeded to give directions to me and my parent partner to get the children in place. I was assigned the odd-numbered chorus members—groups A through F on stage left. I fumbled with my parent binder that contained the cast lists and began to call out names. The children meandered over to me, still talking and laughing on a sugar high from the Valentine's day candy they had been munching on all day.

"What number are you?" I asked, trying to herd about forty of them into their designated spots.

Mrs. Leiter, however, was still not happy. "I see many without a script," she huffed. It was true. At least a third of the cast were not holding the black, *Annie Jr.* script books. Miraculously, Priscilla had hers and sat with her chorus group A. However, about twenty other chorus members from different groups broke ranks, crawled over to their backpacks, pulled out their book, and then returned to the stage.

"Whoever does not have a script, raise your hand," Mrs. Leiter said with an exasperated sigh. This elementary school version of kicking butt and taking names got results when they sincerely promised to bring their scripts the next time.

Mrs. Leiter slapped a new poster board on the stand and shouted out the groupings for the song "It's a Hard-Knock Life." I could not seem to remember anyone's name or number, and so I kept asking *who was who and where do they belong?* Luckily, Mrs. Leiter didn't notice. What I noticed, though, was that Priscilla would go out of her way to avoid Isabella on stage.

The choreography was pretty basic, but at one point during the "Hard-Knock Life" song, the orphans, which included Priscilla, bent over pretending to mimic an ironing board while Isabella "ironed" on their backs during the song. In an effort to avoid Isabella, Priscilla kept turning the wrong way on stage, crashing into other chorus members. Mrs. Leiter shook her head and gave the correct stage direction each time. The little hurts were always there, and Priscilla timed them perfectly. It made me a bit sad to watch. The patterns from home emerged when the two were thrust together.

Ten weeks until the performance...

Isabella was to have the entire play memorized by now. We read through the last few scenes. Every time she didn't know her line, she reverted to a sincere and cute, "Oohh, boy!" It worked some of the time, but I helped her listen for cues to get it right. She sang, "Maybe" and "Tomorrow," and was a bit flat on some of the notes. We enlisted the help of a family friend who was a professional singer for some musical coaching.

When Isabella came into my room to say good night, she hugged me and started to cry. This time Priscilla was not the source of her angst and I was almost relieved. Between sobs, Isabella told me that during study period, two mean boys took advantage of the quiet time to tell her that she "stunk" as Annie. I put my arms around her and hugged tightly.

Five weeks until the performance...

Our family friend continued to help Isabella through some of the rough spots of "Tomorrow" and other challenging vocals. This was just what the doctor ordered as they found the right pitch together resulting in a significant confidence boost. With the opening night right around the corner, the order forms for tickets arrived with the lead roles approved for a few extra tickets.

In her update letter, Mrs. Leiter wrote enthusiastically:

The show is going to be great! We have spent a lot of time trying to get as many seats as we can in the auditorium. Understand that you are welcome to come to the Friday school performance and also are welcome at the dress rehearsals. Thanks for the pleasure of working with your talented, energetic and adorable kids. You are going to be so proud of them!
Love, Mrs. Bobbie Leiter.

Who wouldn't love a teacher like that?

Three weeks until the performance...

Isabella returned home from her singing lesson and told us all about how she would stand on stage in order to get more power from her voice. I did not hear about any more stage mishaps between the girls. However, they still found plenty to argue about—including opinions and observations on the various cast members or appropriate attire for the cast party.

Priscilla transitioned to mopey and quiet as opening night loomed closer. Since it was Easter weekend, we decided a change in scenery would be good for everyone and drove to the shore. Richard had a brilliant idea to hide Easter eggs on the beach. Two hours later we were still digging for them in the hot sun, not knowing where to look because the shifting sand obliterated the markings we made. We recovered about half of the brightly colored plastic eggs but never found the bag of jelly beans. Back at the house, I asked Isabella for some *Annie* songs. Priscilla volunteered to be Sandy, the dog.

Isabella sang "Tomorrow" while Priscilla bounced at her side and performed her best dog imitation. Next, the girls sang "Maybe," my favorite song in the show. Priscilla took her appropriate place stage-left and pretended to be asleep until it was her time to sing the chorus: *"Their one mistake was givin' up me."*

One week until the performance...

Isabella woke up with serious stomach distress, but did not throw up. We calmed her nerves with tea and toast. Richard and I both tiptoed around homework and other activities. Rehearsal schedules doubled, and we had their favorite foods when they returned home. Isabella was a straight "A" student and memorization was almost easy for her. I knew she had the lines down cold and when she wanted to sing a song or two, we listened and encouraged.

Priscilla picked this time to tell us that she really did not want to be on stage and she wouldn't be able to do it because she was so nervous.

Isabella sighed, "Always drama."

The day of the performance...

"This is IT!" Mrs. Leiter's rehearsal schedule note screamed at us from its post on the basement door. I was a nervous wreck when I left for work. Late that afternoon, I rushed home and helped Isabella pin down her hair so the red wig would fit snugly.

"I am SO nervous," Priscilla almost screamed at the dinner table. The girls had a quick slice of pizza before leaving. "This is my first show, my first big production." We laughed as Isabella calmly sat at the table putting the finishing touches on her book report.

"Everybody will be staring at me," Priscilla complained. As one of the smallest members of the chorus, she would be right in front at center stage. I told her that I would be watching and waving to her from the first row.

Grammy, Nana, and Pop-pop, as well as my sister Kathy and her husband Bill arrived at the house and we left hurriedly with flowers and jitters. It made me so happy to have the family together. We took our seats in the front of the auditorium. Parents wished us good luck. Behind us, neighbors slid into the row. One mother looked at me apologetically and said, "I am so sorry. I think I offended Priscilla."

"What?" I responded.

"Well, they were getting ready backstage, and I asked her, 'Are those your orphan clothes?' Priscilla crossed her arms and just stared at me, saying, 'Yes, these are my clothes.'"

"I'm sorry. I wasn't even thinking; I just blurted it out."

I waved her concern away, truthfully not even sure if Priscilla was offended or not. If true, it would be the first recognition from Priscilla that she was bothered at all by someone referring to her as an orphan. In any event, as I heard about Priscilla's reaction, it confirmed my uneasiness about the *Annie* story. I was beginning to think I was a little crazy.

Through the small opening at the bottom of the blue velvet curtain, I saw the rows and rows of sneakers assembled backstage. The sound of young stagehands hurriedly moving set pieces was muffled from behind the curtain, when suddenly it was swept aside to reveal all of the orphans asleep on center stage. As Molly woke from her dream, Annie breezed up the stairs on stage right to comfort her. The other orphans also woke with a chatter. "Pipe down, all of ya. There, there," Annie said to Molly, putting her arm around her.

I barely recognized my own daughter. Isabella's skin absolutely glowed under her red wig. Freckles were spattered on her nose and cheeks. She wore a drab green skirt, a striped shapeless shirt, dark tights, and black ankle boots. Her big brown eyes were intensely focused, and she looked out above the audience and sang:

> *Maybe far away or maybe real nearby, he may be pourin' her coffee, she may be straightenin' his tie.*
>
> *Maybe in a house all hidden by a hill, she's sittin' playin' piano, he's sittin' payin' a bill...Betcha they're young, betcha they're smart. Bet they collect things like ashtrays and art.*
>
> *Betcha they're good, why shouldn't they be... their one mistake was givin up me...*[1]

On cue, Priscilla woke up center stage, yawning and stretching her arms, singing with the chorus, her glasses glinting in the stage light.

I reached inside my purse to get my tissues.

Reflecting on it all after the show, I realized the girls were not as focused on the orphan theme as I was. In fact, years later, Priscilla's memory of the play was that she participated only as a way to qualify for the field trip to New York and a Broadway

---

1. *The musical "Annie" is based upon Harold Gray comic strip, "Little Orphan Annie," music by Charles Strouse, lyrics by Martin Charnin*

show. Truthfully, the storyline seemed to have little significance for either of them. The day-to-day drama in our home revolved consistently around trivial sibling spats, not orphan show plots.

Still, it felt strange watching Priscilla swinging a broom and singing about her hard-knock life. I could still visualize all of the dirty mops and brooms stacked in the corner of the patio at the Cuernavaca shelter while we waited for her to come down the stairs and meet us that first time. At one point during the show, I gave her the promised subtle wave from the front row and she smiled the most beautiful smile at me as she danced off stage. A mother couldn't ask for more than that from the world's most-loved, *former* orphan.

CHAPTER 26

Immersion

E lementary school was still challenging for Priscilla. Her routine of school, daycare, soccer, ballet, and church continued, with behavior issues that were mostly ill-timed tantrums or stubbornness. I wracked my brain to think of ways that would integrate her into family life.

During our first Christmas together, we traveled to Radio City Music Hall for the Christmas show. The girls were nine and ten and although too old for Santa they were still young enough to be excited about a trip to New York. The Christmas show finale, including a live Nativity scene and the beauty of Christ in a manger, brought home some timely inspiration about what the holidays really mean. On Sunday night that weekend after the girls had gone to bed, Richard and I were drinking tea and talking about it all.

"What do you think about having Priscilla baptized?" Ceci told us that none of the children at the orphanage were baptized. I never quite understood the reason why, but this was an opportunity for an official thing we could do to tell the world that Priscilla was ours.

Richard agreed. We had intended to have Priscilla baptized that spring but our pastor transferred to another church. An interim pastor was appointed, and because Priscilla had so many people come and go in her life already, it just didn't seem quite right to have a temp do the deed.

The search for the interim replacement took almost two years, but in the end, Pastor Sanford Hull accepted the calling, energized to do God's work together with us. Tall, wiry, with an easy smile, he captivated the entire search committee, delivering a Sunday sermon of inspiration that touched us all.

It wasn't until the spring of 2007, when Priscilla was eleven, that I approached him during the Sunday after-service coffee and donut social time. I spotted him in the corner of the parlor in his black robe, surrounded by the faithful. We had all met Pastor Hull at his welcome reception, but this was the first time we would talk about a family matter and, for some reason, I was a bit nervous.

"We have a family request that we have put off and now that you are here, it's time." I took a breath. "Will you baptize Priscilla?" I grinned.

Priscilla hovered nearby, trying to hide behind me. Pastor Hull smiled, tousled her hair, nodded, and said, "I'd love to."

I could see that Priscilla's glasses were covered in fingerprints and filmy streaks when she looked up at him. "It's going to be embarrassing," she half mumbled, pushing the glasses back up on her nose.

"It'll be great," Pastor Hull said enthusiastically—as if inviting her to an exclusive club.

During the short car ride home, Priscilla processed the upcoming event and started to squirm under her seat belt behind me.

She whined, drawing out her words, almost crying, "Baptism is for babies. Whhhhyyyy do I have to do it now?"

Never missing the opportunity to provide the parental message, I responded brightly, "If you want to be a member of the church, then this is how you join God's family. It's a wonderful ceremony. Pastor Hull will be blessing you with water on the altar and the whole congregation will be answering his questions, making a commitment to be there for you in your time of need or help you in any way as you go through life. Doesn't that sound beautiful? Priscilla? Hello?"

There was no response and I looked in the rearview mirror to see Priscilla's vacant stare out the window.

"I'm sorry, Mommy, I was not listening. I was thinking about food."

"For God's sake," I sighed heavily and pulled into the driveway.

Pastor Hull is not the kind of person who leaves anything to chance. Since we didn't know what Priscilla's religious education had been up to that point, he wanted the opportunity to speak with her about the deeper meaning of baptism prior to the big day.

Pastor greeted us with hugs as we opened the carved wooden doors leading into the Church lobby. We sank into two large, brown leather wing chairs in his office. Priscilla gave me goofy eyes as we waited for Pastor Hull to return, which he did in five minutes, carrying a large, yellow, glass bowl of water. The water sloshed around as he leaned over to carefully put the bowl down on his massive mahogany desk.

"Now," he said, sitting on the edge of his chair, "Are you ready? Let's talk about baptism."

He turned toward Priscilla who was still looking all around the office, seemingly fascinated or stalling, I couldn't tell. The appointment with Pastor Hull had not exactly been high on her list of things to do that evening. Still, it was probably better than homework so we were there without much protest, thankfully.

"I never been in here," she exclaimed. Priscilla never used contractions and her shorthand English popped up every once in a while. Her feet did not quite touch the ground and she was swinging them, ankles crossed, back and forth as her head kept turning all around the office. Pastor Hull waited patiently as I leaned over and put a hand on her knee. "Honey," I said squeezing gently and making eye contact in a split second that said, pay attention!

Pastor continued. "Priscilla, how many different ways do we use water? Let's all take turns, whaddaya say?"

We moved our chairs closer to the desk and huddled around the bowl. Pastor asked us to put our fingertips into the bowl as we talked. Priscilla immediately wet her hands and flicked water at me. We said things like drinking, bathing, washing, swimming, and playing. Pastor Hull talked about water as the symbol for life and how Priscilla would be welcomed into God's family by being baptized. She nodded, listening intently. Our session ended with homework: read the story of Silas. Who?

Later, snuggled in her room, Priscilla and I discovered the story together. Silas and Paul were in prison because of their missionary work when an earthquake struck, freeing them. However, they decided not to escape. When their jailer realized that Paul and Silas were still there, he asked, "What must I do to be saved?" Paul and Silas then baptized the jailer who was filled with joy because he had come to believe in God. Paul and Silas were then released from prison.

Priscilla sat next to me on the floor, both of us leaning against the bed. Always a bit self-conscious about my limited Bible knowledge, I wanted to ask the oh-so-right and meaningful question as I closed the heavy book and placed it on the floor. Priscilla beat me to the punch, blurting, "After the baptism, am I going to have a party with a moon bounce and lots of food and stuff like that for all of my friends?" Her eyes were just inches from mine, big and pleading, staring right through me.

"I don't think so, honey. The baptism is scheduled in two weeks and there's not enough time to plan. We'll do something special, I promise."

Priscilla sighed, "Okay," as her body went limp in disappointment.

"Grammy will be there and I know she is excited to see this happen for you. Let's think about what the story has to say. You're old enough to really understand the meaning of baptism."

"I wish I was baptized when I was a baby like Isabella."

"I know, sweetie. I love you." We hugged, talked about Silas and how brave he was, and held onto each other for a while. We agreed that baptism is something special. When I suggested that it was time for bed, she gave me one more squeeze and climbed beneath her mountain of stuffed animals. I kissed her forehead and backed out of the room, closing the door softly behind me.

On the Sunday morning of the baptism, nervousness overtook me again. Priscilla had ants in her pants from the moment we sat down. Glancing behind us every few seconds, she kept updating me when any of her friends arrived.

"Mary is here," she whispered, tugging on my arm again. Scrounging around in my purse, I gave her two peppermints to keep her occupied.

"I see Mrs. Leonard, and Debbie is with her," Priscilla announced again in a loud whisper.

The congregation rose and the choir began with "Cast Thy Burden Upon the Lord." *Oh, how appropriate,* I thought. *Lord, I lay this burden at your feet today. Please help me to get Pris through the service.*

Over the choir voices, Priscilla almost yelled, "Mom, how many people do you think are here today?"

I bent down close to her ear so I didn't have to yell. "Oh, honey. I don't know... the usual," I said, waving a hand like I was swatting a fly as if to say "No sweat."

"Please be seated." Pastor Hull was a commanding presence, especially with his microphone-amplified voice. "Today is a very special day. Tomorrow, about thirty from our congregation will be traveling to New Orleans to continue with our mission project. A year ago, we visited a neighborhood destroyed by Katrina, staying a week on clean-up duty. Well, they still need our help. Would our mission trip participants please come to the front here for a special blessing?"

The organist jumped into a lively version of "When the Saints Go Marching In." Priscilla had her head in her hands, rocking back and forth a bit. A group of about twenty-five men and women in bright green T-shirts with "Katrina Mission Trip" emblazoned on the front marched up the center aisle. The church was in full celebration mode as the congregation clapped and the T-shirted group knelt for Pastor Hull's upbeat and inspirational blessing. To my surprise, he ended with, "And let us continue our celebration today as we welcome Priscilla Pamela into God's family," waving us forward to join him on the altar. I had thought the baptism would be in the middle of the service.

Priscilla grabbed my arm harder this time and pulled me toward her. "Mom," she choked, "I'm not going."

"What do you mean, you're not going?" I said, distracted. The organist was playing something peppy as the mission group walked back down the center aisle while the congregation clapped in approval. The guest trumpeter added noticeably to the decibel level and I could hardly hear her.

She crossed her arms and sat back in the pew. "I'm not going up there. Everybody will be watching me. All of my friends are here." She looked like she was going to cry and started to slide down in her seat toward the floor just as Pastor Hull asked us again to come up to the altar and join him.

I had stood up, but now bent down and spoke directly into her ear, insisting firmly, "You're going."

Richard seemed unaware of this recent turn of events and had started up the aisle with Isabella before he realized we had not moved out of the pew. I grabbed Priscilla's arms from the back and pushed her gently out of the pew. We managed to get to the middle of the aisle, at which point I began dragging her up to the altar. By sheer force, I moved her up the stairs like a wooden soldier.

Pastor Hull motioned for us to move in a little closer. "This isn't an inquisition, Priscilla."

The congregation responded with polite laughter, but I was petrified that Priscilla would bolt down the aisle. I gripped her arm and then stood frozen in the silence. All of a sudden, you could hear a pin drop as we turned to face the congregation. Of course, I then had an uncontrollable urge to laugh as I replayed the last thirty seconds in my head. To stop myself, I thought of something serious and depressing, like Hurricane Katrina.

With a nod from Pastor Hull, Elder Ruth began. "On behalf of the Session, I present Priscilla Pamela to receive the sacrament of baptism."

After Priscilla had affirmed her faith in front of the whole church, Elder Ruth added, "Our Lord Jesus ordered us to teach those who are baptized. Do you, the people of the church, promise to tell Priscilla the good news of the gospel? If so, please say, 'We do.'"

The congregation responded as one, "We do."

Pastor Hull motioned for us to move toward the baptismal font. Priscilla froze once again. I put my arm around her and gently moved her to the font where we knelt together as the pastor showered us three times with water.

"Priscilla Pamela, I baptize you in the name of the Father, and of the Son and of the Holy Spirit. Amen."

Priscilla and I stood, and I squeezed her in celebration. Pastor Hull said something else to the congregation, but I could only focus on the wonderful moment, and the catastrophe avoided. I heaved a great sigh of relief as we made our way back to the pew.

Grammy laughed about the scene as we drove to our favorite brunch restaurant. Mimosas and Shirley Temples were ordered all around. "I didn't think you were going to make it," she said to Priscilla, as we looked over the menus.

"I didn't want to do it in front of all my friends, but Mom made me."

"Honey, we had been talking about it for a long time. I know you were scared, but you did a fabulous job and we are very proud of you."

"Congratulations, Prissy," we all shouted and lifted our glasses, clinked, and smiled.

When the food arrived, we hungrily devoured eggs, toast, and pastries.

I looked around at the family scene, taking it all in. We had come so far, but this cute Stitch still had her demons to tame. Priscilla would not hesitate to hurl angry words if she did not get her way or was dismayed that she was caught lying or doing something she was not supposed to do.

~

Priscilla almost never missed an opportunity to communicate with words or deeds that she was hurting, and in turn, would inflict that hurt on us. Angry words like, "You're not my father" to Richard, or "I hate you" to me, stung and we struggled to cope. Richard and I saw those outbursts for what they were —a child's emotional reaction.

One of the most helpful things we learned from therapy was that Pris was maturing at about two to four years behind schedule. When Priscilla was about eight, we were working with a therapist who recommended that we think of Priscilla as a younger version of herself. How would we talk to that child? How would we discipline that child? I was convinced she would grow out of it at some point.

These types of blowups occurred every few weeks. However, gradually, the threats to leave or disown us as parents stopped. Over time, with her Spanish gone and all of the family routines established, Priscilla was settling in, but the lying, covering up, and the antagonistic relationship with Isabella remained.

I tried to bridge the gap, but often felt that I could not reach her. In class at school during that same year, after the girls and boys were separated to discuss changing bodies and growing up, Priscilla came home in tears. When I was finally able to coax the problem from her, Priscilla said that all of her friends knew the story of how they were born. She did not. Priscilla moved closer to hug me and sobbed that she "wished she came from my tummy." I think if at that moment she could have crawled under my shirt, she would have done it. Then in a flash of anger, one of the first and only times I have heard it, Priscilla lamented, "My parents dumped me in an orphanage and now I have to deal with that."

As a mother, you want to be able to solve every issue, but I remember being so surprised at the anger and not knowing quite what to say. As I had done countless times before, I reminded Priscilla of the love of Ceci and *Tía* Vero. She had experienced unconditional love from her earliest days, which made her the great girl that she was.

Then I said, "Your mother made a decision, the best one she could make. Who knows why. You were raised with love then and now, let it in."

It was a confusing message to sort out. We tried to show that our family love was solid, and we looked to affirm it every chance we got. At the moment Priscilla would hurl a hurtful comment, I would steel myself to not react emotionally. Yes, it was upsetting to hear, but I never veered from my love theme. It was the reason that I hung on.

There were plenty of golden moments, too—cooking Mexican lasagna together, opening gifts on Christmas morning, swimming in the ocean on boogie boards, family dinners by the fire. I knew that Priscilla had the capacity to love and did so from the moment she was born. She was able to form attachments and did so successfully with Ceci, Vero, and many children.

Summer arrived before we knew it, and we looked forward to a little downtime. It felt like dejá vu all over again as we joined the same pool as that first summer when Priscilla came to live with us. We had not been back to the club since the summer of her stubborn stand when she preferred to sweat rather than swim. We sought out a lounge chair under an umbrella by the shallow end. It was hot in the bright sunlight and the water looked cool and inviting. I floated off of the steps into clear refreshment, and in an instant, Priscilla was at my side bobbing up and down. "Mommy, do you want to play a game of catch?"

"No, honey, I am going to swim for a while. I need the exercise."

Treading water, Priscilla wondered, "Are you going to get your hair wet?"

"No, I think I will just float and swim around, maybe just do breaststroke. I really don't want to get my hair wet just yet."

"Mommy, watch and see how far I can swim underwater." Priscilla took off and surfaced at the other end of the pool. She jumped out and shouted, "Mom, watch me dive." She plunged in and surfaced once again at my side.

"That was a perfect dive! I can't believe how long you can hold your breath!"

"Mom, do you want to play this game where we close our eyes and swim around?"

"No, I think I just want to paddle around a while."

She shrugged her shoulders "Okay, Mommy. Then I am going to swim with you like a baby whale following her mommy."

With that, she dove under the surface once again and squiggled next to me. Immersed and happy, the water carried us, and we floated easily together under a bright blue sky.

CHAPTER 27

The Dress

The years passed in much the same way as when Priscilla first arrived. There were periods of highs we could not have anticipated—like family vacations where we truly enjoyed being together—and lows, when Priscilla was grounded for what seemed like the millionth time after one of her tantrums of stubborn unwillingness to cooperate with whatever we were doing.

In middle school, which was seventh grade, Priscilla began instruction in Spanish. I had been so eager for that day! At long last, the Spanish language would be part of her daily routine. Priscilla had lamented losing her Spanish many times and asked us why we adopted her if we did not speak Spanish? It was just another thing that Priscilla blamed us for. The truth was that I continued to feel really bad about it. When we first explored the opportunity to adopt from Mexico, the response from those we told about our plan was almost always, "Do you speak Spanish?" or, "I didn't know you spoke Spanish!" When we admitted that we could not speak the language, never did, and never will, surprised silence usually followed. The what-the-heck-are-you-thinking look burned a hole through my head a number of times. Truthfully, the transition to English was the least of our problems.

I responded to Priscilla's Spanish pity party by once again hiring a tutor and saying something inspiring like, "It's up to you now." We'd played enough of the blame game in therapy over the years. There was a glimmer of interest now that Spanish was part of her curriculum and we told her that regaining fluency would be hard and she would have to work at it.

Richard knew many students who were eager to earn some extra money, and so we arranged for Stephanie to converse in Spanish with Priscilla two to three times a week. Stephanie was a graduate student and a Spanish Education major at the university where Richard taught. We thought that a grammar lesson would not be appealing and Stephanie agreed. To stimulate conversation, she gave Priscilla the Spanish versions of popular magazines, other news publications, plus some Spanish music with the thinking that these topics would emphasize conversation rather than grammar rules.

Priscilla never took advantage of this opportunity. The magazines sat piled in the corner of her room. Stephanie came to the house once a week for a lesson, but then Priscilla never called her during the week to practice, and soon Stephanie had to move away. I reminded Priscilla that her Spanish skills would only return if she put in the effort. I didn't have the energy to lecture and, in leaving it to Priscilla, nothing happened.

Unfortunately, it was the same story in her freshman high school Spanish class. Priscilla did not take it seriously and her teacher reported "minimal" class participation. Priscilla herself told me she regularly "blew off" homework such as repetition-type assignments to hand-write verbs and nouns ten times each in columns across the paper, saying that was "just stupid." When Pris handed in the assignment and used Excel to copy and paste the vocabulary words instead of writing them—she was rewarded with detention.

There were family changes, such as my new job, which changed again a short time later when another company took over. It was important for me to be more focused at work, which meant that I could not devote myself the way I used to when

Priscilla had a meltdown. I spent at least two hours a day commuting to work and discovered that there was only so much energy to expend on a daily basis.

In elementary school, Priscilla made significant progress, forging a close relationship with her ESL teacher and mastering the English language to a point where she graduated from the program and, by middle school, took classes at the same level as her peers. Priscilla had come a long way from dreading presentation-type assignments, at one point hiding under her teacher's desk when it was her turn to be the "newscaster" for the day. Now she could hold her own in the classroom. High school Spanish focused more on the spoken word and Priscilla was hearing her native tongue more than she had since her arrival.

Isabella needed a change and had transitioned to a more academically challenging Quaker high school and was thriving. The girls were not in the same orbit and that took the competition down a notch, but not totally. Isabella was also taking Spanish and never hesitated to correct Priscilla's Spanish grammar.

"Priscilla, you used the masculine verb when the feminine should have been used."

"Shut up, Isabella."

When I heard Priscilla speak any Spanish, her accent made me smile. It was full of flavor and rolled right off her tongue. But after venturing a few words, she would shake her head and run out of the room to avoid further discussion. Meanwhile, Isabella was reading and writing complex Spanish book reports but her accent did not produce those magic "R"s that Priscilla could. At least they weren't biting each other.

The first year Priscilla lived with us, we were invited to a *quinceañera* celebration which is part of the Latin tradition to honor a girl's fifteenth birthday. We had never heard the word before, but our neighbors, who are not Hispanic, had lived quite a few years in Puerto Rico and gave the party for their daughter.

Priscilla, who had never had a birthday party, really enjoyed the festivities. We decided right then to give Pris a *quinceañera* as a way to celebrate our crazy and unique family dynamic.

In my mind, the dress was oh-so-important and my research confirmed that fact. The *quinceañera* dress was the centerpiece of the event. It would be what everyone would remember about the event. However, every time I would bring up the S-word (shopping), Priscilla changed the subject or waved me away. What teenage girl did not want to shop for a fancy dress?

Our *quinceañera* exploration also told us that there are many customs associated with this celebration, including a father-daughter dance in which Dad gives his daughter her first pair of high-heeled shoes. There were also religious aspects of the celebration. We asked Pastor Hull, who had baptized Priscilla just three short years before, to give a blessing and he agreed.

When we first came up with the idea for her party, Priscilla seemed eager, but after deciding on a date, she tired of talking and planning with me. Priscilla was a year older than her freshman year classmates and for a while I thought perhaps she did not want to draw attention to that fact. Was I pushing her into claiming her birthright, insisting on it when Richard and I had no connection whatsoever to this type of celebration? Hell, I could not even say it or spell it without double and triple-checking myself.

The fact remained that Priscilla's heritage was important to the family. When this significant birthday approached, I could not ignore it. We worked together to map out the basic elements of a great teenage party: DJ, food, color-coordinated invitations, balloons, and favors. But most of all, there was the dress. My online *quinceañera* investigation showed elaborate long dresses of every color gathered at the waist, with a strapless form-fitting bodice. Priscilla shook her head, insisting that type of dress would not look good on her. She occasionally watched online videos of various parties. There was even a show on MTV about *quinceañeras* that we checked out. What was she thinking as she watched these Hispanic families prepare for the event?

"Look at this," I demanded when I searched for a dress on my laptop one evening as we watched TV. Priscilla would look, nod, then go back to *Full House* reruns. When pressed, her normal response was, "I don't know what I want." We ventured out to local bridal shops and I had to make her try on dresses. She swiped at the dresses on the rack saying, "No, no, no, not right." None of the bridal dresses came close to what I had seen online, so I knew we would have to order something.

There was never a question as to where the party would be. As a ten-year-old, I learned to swim at the "German Club." The *Vereinigung Erzgebirge* was a local social club with an enormous pool where I took swimming lessons, my brother played soccer, and my sister sang "Oh Christmas Tree" (was it in German? I can't remember) at the Christmas festival. On hot summer days, large German ladies would sit by the pool's edge, giving my sister and me the chance to continually annoy them by running along the shallow end kicking up enough water to splash their bulging suits. We were so young and easily entertained!

The clubhouse was dark and smoky but had recently been renovated. It was the perfect venue. However, sitting with the event planner a few weeks before to iron out details, Priscilla was sullen and cranky. Looking around the room, she said she wanted the party to be "fancier." We settled on pink napkins and white table cloths, with balloons to match the invitation color scheme. Once we were outside, however, I read her the riot act. The sabotage behavior I had seen so often was back. Well, honestly, it never really left. No matter what family event was on the horizon, Priscilla would look forward to it and even say so. But as the date drew closer, she would withdraw, subtly at first. Then during the actual event, she would say and do hurtful things that would cause all involved to have stomach pain, a headache, or both. Was this going to be another one of those deep regret moments? Why did I want to have this party anyway? Who was I trying to impress?

Because we had grown so used to the behavior, we let many things slide. Now that she was a bit older, I tried to reason with her about how she affected the family. But just when we thought we had made any headway, the moodiness would appear and we would start the dance all over again. Priscilla never had any explanation and was always promising that she would control her moodiness or just be NICE. The merry-go-round was relentless, and I was always searching for the best way to reach her, concluding that I must be doing something wrong.

Later that evening while again searching for dresses on my laptop, I asked Priscilla to choose from two. We ordered a strapless, long, lime green dress with a huge flowing skirt and lovely lavender flowers with beading on a fitted bodice.

"What music do you want the DJ to play when you walk in the room? How about, *Tonight's Going to Be a Good Night*?"

"I don't like that song."

"Do you want to have favors for the guests?"

"I don't care."

"I thought it might be fun to have a salsa dance lesson for the guests."

"It's up to you, Mom."

And so it went.

~

Sibling rivalry is part of every family dynamic, and my King Solomon skills were put to the ultimate test that summer. July of that year was Isabella's sixteenth birthday, and since a Sweet Sixteen party did not appeal to her, I suggested that we take a special trip to commemorate the event. She chose Ireland as one of the English-speaking alternatives that I proposed, and we had a lot of fun planning what sights to visit.

Isabella was a focused and driven young woman, and at sixteen, with a fifteen-year-old sister, life was different than we both had imagined. The girls were growing apart right in front of my eyes. We cherished time with the girls separately or together, but it was a constant challenge to live peacefully as a family. Whenever one would remove a brick in the sister wall, unfortunately, the other would be sure to cement one in. It was a never-ending struggle.

Children of the same parents can be vastly different. This is what I told myself constantly as the girls grew. Isabella was a tall, curly-haired, and loving daughter who was good at anything athletic or academic. She was serious about school and would often bring home her lessons learned for the family to ponder. I remember hearing about one of her first elementary school introductory science classes. Did we know that a human being passes gas seven to eight times a day she asked earnestly one night at dinner? A straight "A" student, she never needed a homework reminder. Because she was our only child, she had our undivided attention for eight years. Learning about the world made her happy and she loved to try new things. I often joked that she was ready to leave home at twelve years old. As soon as she knew about overnight camp, Isabella asked to go. She participated in weekend church retreats, loved her reading and math Olympics teams, geeked out at the annual science fair, read all the Harry Potter books twice, and went to summer camp in Germany for a month as soon as she was eligible—at age fourteen. Isabella tipped the scale toward the introvert level, but had a close circle of friends and loved to laugh and play all types of games.

Priscilla was a petite, loud ball of excitement that could draw you in for the fun of it or burn you for getting too close. Because of her language transition, Priscilla avoided reading anything. We relentlessly checked up on her homework to make sure that it got done, but she never had anything to share about school otherwise. Priscilla participated in school activities when she was forced to. I still remember her wearing the tie-dyed Reading Olympics T-shirt. The permission slip had been signed and the bus transportation scheduled. After the event, it was apparent that she had not read a single one of the books. Priscilla spent more time avoiding work than actually doing the task. Everyone in school was her friend, yet a close relationship with a "bestie" eluded her. Her temper could be sparked with little notice and students at school saw a bit of that, but for the most part she was fun, playful, and well-liked by her classmates.

~

With Priscilla's entire class, family, and friends on hand to celebrate, I was nervous about some sort of meltdown, but when I saw Priscilla in that gorgeous *quinceañera* dress, all the difficulties getting there were forgotten. The vibrant color looked beautiful against her summer tan. Her straight black hair was curled into long ringlets behind a tiara which is standard attire for any *quinceañera* princess. She looked radiant as she floated into the ballroom, arm-in-arm with two friends. I could tell she was embarrassed, though. As she walked up to join us near the stage, she was talking to her friends, laughing in an over-exaggerated way, not looking at any of the guests. The rest of the family had been introduced first and we waved, clapping along with whatever music was playing.

Pastor Hull's blessing was personal and set the tone. The room grew quiet as he spoke about the love of family, the difficulties getting there, and our joy at that moment. I took the microphone and told our guests about the significance of the setting and how special it was for our family. What a perfect place to celebrate.

When it was time for Richard to speak, Priscilla leaned on her friends and looked away to giggle and eye roll. Dad slipped the heels on her feet, and then *What a Wonderful World* played. As father and daughter swayed stiffly to the music, I could see Priscilla was not happy. She was talking nonstop to Richard and had an exasperated look on her face, her head moving the long curls from side to side as she made her point.

When the music ended, I rushed over to ask what the heck they were talking about during the song. Richard told me that Priscilla whined and complained the entire time about how "annoying" it was to have to dance with him — asking over and over, why she had to do it. I sent Richard over to the bar.

Priscilla's self-awareness had always been zero. We had never been successful at holding up the mirror to show the effect her actions had on the family. It had been seven years since her arrival, and once again, she resorted to a petty tantrum just at the moment we were honoring her. Even at fifteen, she did not understand the right thing to do. Any thought Priscilla had was immediately telegraphed in a multitude of ways. She was embarrassed, uncomfortable, and did not want the spotlight. It was a sad postscript to the event and Richard carried that memory for years.

As the guests got their drinks and mingled, we posed for family pictures outside under the trees. It was a time machine moment for me. Looking around this place from my childhood, now with all of the important people from our life — in-laws of twenty years, my own mother looking so frail and thin, siblings, new neighbors, and old friends — I was grateful and happy.

The photographer lined us up, and I stood back for a moment to watch. "Pops," my father-in-law, leaned into his cane, and Jackie, my mother-in-law, who was stooped over, suddenly flashed me a toothless grin. My mother's hair had evolved into a blazing red color that clashed with her mint-green suit, but she was smiling and happy to be holding the arm of my brother, Sam. Uncle Guy was doing his best to keep up with the conversation, shouting for clarification after each sentence. When did everyone get so old?

The party proceeded without a hint of the sour moment that Richard experienced. The DJ had fun music, including a mother-daughter dance that I had arranged to Third World's "Now That We Found Love." We formed two lines and danced through them with our clapping and laughing guests. Priscilla was reluctant and self-conscious, but I did not let her out of it and pulled her onto the dance floor.

Priscilla's classmates had a raucous time playing the "Priscilla Trivia" game. We arranged for a salsa dancing demonstration for the guests and then a short lesson. The food was good, and she received many gifts and an outpouring of love. We ordered t-shirts with a small sombrero on the front encircled with the date of the *quinceañera* and a large block "15" on the back. I could see Priscilla laughing as she handed out the shirts to her classmates and friends—looking for the right sizes. She cut the cake after a rousing Happy Birthday song, and by the end of the night seemed comfortable and able to enjoy the festivities. The party was a success on many levels—a happy family occasion, so few and far between at this stage in our lives.

As I look back on why we do these things, my answer is always the same: family. Yes, sometimes it is annoying, even contentious to be with any number of family members. The push and pull of family relationships are not always comfortable or easy, but we do it because it's the only family we have. I wanted Priscilla to know that on this happy day of celebration, she is family. She makes us laugh and she makes us cry. Today and every day, we love her.

CHAPTER 28

The Truth

P riscilla has had an issue with telling the truth ever since she
learned English, probably even before then, based on what
the *Tías* told us. We were constantly trying to determine what
exactly was going on behind those big, brown eyes. Because she
lived in a group setting until the age of seven, we guessed that she
was attempting to get away with something about eighty-seven
percent of the time. Talking in circles was perfected. Sometimes,
yes, there were outright lies, and other times, her responses contained just enough plausibility to make me crazy.

Most of our issues were connected to her school activities:
class trips, projects, homework, athletics—so many opportunities to deceive. Maybe deceive is a strong word. After hundreds
of these types of interactions, I had no explanation for them
other than Priscilla did not want us to know what was really
happening... with anything. One thing was for sure, we never
got an answer the first time a question was asked.

"Mom, I need to go to the drug store."

"Why?"

"I need to get something."

"What?"

"A posterboard."

"What for?"

"For school."

"What are you doing at school?"

"Science class."

"What about your science class?"

"I'm doing a science project."

"Why do you need a poster board at 8:00 p.m. on a Sunday night?"

"My science fair project is due tomorrow."

"Perfect."

Richard was with the girls every step of the way, whether it was for school activities or play time. As our resident professor, he supervised homework and all things school-related. His teaching schedule allowed him to drop the girls at school each morning. He also arranged his office hours so that he was available for daycare pickup, ballet lessons, most doctor visits, and athletic events. We both came from families where dad worked all the time and that was not what we wanted for our family. Richard loved playing games with the girls. He spent hours on the beach digging holes, made drippy mud sand castles, played running the bases, or took orders for our favorite foods or snacks. He drove us on many shopping excursions, waited at a coffee shop, and then picked us up when we were ready. Dad was always there when we needed him, and he loved doing it.

In the girls' early years of elementary school, I could assist with homework for all the basic subjects. It only took a few years for me to be completely out of my depth in science and math and I deferred to Richard for accuracy and supplemental teaching. He took his responsibilities seriously and reviewed math and science textbooks, assignments, and tests with a thorough and caring eye. Isabella completed her homework with no issues and as she moved up each year to more difficult math levels such as advanced calculus then to differential equations, she wanted Richard to double check her work.

With Priscilla, however, there were nightly arguments about her assignments as she was convinced that she had completed her homework correctly. Richard begged to differ. The frequency of these arguments did nothing to dampen her enthusiasm for insisting that she was right and that Richard simply did not understand the project at hand.

On a nightly basis the argument would go something like this:

"Priscilla, I have been a teacher for thirty years and there is no way that you are being asked to complete this assignment in this way."

"Dad, you don't understand what my teacher was saying. You weren't there, and we were told to do it this way."

"OK, well I am going to call your teacher and ask why you are doing the assignment this way when it is clearly incorrect."

"Dad, don't call, you are always trying to embarrass me. You think I can't do anything right."

Richard cared about her lesson plan and her comprehension level. He didn't help with homework just to check the box. He cared passionately that Priscilla actually understood what was being taught. As his daughter, Priscilla did not see it that way and thought any oversight was intrusive and unfair. He did not do the same for Isabella because there was no need.

The resentment started subtly at first but as Priscilla realized that Isabella had the advantage for all things connected to school no matter how much we tried to downplay it, Priscilla turned her frustration back to the family and in particular to Isabella. As parents, we were in the difficult situation of praising and encouraging both daughters, but the see-saw was heavily weighted. While Priscilla's homework required intense scrutiny, Isabella achieved effortless perfection without breaking a sweat. I don't say that lightly either. Isabella was an "unusual child" as my friends liked to remind me. At the top of her class in everything, she took it all in stride and sought out new experiences because she loved learning and challenging herself. The end result for the family, though, was extreme angst, unfortunately. While I wanted to be happy for all that Isabella achieved academically, it was always tempered by the reaction that we thought we would get from Priscilla.

As difficult as the school situations were to handle, the behavior exhibited on a daily basis was exhausting. When another Priscilla event reduced me to tears or compulsive donut eating, Richard would take on the role as chief investigator and start questioning her, refuting her answers based on "logic."

Now there was no more logical person on earth than my wonderful, cerebral husband. But in these situations, "logic" played like our constantly out-of-tune, fifty-year-old piano. Priscilla's typical nonsensical answers were not limited to school activities. Most of the time, we never heard the real reason for anything. Her assertions had a way of multiplying and circulating round and round as Richard led the discussion and pointed out all the logical flaws. Priscilla would often begin with one tall tale, only to keep adding to the story to explain each subsequent fabrication—realizing that the sequence of events didn't make sense. Random facts would be given in quick succession in the hope that a somewhat believable one would stick. Sometimes the result would be that we would ask the same questions over and over, then just give up. What fantastic story was I going to hear next from Priscilla's own series of unfortunate events?

I still laugh at an event from middle school. For the first few years of school, I packed the girls' lunches the evening before, plus they were always given lunch money for a snack or drink. When the school converted to an account system, we wrote checks of conservative amounts—thirty to fifty dollars—that the school tracked as cafeteria purchases were made when the girls gave the cashier their assigned four-digit number. The girls started to buy lunch more frequently as my schedule got crazier. To begin the school year in the seventh grade, I gave Priscilla a check for one hundred dollars—thinking it would last until at least Thanksgiving. Because Isabella had moved on to her new high school, she would not be using the account. Around the middle of September, I received a notice from the school that Priscilla's account had a balance of fifty-three cents. When I asked Priscilla about it that evening, she said there was a mixup with the account numbers and that the balance was wrong.

A short time later, when I checked the account balance again, it read twenty-three dollars. After several question and answer sessions, we concluded that Priscilla had given her account number to quite a few students, then when the account was almost depleted, supplemented it with her babysitting money. When I asked Priscilla about these various acts of charity, she vehemently denied them, saying that just her best friend Kelsey had purchased only a single slice of pizza. It made me angry that she had so little regard for the money and the trust we had in her to spend it wisely. We never heard the real story and stopped asking. The school changed its practice after that and so did I. That night, a jar of peanut butter and loaf of bread were on the counter and I never put another dime in the account.

Priscilla always had a story... I mean an answer, for everything. Sometimes she would be waiting for me in my room when I arrived home from work or chase me down as soon as I got out of the car. It seems that Dad was already asking logic questions of some sort due to a school activity or homework issue. Priscilla's answers were not satisfactory, and she would try to make an end run to me with a half-truth to explain it all away. I was forever in the position of peace broker.

Whether the stories were entertaining or had more dire consequences, these incidents resulted in me blaming myself for being distracted at work or on some level not being a good enough mother. One thing we knew for sure was that Priscilla's friends were the most important thing to her. She had a few close friends and frequently hung out with large groups. The bottom line was that they called the shots. Whatever her friends wanted, Priscilla went along with it, even though she knew it would run contrary to what we expected her to do. She craved the attention, and when her friends fulfilled the role of devoted followers, her family did not seem to matter. With the passage of time, some of these stories became legendary in our family and we laughed about them. But there were also some betrayals that stung for years.

Trust me, though, we were not laughing at the middle school parent-teacher conference when multiple teachers reported her homework not completed, book reports that were sloppy, and a chatty and distracted Priscilla during class. On nights when Richard did not check her homework, Priscilla must have figured that was her hall pass not to complete it. Just telling us that she had done her homework made perfect sense to her. Richard resolved the homework issue once and for all by signing up for automatic e-notifications from the school. At 1:00 a.m. each night we received a report detailing the previous day's activity and homework for all subjects including quizzes, tests, and project assignments. Predictably, Richard was up at that time of night and reported going to bed with a bit of heartburn when the notices came in. In the morning, everyone would be talking loudly about the missing assignments, which was not the ideal start to our day.

Priscilla did not limit her creativity to the school day. The thing that amazed me was that Priscilla always thought she would get away with everything. Our little town was the size of a postage stamp and eventually I would hear about any attempt to navigate around the straight and narrow. Weaving great storylines, Priscilla was our own little Pinocchio. We knew instantly when something else was going on. We rarely got to the bottom of it, which made me vigilant and a bit more in her face.

I also had a funny second sense with Priscilla and these various "activities." The exact moment that I thought we were making progress on any level, or if there was ever a hint or a suggestion that Priscilla's days of telling tales were over, I would quickly be made to regret that thought within just a few short hours. Call it women's intuition in reverse or mother-daughter backward bonding but it never ceased to amaze me how wrong I was over and over and over. But just like the kind and elderly Geppetto, I kept going back to my darling daughter and the stories just kept coming. I questioned my instincts all the time and some days I was just worn out.

High school years were a bit of a switch for Priscilla as teachers were not so quick to let things slide. She was a charmer and could talk her way out of most things. But the magic began to wear thin in high school, and the teachers did not let deadlines or standards slip just because English was not her first language. Enough time had passed for Pris to be fully integrated into the school. Her ESL lessons were ancient history. Any grace period previously bestowed was officially over.

The teenage routine for both girls included field hockey, lacrosse, dances, on-again-off-again boyfriends, and sleepovers. Isabella's move to a Quaker high school in Philadelphia meant that she had to learn to drive by her junior year. There were minor skirmishes with Isabella over the years about clothes and curfew but there was never the knock-down, drag-out fights that we had with Priscilla. There was no question that Isabella would get her license and have a car to drive to school. We trusted her, and she earned that trust through many years of being honest and dependable.

Unfortunately, though, we had gotten to that place where the girls did not trust each other. The arguments built up and were reinforced during the week. I tried to establish a practice that, once a particular incident was over with, we didn't bring it up again to prove a point or establish a pattern of behavior. Although I suggested this numerous times, there was often re-treading back to old fights and previous untruths, which made it harder to move forward. Richard and I both tried to referee at the right moment. It was crucial to me that I salvage some semblance of sisterhood. This happened only on rare occasions. When the three of us were in the kitchen, boiling and ricing potatoes, forming perfect pillows of dough, the gnocchi miracle of cooking, eating, laughter, and love would occur for at least an hour or so.

We tried not to leave Priscilla alone in the house, but on the weekends, that was just about impossible. Because Isabella's new high school was in Philadelphia, when friends invited her over, that usually meant that she would be staying in the city overnight. These social events were important for her, and she almost always stayed with friends on the weekend. It was disappointing to me that she was not around that much, but I think the drama Priscilla inflicted during their time together was too much to bear. They were so different and as much as I wanted them to be close, it would not happen while they were in high school.

One weekend in the early fall of Priscilla's freshman year in high school, we were to meet friends for dinner in the city. As we prepared to leave the house, I reminded Priscilla, "Please, no friends over tonight without us knowing about it," as we left through the porch door.

About three hours later, as I inserted my key into the front door, I looked straight into the eyes of an astounded Priscilla. Just after uttering, "What's wrong?" I saw pizza crusts, soda cans, and the pillows from the living room strewn around the floor. We argued with her for about twenty minutes, trying to understand why she did the very thing we asked her not to do. No response. Something seemed a bit off. Sure enough, in

Priscilla's room were three teenage guys scrambling to squeeze under her bed. "Time to go," I said as calmly as I could. Another lesson in parenthood: search the house before you start screaming at your daughter.

Friends would tell me that Priscilla was the perfect balance to our life with Isabella. I guess that was one way to look at it. Pris was goofy at times and always demanding attention by talking everyone's ears off. Isabella's natural state was to stand back a bit and observe the scene. But with Priscilla hogging center stage, Isabella spoke up more and allowed her silly side to show. There was no doubt in my mind that most of the time our family dynamic had improved. Isabella had our attention for the first eight years of her life and was confident in our love. Priscilla was constantly at the ready to challenge us if the scales tipped too far.

The number of times we had the same conversation with Priscilla was maddening. She seemed happy and settled but could still be set off by a hair trigger. We had precious moments of family bonding, but it was a struggle. We had started and stopped with many therapists over the years. However, during Priscilla's second year in high school, I received a call from Mary, the school psychologist, recommending that Priscilla speak to a therapist again. A "friend" of Priscilla's called Mary's office and said that Priscilla was cutting herself. Mary said that she wanted to reach out to me right away and let me know. I held the phone in stunned silence for a second as I tried to take it all in.

My first reaction was one of disbelief. Sure, there were highs and lows. Was it possible that I had misread the cues that pushed Priscilla to this desperate behavior?

Love at the Border

CHAPTER 29

The Bright Side

I gripped the phone tightly and focused on what Mary was trying to tell me. She spoke slowly, looking for the right words to tell me my child was facing a crisis. She relayed a few of Priscilla's behaviors that I knew all too well. Priscilla was a master of blaming others and I interrupted her, "Did Priscilla tell you that or did you hear it from someone else? Priscilla will say just about anything to get attention."

Mary responded, "Priscilla confided in someone that she needs help, and I think we need to listen to her."

"Mary, I think you are mistaken. Priscilla wants attention— but not this way. I just don't believe she is that depressed."

I don't think Mary was expecting outright hostility from me, but that is what she got at 2:00 p.m. on a Wednesday afternoon. It annoyed me that I had been interrupted by this call, which was clearly some sort of hysterical reaction to something Priscilla said. It stung that a stranger possibly knew something about Priscilla that I didn't and it infuriated me that ultimately, once again, the onus would be on me to solve this latest crisis.

It wasn't that Richard didn't care. He did. Deeply. However, he left the coaching to me. Our roles had evolved to the point that Richard was most effective when on a "special teams" assignment, like homework or our family hunter-gatherer: pick-up, drop-off, and shopping. While he stood by me no matter what, the effort to Priscilla's heart was something I needed to lead. He was so hurt by past transgressions and upset that I was in pain. His response to that was avoidance. It was tough for him to start over after each time he felt betrayed by her behavior. He was comfortable in the school setting and I wanted and needed him to manage that completely—which he did. He had his nightly homework routine with Priscilla and her midterm grades were good. Her progress in this area was a real accomplishment.

Meanwhile on the phone, Mary was waiting patiently for me to absorb this latest news about Priscilla. She recommended a psychologist in a town adjacent to ours, whose family therapy practice had positive reviews from some local families. Instead of thanking Mary for this recommendation, I sighed heavily and hung up without much of a goodbye. I made the appointment without asking Priscilla because I knew Mary was right. We needed some outside intervention.

It turned out, however, that my suspicions were correct. Priscilla was not cutting. The "friend" who called Mary's office was actually the one who was cutting herself and probably reaching out for help. Still, some sort of limit had been reached, and I decided to keep the appointment to talk about our own family situation. Priscilla was hardly ever truthful with us, and the girls were still arguing all of the time.

In the car ride to the therapist office, I was in full lecture mode. "Priscilla, this is yours to fix. Dad and I have provided every support in the world. But we are tired. We love you and will do anything for you, but this behavior—rebellious, acting out, disrespectful talk— has got to stop."

"I know, Mommy," Priscilla said without looking at me. She stared straight ahead, expressionless.

We turned off the highway into the parking lot of a four-story, brick box of a building. It was a nondescript suburban office with a blue and white Family Therapy sign on a post in the parking lot. We took the elevator to the third floor and Sherrie came

274

out to greet us almost immediately. She ushered Priscilla to her office while I filled out the paperwork in the waiting room. About thirty minutes later, Sherrie came out and motioned for me to join them. Having been down this road many times, I was prepared to tell my side of the story. Whatever was happening that got us here was (probably) the result of something I was or was not doing and I could just not hear that song and dance again, as my father used to say.

Sherrie's office was casually furnished with a small sofa and a few chairs around a coffee table. I sat on the edge of the sofa next to Priscilla, who was slumped in her chair. Sherrie had a calm and smooth voice that made my shoulders fall about six inches the instant she started talking. She announced that Priscilla had agreed to return for a few visits to talk about school, family, and other things that were important to her. Sherrie wrote a few notes, looked up and then asked Pris to step out so that she could chat with me. When the door closed, I let fly my Priscilla list. I was so happy that we were not going to have a confrontational talk, and now that I had a turn all to myself, I couldn't stop talking.

"Sherrie, I am not sure if Priscilla told you, but were you aware that she has lied to us, deceived us, and treated us disrespectfully? We are pretty sure that she has never told us the truth about anything."

I shared our desire for Priscilla to be honest with us. After all, we had the "proof" many times over and we wanted to make it right. I ended with, "What did Priscilla say? Did she blame us for everything? Is she really depressed or just wanting attention?"

Sherrie looked at me and put down her notebook. "It may not be helpful for you to keep questioning Priscilla in this way."

"What... why," I asked?

"If you know something is amiss, why keep asking her?"

"Because I want her to admit it and come clean. I want her to tell me what really happened and what is going on in that head of hers."

I could feel myself beginning to boil again. How was this my fault? Isn't telling the truth one of the commandments? Isn't this country built on honesty? What about that cherry tree? Heck, this was the only thing I thought that we were doing right and now this woman was telling me that it's wrong? The advice went against my rule-focused upbringing. I asked Sherrie, "Don't we have a right to know what goes on in our own home?"

Sherrie responded, "In the process of all the questioning, you are breaking down what you are trying to build up." Sherrie paused and shifted in her chair to face me directly.

"You might want to share what you know, then tell Priscilla that she can come talk to you when she is ready. In the meantime, you should try and react to what is in front of you but do it in a way that involves her, that tells her she matters to you."

I sat back in my chair to let it all sink in. This five-minute, end-of-the-appointment advice was a bit of a jolt for me. My parenting skills had been called into question. Sherrie presented an alternative strategy to me in such a way that really made me stop and think. Was this the right time to reconsider our tactics? Or maybe it was advice that Sherrie gives all frustrated and angry parents: dial it back a notch. I had arrived at the session ready for a fight. Was Priscilla realizing what was happening to us as a family and feeling depressed? I sensed all of us going in different directions, which felt isolating and lonely. But if there was ever an example of actions speaking louder than words, this was it.

We took Sherrie's advice, and when we suspected a Pinocchio event, we did not push for what actually happened. We waited. Sounds easy, doesn't it? Well, it was almost worse on my gut than the fighting. I had to keep Richard calm as he was convinced that any number of adventures were happening behind the scenes. My strategy to let it go was a deliberate shift in the conversation. It felt fake in the parental rhythm of daily life, but it cut down the drama big time.

Sherrie also suggested that Richard stop assisting Priscilla with her math and science homework. Talk about a difficult adjustment. I was not excited about bringing that bit of news home. He had taken her education personally and felt responsible for her knowledge. We managed this by maintaining the ability to see assignments and test scores on the school's parent portal. Richard gave up the nightly battles and we agreed to a student tutor and extra sessions with the teacher after class. This turned out to be a major step for all of us. Priscilla was able to pass all of her coursework at the end of the year, and that was all that really mattered.

As we were trying all of this out, we saw Sherrie together again in a few weeks. I didn't know what was on the agenda but was content to have Priscilla and Sherrie work it out while I distracted myself with a People magazine. After only about ten minutes together though, Sherrie called me in and said that Priscilla was intent on recounting everything that was not equal between her and her sister. After I listened to Priscilla's complaints such as Isabella could drive, had gone abroad to summer camp and attended private high school, I began to count everything that Priscilla did to destroy our trust, such as not doing her homework, having parties at the house, taking Isabella's clothes, and not showing up where she needed to be. Sherrie cut into my naughty list and began asking me the kinds of things I usually do with Isabella for fun.

Priscilla did not give me a chance to answer and said, "You always watch *Grey's Anatomy* with Isabella and never watch TV with me."

I turned to look at her, sitting back a bit in my chair. "Priscilla, I don't even like *Grey's Anatomy*. I watch it because Isabella likes it and it's something we can do together."

Priscilla continued her train of thought, "You are always doing things with Isabella and not with me."

Now it was Sherrie's turn to take over, "Priscilla, did you hear what your Mom said? She doesn't even like *Grey's Anatomy*, but does it to be with Isabella."

I added, "Honey, I have asked you many times to watch it with us or watch something different with me, but you are always in a mood or just mad at someone in the family."

Sherrie did not let her off the hook. "Priscilla, what do you have to say to that?"

Priscilla was suddenly fascinated by the pillow on her chair and looked down to pull at the fringe.

I asked Priscilla, "Why are you always so angry?"

Then Sherrie took the words right out of my mouth and said quietly, "Priscilla, how long do you think all of this... will go on?"

Priscilla muttered under her breath, "I don't know."

Sherrie then spent quite a bit of time talking about how we do things for people even when we don't want to, and that it's important to act in certain ways if we truly love someone. Sherrie used the TV example and then addressed the angry behavior directly, asking Priscilla to own up to it and try to do better.

It wasn't quite the *"Good Will Hunting"* moment, but Priscilla had been rocked. She went back to visit with Sherrie alone for a few more times after that, and, as a family, we slowly gained a bit of ground. We started off with TV, which was not the worst place to begin building—watching more movies together, just the two of us, making an effort to be together. It sounds simple enough but after school, work, sports, dinner, and homework— it all took planning to arrange. Plus, the relationship repair work needed was so much more than passive TV watching. In order to build the trust that we so desperately needed, it was necessary to be actively engaged. We did a little something together most evenings—just the two of us. It was my hope that this effort would expand to Isabella and Richard and, to a small extent, it did.

During this time, I continued to read books about the adoption experience. The one concept that resonated with me was the "primal wound," which holds that *"severing the connection between (the child) and the biological mother (through adoption) causes a primal wound which often manifests in a sense of loss (depression), basic mistrust (anxiety), emotional and/or behavior problems and difficulties in relationships with significant others... affecting the adoptee's sense of self, self-esteem and self-worth throughout life."*[1]

In her book, *The Primal Wound: Understanding the Adopted Child,*[2] Nancy Verrier further explains that those who have been separated from their biological mothers at birth experience abandonment and loss, creating this primal wound—interrupting the "natural" evolution. There were so many examples of these coping mechanisms in the book that were spot on to our experience: saying hurtful things, sabotaging family events, always being mad, lashing out and not knowing why. Finally, I had the validation that I had been looking for. Priscilla had been separated from both her biological mother *and* her *Ministerios Mothers*—Ceci and *Tía* Vero. However, I don't think I understood the true depth of these angry feelings and was often caught up in dealing with how the resulting behavior was affecting the rest of the family. There probably could have been a better balance of all of these forces, but the day-to-day routines rolled on. We had

---

1. *Dawn Davenport, What Adoptive Parents Need to Know about the Primal Wound, creatingafamily.org, 2017.*

2. *Verrier, Nancy Newton, The Primal Wound, Understanding the Adopted Child, Gateway Press, Inc.,1993*

made progress and I was constantly optimistic that we would continue to build on that. On some days, there were victories, other days it felt like we were in a bottomless pit from which we would never see the light.

~

During her elementary and middle school years, Priscilla struggled with English class and reading. Spanish and all her studies continued to be difficult. Starting in her junior year, Priscilla's Spanish class was taught by a wonderful man named *Señor Hernandez* who was about as tall as Priscilla, with thinning grey hair and wire rims. From the beginning, they clicked.

Priscilla would often report that he spoke to her after class. Up to this point, she was so reluctant to speak Spanish aloud. He must have done or said something encouraging, because for the first time in forever, Priscilla said she enjoyed speaking Spanish. When I asked to hear a few sample sentences, she just shook her head. Even when I would beg, cajole, and plead, "Please, just pretend that you are asking me about the weather or something." Nothing doing.

Our small town high school only had Spanish and French, so at least half the class was attempting to learn Spanish, yet *Señor Hernandez* was beloved by all the high schoolers. Sometimes I would see him out of the corner of my eye at the edge of the bleachers at a field hockey or lacrosse game. Priscilla was more than just showing up at Spanish class—she had a perfect record and was asked to join the Spanish Honor Society. When Priscilla heard about the Spanish class trip to León, Spain, she could not stop talking about it. This exchange program had the Spanish students arriving in September, staying with local families. The students from the U.S. would travel to Spain in the spring and stay with those same families. We held out support for the

Spanish trip, telling Priscila that she could go ONLY if we saw good behavior and good grades.

Always a super-picky eater, Priscilla began to show interest again in Mexican food and candy. When we visited the city, we would make a special trip to South Philadelphia to buy chili-coated lollipops and other spicy treats at any one of the many Mexican grocery stores. I have a sweet tooth but could not tolerate anything chili-coated for even a second. Sometimes I wondered if the pepper didn't fan her flame. We found a Mexican cooking show on the food network and would sometimes watch that together.

Despite the progress that we were making, there was backtracking. Petty bickering between the girls persisted. At dinner, when I didn't excuse her from the table fast enough, Priscilla would see that one offending item on her plate and start to make a fuss. Then Isabella would get into the act.

"Priscilla, just eat it."

"Shut up."

"No, you shut up."

"I hate you."

"Suck it."

Priscilla usually ended up losing her phone or other electronics (again) during these exchanges. Afterward she would pout. "Why is it always my fault?" Honestly, the answer to that question was that she was the one that always started it by complaining about food or taking any minor disagreement too far with cursing, launching insults, or hitting Isabella; she was our built-in appetite suppressant.

Priscilla continued to demand all of our energy and it was wearing everyone down. Isabella rarely provoked Priscilla and detested conflict of any sort. After all we had been through, she just wanted the antagonistic behavior to end. Verrier had a comment about that, too, noting that biological children raised in the same home with an adopted sibling feel as if they are living with a child who has a disability, who needs at least ninety percent of parental attention.

We still had the Spanish exchange program as an incentive, and I reminded Priscilla of the stakes repeatedly. When Priscilla was still in middle school, we hosted a girl from Mexico who was part of Isabella's Spanish program. Carla was lovely, but so extremely shy that she did not utter a complete sentence (in Spanish or in English) during the three weeks that she stayed with us. We tried so hard to encourage conversation. For a few nights, additional Mexican students also stayed with us and, even in a crowd, talk was almost nonexistent. It was frustrating, as I had hoped that Priscilla would try some Spanish during that time, but no dice.

In the fall of Priscilla's junior year, we eagerly anticipated Tanya's arrival for the exchange program. Tanya, from León, Spain, was a lively girl with long, light brown hair and braces which meant that she would not smile for pictures. She hit it off with Priscilla immediately, laughing, then quickly covering her mouth. I watched from afar, not wanting to discourage the banter, as the two bonded, staying up late and talking easily in Spanglish. Most of the conversation was in English, but occasionally I could hear Tanya explaining something to Priscilla in Spanish because her English would not suffice. I am not sure how much was understood, but the two of them sat in our family room wrapped in quilts, laughing, eating junk food, and talking like old friends.

It was just the two of them as Isabella left for college that fall, on her way to becoming a mechanical engineer. You know what they say, absence makes the arguments less frequent. It was a different Priscilla who had her parents all to herself and everything was quiet for the most part.

Priscilla stayed with Tanya's family in León later that spring, loving every minute of it. Something really kicked in because of this experience. Priscilla saw a new part of the world, heard her native language, and it softened her. She maintained excellent grades in Spanish class and, according to her teacher, was one of the more proficient students. She started to listen to Spanish music and was connected to all the Spanish students on Facebook.

Priscilla had also developed the habit of saying, "Look at the bright side" in response to just about anything. If it was raining outside, Priscilla would chirp, "Look at the bright side, Mommy, now you don't have to water the plants." If I was running late for an appointment or couldn't decide what to buy or what food to serve, Priscilla would add, "Look at the bright side, Mommy," then add an alternative optimistic view.

I didn't even notice it at first, but then I started hearing it all the time when the two of us were planning or doing something. I never said anything to her about it, but when Priscilla added that helpful note to our conversation, it always made me smile. Where did that even come from? Was this my daughter who was so depressed two years ago that the school psychologist had to intervene? Was this the girl from the hard-knock life who was now always cheerful, giving me a more positive view for whatever I was complaining about?

We visited Isabella during her freshman year of college and attended her field hockey events. The girls stayed together in Isabella's dorm with Pris tagging along to a frat party. With the day-to-day pressure of living together gone, the girls had fun and it made Priscilla think about her own future. Between the two, a new level of tolerance had been reached. Priscilla thrived as our only child and began to confront her demons for the first time ever. Without Isabella, Priscilla had to take more responsibility for her behavior. It had been convenient to attribute her disrespectful and dismissive behavior as some sort of payback or adjustment for all of the injustices she experienced when compared to Isabella.

Clearly we had turned a corner, but nothing is ever that easy or that straightforward. At home, it was evident her actions had to stand on their own for what they were: acting out under the influence of her friends. Despite our progress, Priscilla still craved their attention. She did not as yet have a mind of her own and her clique continued to influence her behavior. We saw glimpses of a mature young woman emerging, but she still had so much more growing up to do.

CHAPTER 30

Mexican Reunion

*I have a great respect for the past. If you
don't know where you've come from, you
don't know where you're going.*

—*Maya Angelou*

Sometimes when the stars just align, a single decision or chance circumstance produces just the right outcome at the exact right time. At the end of Isabella's freshman year in college, the sisters would make these discoveries together.

One of the college programs Isabella was most excited about was summer abroad. She had her heart set on going to Spain, but when that did not work out, she was offered an opportunity in Mexico. Her Spanish was good and this was a chance to improve it even more while also giving back to the community. In discussion with her advisor, Isabella learned that one of the organizations where she could work was *Ministerios de Amor* — the very same one that delivered Priscilla to us! When Isabella mentioned our family connection, the arrangements were made. Isabella would be responsible for teaching English and math and assisting at the girls' shelter in Cuernavaca. It would not be the same location where Priscilla lived. That location had been sold.

The year before, around Priscilla's birthday, *Tía* Vero had reached out via Facebook and posted pictures of Priscilla as a toddler. Facebook had changed Priscilla's life in a big way during high school. I remember that evening when Priscilla ran into the family room and excitedly opened her laptop next to me on the sofa. On the screen was a tiny Priscilla, about age four in a purple bathing suit with a pink ruffle, standing at the edge of a fountain. With the water splashing high, she stretched her arms out wide and held a white towel behind her like a superman cape. Her best friend Rosie, in a crazy print yellow and green suit, stood next to her in the exact same position. Two super-girls with silly grins posing for the camera.

In another photo, Priscilla looked no more than two years old, standing on a bathroom counter dressed in a red and white zip-up pajama. She was clowning for the camera, combing her hair. Other photos were group shots at the shelter. The most precious image was of Priscilla in a red sailor dress with a huge white bow, barely able to stand and holding on to a tree.

I pulled Priscilla close on my chair and put my arm around her asking, "What's it like, honey? You are seeing yourself as a baby for the first time!"

"I know. I can't believe it."

"Look at how you cute you were—and you know what? You still are."

Tía Vero may have had those pictures for a while, I don't know, but sharing them with Priscilla was a precious time capsule moment. Can you imagine growing up never having seen an image of yourself as a baby? We don't even think about these things, but for children adopted a bit later in life, it's a huge piece of the development puzzle. "How did I grow to be the person that I am?" "What was I like as a baby?" How fortunate for us that Vero stayed connected, giving my daughter some precious memories.

For months now, Priscilla had been reaching out to her *Ministerios* friends on Facebook and was having online conversations with them. Richard and I were the last to know this of course, but given the timing, it all made sense. Priscilla made the connections and she now knew what happened to them after her departure nine years earlier.

The fact that Isabella would spend a summer in Mexico was not easy for Priscilla to hear. Mexico was her thing—why did her sister have to take that over, too? We had been planning our own reunion trip at some point in the future—but the timing never seemed right. The rollercoaster of emotions we felt daily never stopped long enough for me to plan a trip that would require a significant investment—and I am not talking about money. I had been looking for a stamp of approval, a feeling that our family felt "established." Now, without warning, the opportunity was in front of us. We made plans to visit Isabella later in the summer.

Our summer itinerary began to take shape. We confirmed Ceci's schedule first, and agreed on a date to meet at the Cuernavaca shelter. *Tía* Vero also was available to spend the day with us in Mexico City and would come to our hotel the morning after our arrival. Here was the chance for Priscilla to be reunited and have some closure with the women whose decisions changed the course of her life. Were we ready?

Emotions leading up to this trip felt different this time. I was proud of the family that we had become, yet was hopeful that the trip could bring our daughters a bit closer together.

Isabella left for Mexico shortly after Memorial Day. She would live at the girls' shelter in Cuernavaca during the week and then on the weekends in an apartment in Mexico City near the Mexican *Tecnológico de Monterrey University*, her summer abroad program sponsor. Richard, Priscilla, and I arrived in Mexico City in mid-July and were unpacking at the hotel when there was a knock at the door. Isabella, looking tan and relaxed, was full of news about the experience and eager to show off her Spanish. We went to dinner at Sanborn's, one of our favorite restaurants from our trips years earlier. Isabella ordered our meal. We were excited for our favorite foods including *posole* soup, tacos, and empanadas topped with *queso fresco* cheese. Before departing for the kitchen, the waitress pointed her pen at Priscilla and asked in Spanish, "Do you speak Spanish?"

Priscilla sat up straight, surprised by the question but then immediately looked down and shook her head. She smiled and said, "No, no, no... " Her voice trailing off as she looked away. The waitress paused for a second waiting for an explanation and looked like she wanted to say, "You look Mexican, why not?" But she didn't say anything else. My heart went out to Priscilla who was probably going to find herself in this pickle during the trip. Isabella was only too happy to oblige in the Spanish department while Priscilla sat there looking blankly at her. Priscilla had dipped her toe in the Spanish-speaking pool when Tanya visited, but was not confident enough to say anything aloud to those who would judge her, especially in Mexico!

We had arranged for *Tía* Vero to spend the next day with us, starting with a late breakfast then sightseeing around Mexico City. As I paced nervously around the lobby, I thought back to her letter and their tearful goodbye over ten years ago. Priscilla waited months to give us the letter that Vero had written. It had been tremendously difficult for Vero to say goodbye. Priscilla loved her like a mother and I remembered how Vero calmed her on the phone during those first few weeks. We could not have made it without her.

Priscilla spotted Vero getting off the elevator and rushed over to hug her. Vero pulled back to make eye contact with Priscilla who smiled and hugged her again. Vero was a petite woman, just a tad taller than Priscilla, dressed in jeans, a crisp white summer cotton shirt and a black vest of colorful embroidery. We embraced and kissed cheeks. Over eggs, toast, and juice, Isabella translated Vero's news. I could tell Priscilla was concentrating, listening to Vero's Spanish then looking to her sister for verification. Vero left *Ministerios* about seven years earlier and decided that she wanted to teach children. She was unmarried, but there was a large family that filled her life. Priscilla and Vero did not seem to mind the awkward translation pauses and just kept looking at each other and smiling.

After breakfast, we set out under a glorious sun to see the enormous Mexican Monument of the Revolution, just a few blocks from our hotel. Posing for pictures around the observation deck, Priscilla and Vero stuck close, occasionally arm in arm. We made our way to the *Zócalo* next, barely squeezing into a subway car. The *Zócalo* was as crazy as I remembered it to be with hundreds of vendors, tribal dancing, and tourists all milling about the Cathedral plaza.

Isabella was excited to find fresh *elote*. We jumped in line as she explained that *elote* is an ear of corn, hot from a steam bath and slathered in spicy mayonnaise and cheese. After Isabella and I had two delicious bites, I gestured to Richard so that he could also purchase one, but he was busy taking pictures. However, the vendors, scared that the police were nearby, had packed up the entire operation with lightning speed and disappeared into the crowd. We laughed as we searched for our pop-up chefs but they were nowhere to be found!

As the afternoon sun began to set, Priscilla's sad puppy face emerged because our time with Vero was coming to an end. On the way back to the hotel and to Vero's bus, we suggested coffee and dessert as a way to extend our time together. The shop was cool and quiet, serving gourmet ice cream and coffee concoctions. Vero and Priscilla sat close mostly in silence. When the time came to say our goodbyes on the sidewalk, Priscilla started to cry in huge sobs. Vero drew her close with a long hug, kissing her hair, and whispered some things in Spanish that I could not make out. She held onto Priscilla who stood there stiffly, crying silently now. We gathered around Priscilla as Vero disappeared down the street.

I pulled Priscilla close as Vero became smaller and smaller on her walk down a bustling *Paseo de la Reforma* toward her bus stop. My mind flashed back to the orphanage eleven years ago when we stood outside the huge metal gate to say our goodbyes to Priscilla on our very first trip. The sun was as bright then as it was at that moment. *Tía* Vero must have been holding Priscilla's hand as I bent down to hug her. She was tentative and uncertain but returned my hug with a quick kiss, plus one for Isabella. Priscilla's big brown eyes were staring a hole through me, and when I pulled her close, I was struck that she did not smell like the "baby smell" I was anticipating. I kissed her cheek and she tasted different. *It must be all that spicy food,* I thought. As our car sped down the road away from the shelter and Priscilla's image in that orange smocked dress became smaller and smaller in the rear window, my gut was twisted with worry. Could I love this girl as my own?

Standing now in the middle of Mexico City and seeing her in pain, all I wanted to do was to protect her from hurting anymore, and I hugged her tightly, then kissed her cheek. As it turned out, the answer to my question was a resounding yes. It had not taken any time at all for this little girl to find her way into my heart. But then I agonized incessantly as to whether she would ever love us! Some days, I was not so sure. Now that Priscilla was back in Mexico, I wondered if she pictured herself here. Having declared she would "move back" so many times, is this where she thought she belonged? I held on to her and reassured her that Vero would always be there for her. After a few moments locked in our hug, she looked up at me and said, "Let's go back to the hotel, Mommy."

~

The next day we were on a mission to visit the girls' shelter where Isabella would show us firsthand where she had been living and working. We hired a driver for the day as Cuernavaca was quite a distance from Mexico City. After several hours of winding roads, we stood outside a high metal gate on a small side street and rang a bell that prompted squeals and footsteps on the other side. We could hear the girls running toward the gate, but when it opened we were greeted by Pedro and Carla—a married couple who managed the shelter. About thirty girls ages seven to mid-teens lived there and traveled by bus to a nearby school for lessons each day.

On the way to the shelter, Isabella told us about getting the girls ready for school each morning. The school schedule is year-round so they are used to the routine which includes getting everyone up and dressed and packed. Then there is breakfast and chatter, jokes and songs on the bus ride. Isabella mentioned that last week, Carla asked one of the girls about carrying her books. Where was the plastic bag that she used yesterday? When the girl responded that she had thrown it out because it had a hole in it, Carla reminded all the girls to keep their bags with them so that they had something to carry their books and lunch. "Can you believe it," Isabella said, "They don't even have backpacks or anything to carry their books and stuff for school."

Isabella was greeted warmly by the girls who were full of questions about who we were and why were we there with another Mexican girl. Isabella explained in Spanish that we were her parents, which was of course believable. But when she said that Priscilla was her sister, they shook their heads and made puzzled faces. Priscilla nodded yes, but the girls were not convinced. Then Carla announced that it was time for lunch, which meant delicious meat, beans, and juice served in a cavernous room that looked like a converted garage. The girls sat in rows of picnic tables, talking and laughing as they ate, stealing glances our way.

During our Skype sessions with Isabella earlier in the summer, Priscilla learned that Ann also worked at the shelter. Ann had cared for Priscilla as a toddler, and when she joined Isabella on camera, Priscilla screamed and ran out of the room. When Priscilla is feeling a new emotion that is not comfortable, she looks for an escape route. As Ann came over to our table now, Priscilla broke out into a huge grin. Ann extended her arms and said, "I remember you!" At lunch, she proceeded to tell us about daily life at the shelter, then offered to take us on a tour.

After clearing our dishes, we walked down to the main part of the grounds accompanied by some of the girls. Behind the huge steel walls were several houses used for various functions. There was a courtyard in the center of it all with a fountain that had long since stopped working. It was a lovely five-tiered structure of larger-to-smaller round basins painted a clay color, trimmed in turquoise. The fountain sat against a yellow wall on a patio of stones and concrete. It was beautiful yet sad—the wall was in such disrepair, the paint discolored and broken clay pots lining the edge. The overall condition of all the buildings was a bit run down, but it was easy to see that the girls were loved and cared for. The bedrooms were neat as a pin, with dozens of stuffed animals piled on each bed. The girls were enthusiastically showing us their favorites and competed for our attention, calling Isabella and Priscilla to "look at this, look at this!"

One little girl in a pirate hat was standing off at the edge of the group. She was dressed in a pink t-shirt and flowered shorts with a long-sleeve pink jacket on, even though it was July. I must not have noticed her at lunch, but she hurried to catch up with us as we left to see Isabella's room. The hat was black with crossed pistols in the front. A gold eye patch with a red band covered her right eye, and when we tried to joke with her about the costume, she said nothing, crossed her arms, and just kept her eye on us. We posed for many pictures, but when I look at the photos now, I see that the girls are unsmiling. Pirate girl is off to one side, not sure if she should join the picture or not. Two girls, about seven or eight with jet black hair combed down almost into their eyes are in a hug with Ann—one in pigtails, the other in a pixie cut looking out from under long bangs with no expression at all. Priscilla and Ann have arms around each other and one of the girls is clinging to the other arm of Ann. There is a dirty rag mop stuck in the fence behind them.

Isabella and Ann's room were separate and apart from the girls in a low-structured building painted turquoise with a terracotta roof surrounded by clay pots—some with plants in them, while others contained dried-up ferns. Isabella's room was small with a musty smell—a cot, two folding chairs, and a small table filled the space. There was a sink at one end and the walls were painted half spice orange and half a golden color. Isabella plopped down on her cot for us to take her picture. Immediately, a few of the girls jumped on her and she playfully tickled and hugged them.

As a family, we had discussed an appropriate gift to give. Hearing the story of the girls carrying their books in plastic bags, we decided that backpacks would be useful for everyone. With the tour over, we told Pedro and Carla of our shopping plan. They were delighted and said the girls would appreciate them. Our driver took us to a department store that looked like something between a Macy's and a Target, about thirty minutes away. The girls worked together to pick out forty backpacks, loading them into a cart. I asked Isabella if she felt comfortable enough to request a discount as they were going to be donated, which she did. Her Spanish was good enough for the saleswoman to immediately shake her head and answer, "No."

There was one thing that would make the gift even sweeter and that was candy. We bought large plastic bags of licorice, sweet tarts, and other assorted chili candy, and we stuffed each bag. In assembly-line fashion, we wrote the name of each girl on a tag, and Priscilla handed them out. Truthfully, I think the older girls felt that the bags were too young for them and not quite what they would have liked to carry books and belongings in, but they all thanked us and posed for pictures. The little ones were especially clingy to Isabella and Priscilla, telling them that lots of people visit and say they are going to come back but they never do.

We had many of those types of moments during the week. Glimpses of a life that was hard through no one's fault, but difficult just the same. We dropped in for our feel-good moment but then would leave just as others had done. The things we take for granted every day did not exist for these girls. Who cares about them? Who will listen to all the things teenage girls like to obsess about? Carla and Pedro seemed to have an endless supply of patience, but how does that work with thirty girls?

Through all of this, Ceci was never far from my thoughts. Ceci was the constant. Ceci was the one who would never leave them and it made perfect sense why the children all called her "Mommy." It has taken me over ten years to fill her shoes and appreciate how high that mountain really was.

The next day we met up with Ceci herself at the younger children's shelter. Boys and girls under the age of seven lived there together. When we arrived, Ceci was holding a prayer meeting, but stopped to welcome us. The group made room around a huge rectangular table set in an outdoor patio area. Ceci was all business that day, dressed in a monochromatic blue silk blouse and pants. Her Bible and assorted papers and folders were nearby.

Ceci began with, "So, how are you?"

I laughed a bit as the answer was so big. My mind scrambled to say something that would sum up the past ten years in a few sentences.

"Well, there have been ups and downs, but of course we have so much love for both of our girls and are proud of them."

Ceci trained her gaze on Priscilla to ask about how she was doing. Priscilla was instantly embarrassed and nervous, looking at her nails, flinging her hair behind her head over and over saying, "Well, things are good... " Her voice trailed off.

Ceci stopped Priscilla mid-sentence to ask, "Are you keeping up with your Spanish?"

Priscilla responded with more hair twisting and muttering.

"You have got to practice your Spanish with your sister," Ceci directed, which was probably the last thing Priscilla wanted to hear. Ceci needed to conclude her meeting and asked us if we would help with lunch and then join up with her group again for a Eucharist service. We said yes and left the porch for the main house where lunch was being prepared. We helped set the picnic tables. As the meal was being cooked, Ceci's son showed us to another play area in the back of the house. On a basketball court-sized paved surface, the boys were kicking a soccer ball and there was general horseplay. The girls crowded around Priscilla and Isabella chattering, asking questions, jumping on their backs for piggyback rides, trying on their sunglasses, and playing with phones. It was a bit chaotic, but Priscilla was in her glory, holding and hugging the children, and speaking to them in broken Spanglish. I think they were intrigued because Priscilla looked like them, but they asked over and over who we were. Priscilla explained that we were her family, but they laughed as if it were a joke.

Ceci had stopped all adoptions years before because the regulations in Mexico had changed. All adoptions were now handled by the State System for the Full Development of the Family (DIF). *Ministerios* was a private shelter system and now the DIF was Mexico's "Central Authority" for all states within Mexico. Currently, prospective adoptive parents are told to be prepared to spend at least three months in Mexico, which includes a two-week trial period where they will live with the child. Ceci also mentioned how difficult it was to let them go—only three others from *Ministerios* had been adopted internationally, and two of them were siblings.

We watched the boys and girls dive into lunch. Tavo, a handsome teenager who lived and worked at the shelter, had a special bond with the boys and they followed his direction. Priscilla explained that he lived at the children's shelter when she was a toddler and she had reached out to him via Facebook before our arrival. Priscilla helped him clear the tables.

At the Eucharist service, the prayers were solemn but joyful. We held hands in a circle while Ceci affirmed the power of Jesus' grace and love. At that moment, I was grateful for the divine intervention that had brought us to that place. I gave my silent thanks to God and this woman for bringing Priscilla into our lives. As the group was breaking up, Ceci asked if we would like to have dinner with her family, which we gladly accepted. Her son drove their SUV and we followed them through twists and turns in Cuernavaca, at one point sighting the town plaza where we first took Priscila all those years ago.

Priscilla managed to crack us up a few times during that first meeting, showing her spitfire self even then. I remember at our alfresco lunch on that same square ten years before being so excited to take her to the bathroom. How very "new mommy" I felt all over again! It may seem funny to talk about it now as she is a grown woman—but I remember being ready with the toilet paper, so eager to help her. In a flash, while still sitting on the potty, she raised her hand in my face with her index finger pointing up, as if to say, "Hold it right there, Mamma!" She did not want me to help her or invade her personal space in any way and took care of her business all by herself. With a satisfied smirk, she flushed the toilet and went over to the sink, washed and dried her hands, then turned to face me. "Seen enough, lady?" her face seemed to ask. I knew then she would be a challenge, but I smiled thinking, *This kid has spunk!*

We arrived at the restaurant, which was a botanical oasis. Walking through the main dining room, I could see that most diners were outside under enormous umbrellas on the patio that overlooked a sweeping lawn and garden. Peacocks strutted among exquisite, colorful native flowers. It had been a long day and we sank into lawn chairs to sip drinks and eat a few appetizers. Ceci told us of her joys and difficulties running five shelters and her struggle to raise funds. Priscilla asked about her friend from the poolside pictures that Vero had sent. The news was not good as Rosie had been asked to leave the shelter. There was a boyfriend tangled up in the story which ended with Ceci begging Priscilla to stay in school.

Priscilla nodded solemnly and promised to do so.

I could see her sadly taking in the news that her friend had a difficult path. Years ago, she used to tell me stories of their adventures. Rosie was her first "best friend" and Priscilla spoke many times of them being reunited. We had been seated for dinner by that point and I looked across the table at her face. She seemed close to tears. The others were talking around us in multiple conversations. The news of Rosie had taken her away. When Pris met my "mom gaze" across the table, I silently raised my glass and gave her a subtle air kiss along with an encouraging smile. She smiled back, nodded, picked up her *Jarritos* tamarind soda, and drank with me. Priscilla had many hurdles these last few years and cleared them all. I think that is why Ceci chose her as the first international adoption from *Ministerios de Amor*. Strong and resilient, Ceci knew Priscilla would thrive.

While we ate a delicious meal of chicken, beef, rice, and vegetables, Priscilla told Ceci that she wanted to help. Could she come back next summer and work at the shelter? I stopped mid-swallow to hear the answer. Ceci smiled at Priscilla and said, "The best way for you to help me is to raise money. Ask your friends to run a race or have a contest and organize a fundraiser. You don't need to come to Mexico to help us."

Priscilla shook her head and said that she understood. It was not the answer Priscilla was expecting. I know she wanted to do what Isabella was doing. Priscilla wanted to be hands-on and in the thick of things. Anything less was a disappointment and I could see it on her face. I offered to help Priscilla think of more fundraising ideas when we returned home.

When it came time to say goodbye, Priscilla and Ceci stepped away from the tables and onto the lawn for a bit of privacy. Ceci smoothed Priscilla's hair then held her face, looking right into her eyes. I could see Priscilla nodding in agreement with whatever Ceci was saying, and then Priscilla walked over to where Isabella and I were standing. Her eyes were teary as her sneakers scuffled along the sidewalk, dragging with each step.

As I watched her come toward me, I had a moment of clarity about our entire journey leading to that moment. When Richard and I announced that I was pregnant and that we would not be pursuing an adoption after all, friends and family members were quick to tell me, "Good thing because you know with an adoption, *you just don't know what you are getting*." At the time, I pushed the thought out of my mind, pressing my hand to my expanding belly. The phrase roiled me for years, and as we returned to the world of adoption, I tried to get past those who said it carelessly, thinking they were giving me sage advice, when really I considered it highly insensitive and rude. I know many parents who struggle to make sense of relationships with their biological children. They didn't know what they were getting either! But as I pulled Priscilla close and thought of all that we had been through, I realized that in the most magical of interpretations... they were right.

On the plane ride home, Priscilla leaned her head on my shoulder. No, I certainly did not know that I would get all the love and feeling of immense satisfaction we had in creating a family that bridged two countries. No, I did not know that I would get the opportunity to improve everyday as a mother and as a human being in this diverse and complicated world. There was no doubt in my mind that Priscilla's Mexican connections would be for life, and that she would return to do something special.

CHAPTER 31

Home

When we returned home, no fundraising ever materialized but something ignited in Priscilla as she continued to connect on Facebook with many people in Mexico. She started to listen to Mexican musicians and, within a short period of time, knew every popular Latin artist and their music. I would catch her singing along while the tunes played on her phone during homework. She knew all the words and translated them for me.

She started watching Spanish/Mexican TV *telenovelas* and explained the plot lines of romance and adventure when we asked. She discovered Mexican TV shows that she used to watch as a little girl in Mexico, such as *El Chavo del Ocho*, along with Mexican game shows and talk shows.

But just in case we thought Priscilla had given up her covert and mysterious ways, one night early in her senior year, she arranged for a big party at our home when we were away for the weekend. Once again, there had been so much progress, and then wham! It was a doozy of a get-together, too, with broken furniture, damaged electronic equipment, excessive alcohol consumption, and a violation of our personal space in a weird and disturbing way. We were disappointed to have gone backward after such a promising summer. It was now my turn to tell Priscilla that the bright side of this adventure would be the enormous amount of time she would have to concentrate on her college applications and essays during the upcoming months while she was grounded at home.

As we thought about college, we were dealing with the fact that her SAT scores were at the middle of the pack, creating uncertainty as to where she would be accepted. Together, Priscilla and I had been through the book of colleges and settled on about a dozen that we felt were right for her.

Priscilla talked about majoring in Spanish. I knew that she was excellent at casual conversation. In fact, the daily report from Spanish class was that she and *Señor Hernandez* talked quite a bit one-on-one during the class. As spring approached, we were surprised and honestly thrilled that she had been accepted to every school to which she applied. When we attended accepted students' day at one of the universities, we learned that language majors were required to spend a year abroad. That sealed the deal for Priscilla, and she signed on the dotted line for a small liberal arts school in rural Pennsylvania.

As a senior in the spring semester of high school, Priscilla had the option of signing up for an internship, which was essentially one month of volunteer work that would sponsor her learning. Priscilla came home extremely excited one late April day to say that she spoke to our neighbor, Sofia, who worked at a Philadelphia women's shelter which also provided education and outreach to the Hispanic community. Sofia agreed to sponsor Priscilla for this internship. During her last month of high school, Priscilla accompanied Sofia to schools, community centers, and civic events to spread the word about resources for women, signs of abuse, and self-defense training. Priscilla told us that her Spanish use was somewhat minimal but she was so excited to be included in the program, and it didn't faze her.

We encouraged Priscilla to continue with her volunteer work after graduation, but when she applied at the agency that had sponsored her internship, she was told that her Spanish was "too slow" and that they would not be able to use her. Priscilla took that comment hard, hanging her head when she told me.

College began, and after a rough first semester of her freshman year, dropping one of her Spanish requirements, Priscilla did not say much about her language progress. It seemed as if we always had to pry the details out of her. She shared that she was busy writing reports and expanding her Spanish reading, but I honestly did not know what to believe because Priscilla was so reluctant to speak any Spanish in front of us.

Gauging Priscilla's Spanish at this point was a bit like the old days. I had to ask a thousand questions to get even a hint about what was really happening, so I retreated but never lost hope. During one weekend home near the end of her first year, Richard, Priscilla, and I found ourselves at one of our favorite Colombian restaurants. All the wait staff are Hispanic. We sat down to delicious garlic bread as the after-work crowd bustled loudly around us. Friday evenings started early with a happy hour and half-priced drinks. I ordered a Margarita.

"Do we want the fried plantains?" I asked.

"Yes," Priscilla said.

"I think my standard chicken and rice is just what I am in the mood for."

"I am so happy not to be in the cafeteria," Priscilla added.

When the waiter came over, I ordered our appetizer first, then nodded to Priscilla to order her dinner. Priscilla put her menu down on the table and pointed to the *Jarritos* sodas list and *asked in Spanish* if they had mango flavor. The waiter answered, *"Sí."* Then Priscilla proceeded to order the rest of her meal *in Spanish!*

The waiter left, but we sat there open-mouthed, staring at Priscilla who smiled ear to ear. I screamed. Priscilla shushed me.

"What a perfect surprise," I told her.

"Yep, I knew you would like that."

We talked about her Spanish miracle the rest of dinner. Priscilla had become close with a number of other Hispanic students at school who encouraged her and provided a safe place to converse in Spanish. From there, conversations started to fly! After all the years of starts and stops to use her language skills, the timing was perfect. She had done it. Seeing her with the confidence to speak Spanish in public was huge. It was so noisy as the restaurant continued to fill up, but it didn't matter. We raised our glasses to toast a beaming young woman who had recovered what she lost all those years ago. I looked across the table at a self-assured Priscilla who was ready to take on the world and begin her journey again.

CHAPTER 32

Epilogue

P riscilla left for Mexico in the second semester of her junior year to begin her study abroad requirement. This was a tremendous accomplishment. When college began two and a half years earlier, Priscilla was so tentative with her Spanish that I had serious doubts as to whether she would be up to the task. It's not a matter of just visiting a country. Priscilla needed to be proficient enough to enroll in coursework at the university level. She was already a semester behind her classmates, due to the dropped Spanish class from her freshman year—because the teacher spoke Catalan. At the time, this made me furious. Priscilla seemed to make no effort to adapt to this professor's dialect. It was only after she dropped the course that she told us about it. Priscilla then spent the Christmas holiday taking a Western Civilization history class in order to make up the credits.

She seemed to adjust to school in many other ways, playing lacrosse during her freshman year, going to parties, and learning about the school's traditions. Of course, there was a bit of drama in the dorm with some mean girl activity. Priscilla emerged unscathed for the most part and formed a reasonable number of good friendships from her time on campus. Priscilla applied to several different study abroad programs, ultimately settling on a large state university in Mexico. Students were assigned to live with a family for the full immersion experience.

Richard and I visited her new hometown, amazed at Priscilla's language fluency and the ease with which she adjusted to life in Mexico. She was also able to reconnect with Ceci, who invited Priscilla to *Ministerios de Amor*'s thirtieth- anniversary celebration. Priscilla even spoke to the crowd in Spanish about her experience. Ceci called Priscilla one of her "success stories." Later in the semester, Priscilla spent a weekend with *Tía* Vero, attending church together and meeting Vero's extended family and friends. Priscilla's questions about Vero's life were answered on a much deeper level than their last meeting four years earlier.

Priscilla loved her Mexican family, coursework, and the community. After classes, she volunteered with two organizations that specialized in helping the most destitute women and their families. She was happier than I had ever seen her. In one Facebook posting I saw, she was joyously jumping up in the air in front of some ancient ruins with the caption: "I fell in love with this country," —in Spanish of course.

Priscilla decided almost immediately to return to Mexico for her second semester requirement. However, about a month after she arrived, three decapitated bodies were found in a park near the home where Priscilla was living. Thankfully, she was out of the house when this happened. Needless to say, we were terrified that our child had come close to such violence, never imagining that something like this could happen in a normally peaceful small town.

At the same time, without warning, my Human Resources career came to an end due to budget cuts. I was told my position was eliminated, but then it was posted four salary grades lower within a few weeks. The interview for the "new" position was scheduled for the exact same day as Priscilla's emergency evacuation from Mexico. My priorities were clear. Still, it was a difficult transition for both of us. For Priscilla, her sudden exit from Mexico was a heartbreaking echo of the separation all those years ago. For me, it meant leaving a role that I had built from the ground up and finding a new path after over thirty years in corporate America.

Because the school was concerned for the safety of the students, the study abroad program was immediately discontinued in Mexico. The six American student participants were transferred to the University of Barcelona, where the fall semester had not yet begun. They were given only a day to pack their belongings and say their goodbyes before departing. Priscilla was so comfortable and much loved in her tiny Mexican town, but now in Barcelona, she had to contend with a tangle of metro lines, a huge university setting, and a family that was not so welcoming. Priscilla got lost on the Barcelona metro system numerous times and it took a while to get acclimated to new school work. We spent many hours on the phone encouraging a sobbing and devastated Priscilla who wanted to come home.

Our response was a tough love message, telling her that it was not possible to return to Philadelphia. The tuition had already been paid and she would not have enough credits to graduate on time. An upside to my situation was that I now had the time to visit a broken Priscilla who was still crushed by the events in Mexico. We had a lovely stay together in Barcelona, and gradually the healing process began to take hold for both of us. Priscilla was a great tour guide. We visited museums, took long walks, engaged in retail therapy, and ate scrumptious food. The Catalan region of Spain was embroiled in its own struggles within the independence movement. During my visit, we talked a lot about the political climate at home and abroad and its influence in our lives.

Isabella graduated from college and moved to the West Coast, so the girls see each other only on holidays and summer vacation, yet still manage to engage in the occasional skirmish.

Out to dinner for Isabella's July birthday, Priscilla reverted to her pouty ways. She picked at the Israeli food, saying that she didn't really like it, and did not take part in any of the conversation. This scene has been repeated many times over the years. Priscilla's anger at some insignificant distraction or throwaway comment would often take over the entire evening—the celebration spoiled, precious family time never to be recovered.

I have devoted multiple hours to devising possible strategies to prevent these digestive hurdles. It's clear that these are remnants of her coping mechanisms, but the fact that they have persisted for so long is a mystery to me. Ultimately, I have concluded that there is no amount of begging, pleading, or preparation that would make the evening turn out differently. Many techniques have been tried over the years with the optimistic thought that I would get better at handling these situations. Perhaps my motherly wisdom will speak to me, resulting in a magic utterance that would have us all laughing, clinking glasses, and eating fried calamari. But it rarely happens. Sometimes, if I am determined, I will attempt to continue the conversation around Priscilla's refusal to talk, reluctance to eat, and snub of the entire family. But this is a tall order as I need to pretend that it does not matter to me that my two daughters don't like each other much. And that hurts. A lot. It's also difficult to eat with a lump in my throat. Of all ironies, sitting right in front of me, we adopted Priscilla so that Isabella could have a sibling and the two of them cannot exist for very long without getting on each other's nerves... still!

Individually, I could not be more proud of both girls. Isabella was hired by a technology firm in a competitive environment, one of the few women in this role. She has global responsibilities and has already been promoted. She continues to be active, staying in shape by hiking and playing lacrosse, and has taken up cooking with a passion. We trade recipe ideas, and I send her favorite cookies from time to time.

In preparation for writing this book, I reached out to Ceci who told us, among other things, that when she was a little girl, Priscilla actually asked to be adopted. Priscilla did not remember this request from her childhood. At the time, it took Ceci by surprise and she told us both in one of our phone calls, "I received you when you were two days old, and I changed your Pampers many times. You were a beautiful baby."

Priscilla approached these calls hesitantly, expressing doubts as to whether she wanted to hear more from Ceci about her early days. Ceci responded, "No one can steal your memories."

Pris said, "But I am still struggling to figure out who I am."

Ceci said, "All of my stories have made me the person I am. Imagine your story and (think of) all of the things that God provided for you. It was God that brought your family to us. I didn't like that you wanted to be adopted. But I knew that you were in the best hands. There are billions of girls that want to have what you have."

I remain optimistic that Priscilla and Isabella are not yet finished learning and growing as sisters. On a freezing February day last year, Pris took a break from school, Isabella grabbed a flight home, and our family came together to celebrate the Super Bowl victory of the Philadelphia Eagles. It was a spirited parade, a joyous celebration of the underdog, and the girls enjoyed it immensely together. So, there is hope.

Truthfully, my faith has waxed and waned over the years. I still consider myself to be a spiritual person and continue to pray for our family. When I needed Mary's intercession, she was there in a big way, providing an opportunity for me, not only to have a child, but to influence the life of another. I remain grateful for both of these experiences and would not trade them for anything.

Without a significant male figure in her life for her first eight years, Priscilla's relationship with her father has developed at an agonizingly slow pace. I see it in fits and starts, and I help it along whenever I can. Richard had a big role in her final college course. It was a difficult few weeks as they plowed through Statistics. They did it successfully, together.

~

Priscilla graduated from college in the spring of 2018 after one final semester back on campus and is looking for the best way to contribute to this crazy world. Although ties to her Mexican heritage are stronger than they have ever been, she tells me that she is firmly rooted in U.S. soil and that she is grateful for the close mother-daughter bond that we share. Her time in Mexico has solidified her identity and increased her confidence in ways that surprised her. Our current unpredictable and intolerant culture, with significant prejudice leveled specifically at Mexicans, has spurred her on to pursue a career utilizing her talents to benefit the Hispanic community. Priscilla says that she has been "called" to do this work. We have grown closer as mother and daughter, united as a diverse family.

Adopting an older child from another country changed our family in a way that I did not expect. While the perfect best-friend relationship has eluded the sisters, I have realized that it was not the result of poor mothering. Adapting to a culture, no matter how welcoming or loving, is not something that can be forced on a timetable, and as much as I wanted to manage every situation, I had to let certain things play out. The playing field was never even, and Priscilla needed so much more time to find herself. With her return to Mexico, a self-assured woman who is ready to meet the world has emerged.

Epilogue

It's been over fifteen years since our Mexican adventure began. Motherhood the second time around was a completely different experience, one that tested me in ways I could not have predicted. I have learned lessons of love, loss, trust, and survival. Our story is a powerful testament to family and our need to belong. Today, the world is a different place than when we first crossed the border. Her love for us has approached that border so many times that I have lost count. My hope for Priscilla is that in re-discovering and understanding the love of her past, she will find the key to her future and the love she wants and deserves.

Acknowledgments

T his book would not have been possible without the efforts of so many. To all those that offered advance reading, editing, and encouragement along the way: Diane Bones, Liz Abrams Morley, Wild River Consultants, Pidge Molyneaux, Terri Gelberg, Carol Cunningham, Paulette Gabriel, Robin Neifield, Irene Levy Baker, Karen Cheney Avril, Tom Avril, Cindy Cox Roman, Linda Karp, Bobbie Leiter, Kim Mehler, Jean Brubaker, Vicky Kauffman, and Michele Nowlan—thank you for your assistance and valuable feedback. Thanks also to Joyce Clark for haircuts and motherly wisdom.

Thanks to the Margate Public Library for providing a beautiful space for the writing of the first draft. Thanks to the Philadelphia Free Library for providing a vehicle for authors to share details of their process and struggles thus giving me endless inspiration. Many thanks to Rachel McCracken and her editors Jaime Lea and Jean Pace at Chasing Kites Publishing for making it possible for me to tell my story. You are a rare find in this publishing world. Thank you also to Nancy Verrier for her generous support. A great big thank you to my launch team of family and friends who gave feedback and support along the way. I have talked about this book for so long. Thank you for not saying, "Are you ever going to finish that thing?"

Thank you to all friends, neighbors, family, teachers, Philadelphia and Jenkintown communities, Grace Presbyterian Church, *Wonder Women*, TTN and *Read Between the Wines* Book

Club, that were part of a special "village." It does take a village and your help in a million different ways ensured success in this adventure. Thanks for being there along the way.

Thank you to my girls, Isabella and Priscilla who tolerated endless discussions about this book. In sharing so much about our family story – I have really pushed the envelope of tolerance and I thank you for not protesting too much.

Finally, none of this would have been possible without my best friend, editor-in-chief, tech guy, and all around supportive partner and husband, Richard DiDio. You shared this adventure with me from the beginning, provided just the right boost when I was stuck, and offered endless encouragement and excitement around this project. You have been a constant source of feedback and pep talks and your vision of this book kept me motivated during the many years it took to write it. You never faltered in your support and encouragement. I am lucky to have you in my corner and love you so very much.

About the Author

F or over twenty years and counting, Anna Maria DiDio has devoted her time and talents to many non-profit organizations focusing on women, girls, and families. She is the mother of two young wonderful women and loves to cook, shop, and watch movies with them – together or separately depending on any number of mitigating factors. Anna Maria is at her most creative when she is traveling and experiencing new people, places, and things to eat – then writing about it! She will never say no to a chocolate chip cookie and lives with her husband Richard in Philadelphia

www.amdidio.com

Twitter: @amdidio
Medium: @AnnaMaria.DiDio

Made in the USA
San Bernardino, CA
17 December 2019